Mystic and Pilgrim

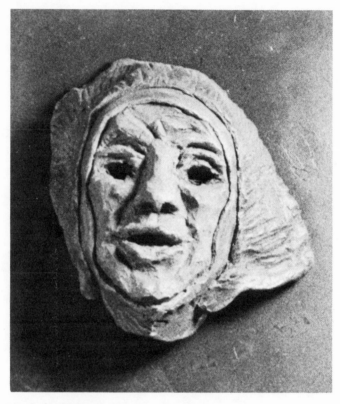

Head of a medieval woman, inspired by Margery Kempe.
Terracotta by Elizabeth Hogeland, 1980. Photo by Meg Atkinson.

Mystic and Pilgrim

The *Book* and the World of Margery Kempe

by

CLARISSA W. ATKINSON

Cornell University Press

ITHACA AND LONDON

First published 1983 by Cornell University Press.
Published in the United Kingdom by Cornell University Press Ltd.,
Ely House, 37 Dover Street, London W1X 4HQ.

International Standard Book Number 0-8014-1521-7
Library of Congress Catalog Card Number 82-22219

Printed in the United States of America

Librarians: Library of Congress cataloging information appears on the last page of the book.

Photographs by Nick Adler unless otherwise credited.

The paper in this book is acid-free and meets the guidelines for permanence and durability of the Committee on Production Guidelines for Book Longevity of the Council òn Library Resources.

To my father
and
in memory of my mother

Contents

Contents

Preface

WHEN I encountered *The Book of Margery Kempe* in 1976, I was first intrigued by Margery Kempe herself and then by the notes to the work written in the 1930s by Hope Emily Allen. I looked around for more: for the "Volume Two" promised by Allen and the Early English Text Society, and for interpretations of Margery Kempe and her book by scholars of medieval religion and society. For complicated reasons (discussed in Chapter 7 below), none of these materialized; Allen never wrote "Volume Two," and scholars—with significant exceptions—had ignored or (I believed) misunderstood Margery Kempe.

In the late 1970s I began my own study of Margery Kempe, intending to bring "this creature" (as she called herself) to the attention not only of scholars, but of "general readers"—particularly readers who were looking to the past with a new curiosity about the history and experience of women. My book is an introduction: an attempt to look at a complex historical figure in a variety of contexts, and to suggest several possible approaches to an interpretation of Margery Kempe and her autobiography. Because this work is intended for general readers, and not exclusively for scholars, I have quoted from the translation of Margery's *Book* made by William Butler-Bowdon, the original owner of the manuscript. It is impossible to appreciate Margery Kempe without reading a great many of her own words, but the Middle English text is not accessible to everyone who will (I hope) wish to read this introduction. The text, edited by Sanford B. Meech and Hope Emily Allen, was published as Volume One of *The Book of Margery Kempe* by the Early English Text Society in 1940.

Since I began my research on Margery Kempe, and at an accelerated pace in the 1980s, scholars have published rich and exciting works in medieval religion and women's history. The discussion of that elusive quantity "feminine piety" grows broader and deeper every year. I am profoundly indebted to many persons who are credited in the text and notes below, and I particularly want to thank those who have shared unpublished material with me, including Susan Dickman, Richard Kieckhefer, and Mary G. Mason.

In search of "Volume Two," I made two visits to the collection of Hope Emily Allen's papers in the Bryn Mawr College Library, and one to the Van Pelt Library at the University of Pennsylvania. I was assisted in my initial access to the Bryn Mawr Archives by my lifelong friend and sponsor, Mary H. Chase. On one delightful visit to Philadelphia, Nita Baugh shared with me her stories and memories of Hope Emily Allen. The Allen Papers were useful as well as inspiring; they were studied and have been quoted by permission of the Bryn Mawr Archives. Quotations from the Butler-Bowdon translation of *The Book of Margery Kempe* (copyright © by W. Butler-Bowdon 1944) are reprinted by permission of the Devin-Adair Company, Old Greenwich, Connecticut.

In 1977–1978 I held the Bertha S. Adkins Fellowship of the American Association of University Women, which made possible the full-time work on Margery Kempe from which this book was developed. For their kind and careful attention, I owe thanks to my teachers and advisers, especially William M. Daly, Jocelyn N. Hillgarth, Eleanor C. McLaughlin, and Samuel J. Miller. My research was made pleasant by discussions with many friends and colleagues, including Dorothy Austin, Dorothy C. Bass, Elaine Huber, and Paul Russell. Later I profited from the advice and companionship of colleagues at the Harvard Divinity School, and especially from the example of scholars in its distinguished program in Women's Studies in Religion. I am particularly grateful for the friendship of Constance H. Buchanan, Marilyn Chapin Massey, and Margaret R. Miles.

Friends and family make it all possible. Pat Rathbone tried hard to explain the "intentional fallacy"; Elizabeth Hogeland and Eleanor Shakin endured and cheered all versions. Holley, Meg, and Matthew Atkinson grew up while this work went on and on, but they never ceased to urge me to turn my attention to a murder mystery. I am grateful to them all.

CLARISSA W. ATKINSON

Weston, Massachusetts

Apotheosis of Tyana   in content of spirit

shows
divine is content
self   of
        divine
        spirit

exorcism

Mystic and Pilgrim

1) It is rare that a woman be a shaman

2) Apollo / Socrates / Plato / Plotinus Augustine

3) verbal but not the distinction between mystic / shaman
   - analogous (Aristotle, Owen)
   - pluralism, pluralists

[logical] [diversity] → shaman model
(grace is [unperishable])

these analogies   similarities / differences

→ 4) what insight? → approach as a back-ground for dialectic

[must] 5) mathematics / geometry?

[grace] 6) is not Plotinus under control? like shaman
         Augustine under control like shaman

Chapter One

"A SHORT TREATISE AND A COMFORTABLE"

"The Book of Margery Kempe"

MARGERY KEMPE, an English woman who lived at the turn of the fifteenth century, was a middle-class housewife of King's Lynn who became a mystic and a pilgrim. In her early twenties she began to live on terms of extraordinary intimacy with Christ and discovered (with divine assistance) a singular vocation. She was called to weep and to pray for the souls of her fellow Christians, and to do so not in a cell or convent, but in the world. Her vocation required her to separate herself from husband and household, impelled her to travel all around England and as far away as Jerusalem, and transformed her existence into one of continual struggle, commotion, and intensity. She was illiterate, but in old age she dictated to scribes an autobiography that recounted the trials and triumphs of her pilgrimage in the world and of the spirit.

Margery Kempe's remarkable vocation and unconventional way of life disturbed and occasionally alarmed her neighbors and acquaintances, some of whom accused her of insanity, heresy, or hypocrisy. She had loyal friends and supporters, but she did not fit comfortably into the social and religious patterns available to women in her time and place. Later historians as well as her own contemporaries have been puzzled, and for similar reasons: received categories of social and religious history do not easily accommodate Margery Kempe. Her personality remains troublesome; she had aspirations to holiness, reported special favors from God, yet does not seem very "saintly" in character or disposition. Her book was written down by scribes, complicating its authorship, and her vocation was highly unusual. Certainly she was not typical of her family or class. Her interactions with her Church and community were various and sometimes troubled, and her spiritual experience strikes some critics as "extreme" or egotistical. Models and precedents for her behavior did exist, but they must be sought outside her immediate environment. To appreciate and interpret the life and activities of Margery Kempe, one must consider a number of perspectives: the character of her autobiography, her ways of knowing and following God's will, her social environment, her relations with her Church, the tradition that shaped her piety, and the context of female religious experience in the late Middle Ages.

In one of the extended colloquies that characterized her communication with God, Margery was told that she was "ordained to be a mirror" to her fellow Christians, "to have great sorrow so that they should take example by thee, and have some little sorrow in their hearts for their sins."[1] The image is significant, for a mirror may distort as well as reflect what it makes visible. What appears in the glass is determined in part by the position of the beholder. Those who knew Margery Kempe in her lifetime, as well as later readers of her book, have seen a great variety of reflections. Their responses and reactions provide, in the first instance, valuable information about English religion and society in the later Middle Ages; in the second, significant insight into our own attitudes toward the past.

Margery Kempe was born in King's Lynn (then Bishop's Lynn) in the county of Norfolk in about the year 1373. Her

1. William Butler-Bowdon, ed., *The Book of Margery Kempe* p. 169. Unless otherwise noted, quotations from *The Book of Margery Kempe* are taken from this edition and followed by a page number in the text.

father, John Burnham (or de Brunham), was a substantial citizen: five times mayor, alderman of the merchant guild, six times Member of Parliament, coroner, and Justice of the Peace. Nothing is known about her mother, who is not mentioned in the *Book* and does not appear in the public records of the city. When Margery was about twenty years old, she was married to John Kempe, also a burgess of Lynn, but a less notable figure than his father-in-law. Kempe, son of a trading family, was probably a brewer by trade. He was elected one of four city chamberlains in 1394; his father, another John Kempe, had been a chamberlain in 1372.[2]

Soon after her marriage Margery became pregnant "as nature would" (p. 1). She was very ill, the birth was difficult, and she feared that she would die. Sending for her confessor, she tried to tell him of a sin (not disclosed) which had troubled her conscience for a long time. The priest was stern and abrupt, she could not bring herself to confess to him, and "for the dread she had of damnation on the one side, and his sharp reproving of her on the other side, this creature went out of her mind and was wondrously vexed and laboured with spirits for half a year, eight weeks and odd days" (p. 1). Her description of her condition abounds with vivid and horrifying details. She was self-destructive and had to be restrained from injuring herself and others. From this terrible illness she was rescued by a vision of Christ, who said to her: "Daughter, why hast thou forsaken me, and I forsook never thee?" (p. 2).

Reassured and recovered, Margery resumed her household responsibilities and determined to serve God. But she could not give up her worldly attachments, and particularly her habits of pride and vainglory. She continued to wear splendid clothes and to boast about her family, and when her husband chided her, she "answered shrewdly and shortly, and said that she was

2. References to John Burnham and John Kempe in the municipal records of Lynn are described by Sanford Meech in Appendix III of *The Book of Margery Kempe*, edited for the Early English Text Society by Sanford Meech and Hope Emily Allen, pp. 359–368.

come of worthy kindred—he should never have wedded her—
for her father was sometime Mayor" (p. 3). Out of pride and
greed (as she believed), she set up her own brewery, but the
business failed after three or four years. Still she could not give
up her ambitions, and "bethought herself of a new housewifery"
(p. 4). She became a miller, but the horses would not pull,
the driver left her service, and it was widely believed that
Margery Kempe and her ventures were unlucky or worse.
Chastened, she asked God's forgiveness and resolved to reform
her life.

During the period of penitence that followed, Margery went
through an experience of mystical conversion which radically
altered her understanding of herself, the world, and her relationship to God. Her conversion was the first step in a lifelong
struggle to identify and live out a unique religious vocation.
She believed that her new existence required celibacy but for a
long time could not persuade her husband to agree, and she
gave birth in all to fourteen children.[3] Long before she was
allowed to be celibate, she adopted strict ascetic habits of
fasting and prayer, which she followed through years of married life and continual childbearing.

Persistent in her efforts at holiness, which aroused considerable hostility among her neighbors, Margery was reassured and assisted by comforting speech with God and the
Virgin. She began to visit holy persons (anchorites, friars,
and others) to talk about her visions and "feelings," and
was encouraged to continue in her way of life. She had mar-
velously vivid meditations, in which she participated in the
life of the Holy Family and discussed with Christ the require-

3. The *debitum conjugale*, or "legal" right to sexual intercourse within
marriage, was maintained in canon law and ecclesiastical practice for both
men and women throughout the Middle Ages. The consent of both parties was
required for voluntary abstinence, justified by 1 Cor. 7:3–5. For a clear summary of this question, see Elizabeth M. Makowski, "The Conjugal Debt and
Medieval Canon Law." See also Thomas N. Tentler, *Sin and Confession on the
Eve of the Reformation*, pp. 170–174.

ments, penalties, and rewards of her singular vocation.

Finally—after about twenty years of married life—John Kempe agreed to go with his wife before the bishop to take a vow of chastity in exchange for Margery's promise to eat and drink with him on Fridays (her usual fast-day) and to pay his debts before she left England on pilgrimage. The setting and style of their agreement is characteristic of the homely tone of Margery's reminiscences: "It befell on a Friday on Midsummer Eve in right hot weather, as this creature was coming from York-ward carrying a bottle with beer in her hand, and her husband a cake in his bosom ... " (p. 16). They sat down under a cross on the way to Bridlington and worked out the details of an arrangement that both symbolized and made possible a new life for Margery Kempe. At about forty years of age she won the consent of her husband and her Church to an existence apart from her family; from that time on, she was free to go wherever she believed herself to be sent by God.

Margery's first destination was the Holy Land, and in 1413, the year of her release from family life (and also of her father's death),[4] she set forth on her longest journey. Traveling east by way of Switzerland and Venice, she visited Jerusalem and the Holy Places, and she spent the winter in Rome on the way home. In the Holy Land she received "the gift of tears"— a gift of the Spirit, but not always a comfortable or convenient one; from that time on she cried and wept uncontrollably when reminded of Christ or the Passion. Later she made separate voyages to Spain and to Prussia and traveled extensively in England, visiting shrines and holy persons and listening to gifted preachers. She was several times arrested,

---

4. See E. I. Watkin, *On Julian of Norwich and In Defence of Margery Kempe,* pp. 37, 40. Watkin points out that money inherited from her father may have enabled Margery to settle her own debts and her husband's and to pay for her voyage to the Holy Land. I suspect that his death may also have removed a restraining influence, making it psychologically as well as financially possible for her to leave Lynn and her family.

imprisoned, and examined for heresy, but never convicted. Margery was frequently ill, repeatedly misunderstood, and attracted violent animosity as well as loyal support. She did not live with her husband again until about 1431, when he became paralyzed after a fall and she came home to look after him until his death. She began to work on her book during this period, and one of her sons, with his wife and child, came home from Germany and lived with her for a month before he also died. Her last (recorded) voyage took place in 1433–1434; after that she returned to Lynn, where she died some time after 1438.

The Book of Margery Kempe is a most unusual autobiography, not least because the author could not read or write; she dictated the book to two scribes. She was more than sixty years old when she began, looking back over half a century of tumultuous experience. Hers is the first autobiography in the English language, and in many ways is even more enigmatic than most works in that complicated genre. But it is our sole source of information about Margery Kempe, for unlike her famous contemporaries, such as Catherine of Siena and Joan of Arc, she left very little public record of her existence and no substantial group of followers to press her claims and to maintain her memory.

This single source seems especially fragile because the original manuscript is lost. The book exists in one fifteenth-century manuscript, which was discovered in 1934 by its owner, Colonel William E. I. Butler-Bowdon, in his family home in Lancashire. It bears two important identifying marks, the first indicating that it was copied (presumably from the original) by a person named Salthows, who signed his name at the bottom of the last folio. Salthows was not one of Margery's scribes, but he worked soon after them; his handwriting and paper belong to the middle of the fifteenth century. Sanford Meech, one of the first editors of the *Book*, believed that since Salthow's spelling, style, vocabulary, and so forth are perfectly consistent, he was an unusually faithful copyist or else he shared the scribe's language almost exactly—indicating a very early copy.[5]

The second useful mark of identification is the inscription "Liber Montis Gracie. This boke is of Mountegrace" in a late fifteenth-century hand on the binding leaf, indicating that in the century of its creation, Salthows's copy belonged to Mount Grace, a Carthusian monastery in the North Riding of Yorkshire. The manuscript was also marked by several other persons; Meech found four separate sets of annotations. Most of them correct omissions or direct the reader's attention to certain words or ideas, but some comment upon Margery Kempe's mystical experiences in relation to those of two Carthusians who were active at Mount Grace in the late fifteenth century. The markings shed some light on the uses made of the *Book* in the years following the author's death.[6]

Seven pages of extracts from *The Book of Margery Kempe* were printed in a pamphlet by Wynkyn de Worde in about 1501. The selections were taken largely from the quieter (less eccentric) colloquies of Margery with Christ or the Virgin; none of them concerns her life in the world, and they offer a rather colorless and misleading impression of author and book. The extracts were reprinted by Henry Pepwell in 1521 in a small volume of selections from mystical writings. Until the manuscript was discovered in 1934, these pamphlets were the sole source of information about Margery Kempe, who was mistakenly identified as an "anchoress" of Lynn.[7]

The various marks and annotations on the manuscript indicate, then, that it was sufficiently valuable or interesting to be copied at least once within a very few years after it was written down. Salthows's copy, which may have been

5. See Meech and Allen, *Margery Kempe*, pp. xxxii–xxxv, for Meech's description of the manuscript and its provenance.

6. *Ibid.*, pp. xxxvi–xliv. And see also James Hogg, "Mount Grace Charterhouse and Late Medieval English Spirituality."

7. Meech and Allen, *Margery Kempe*, pp. xlvi–xlviii.

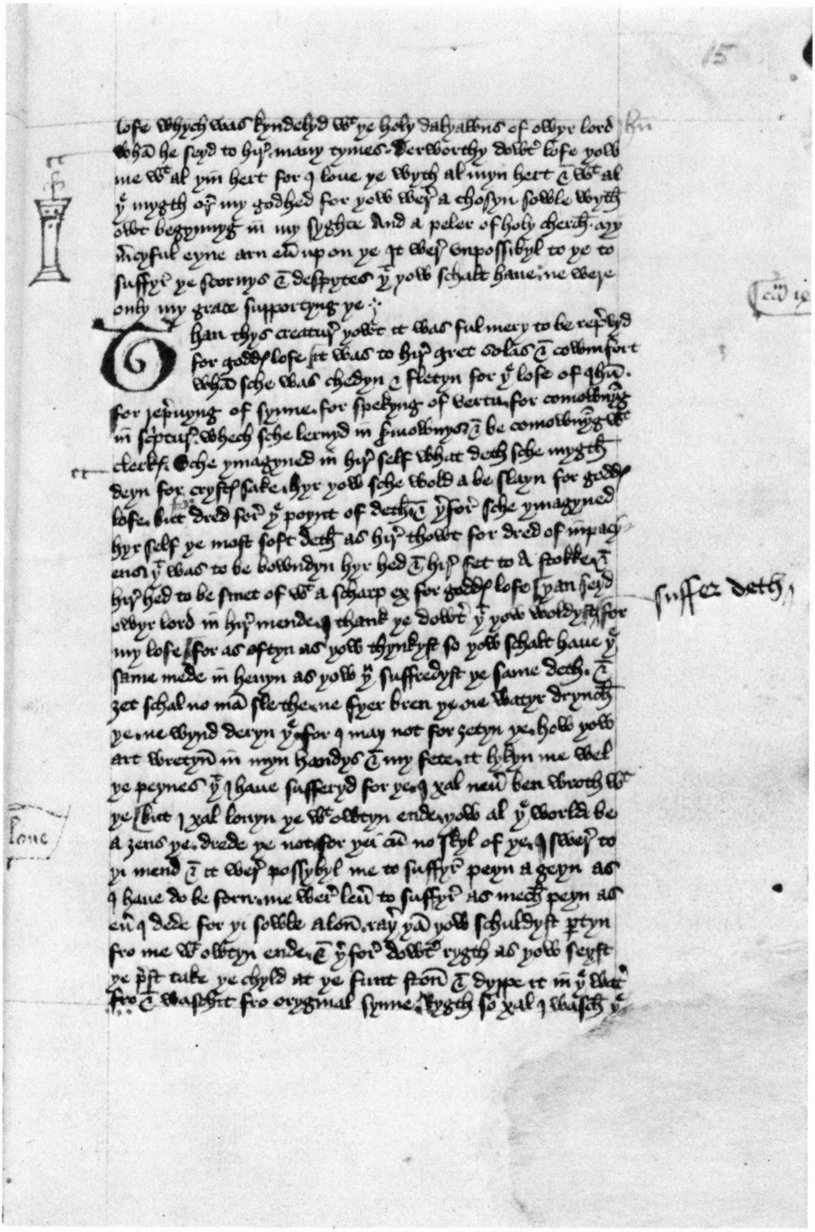

Folio 15a from the original manuscript of *The Book of Margery Kempe*. The drawing in the left-hand margin illustrates "a pillar of Holy Church." Courtesy of The British Library.

commissioned by someone at Mount Grace, was in the monks' possession before the end of the fifteenth century. There is no evidence of its removal to the Butler-Bowdon family; the book-plates of Henry Bowdon (b. 1754) provide only a very late *terminus ad quem* for the transfer. Colonel Butler-Bowdon commented on that question in an article in the London *Times*: "It may be remembered that we are a Catholic family and I believe that when the monasteries were destroyed, the monks sometimes gave valuable books, vestments, etc., to such families in the hope of preserving them. . . . this may have been the case with Margery Kempe's manuscript, and the Carthusians of Mount Grace may have given it to one of my family."[8] *The Book of Margery Kempe* may have played some small part in the drama of the English Reformation, but unfortunately we have no information about the manuscript or its owners and readers between the sixteenth century and the twentieth.

At its simplest, autobiography is the story of a life told by its subject; formally, subject and object are one. Margery Kempe consistently referred to herself as "this creature" in deference to her Creator—a fairly common medieval usage, which nonetheless serves as a constant reminder that the book was not "written" by Margery Kempe, who was illiterate. It also raises the question: was the book written by her, or about her? Is it biography or autobiography? The resolution of that question concerns the role of the scribes but also depends on our understanding of the nature and purpose of autobiography.

Literary historians and critics vary widely in their opinions as to when and under what circumstances "real" autobiography first appeared. Georges Gusdorf ties its beginnings to the invention of the mirror, which he says "would seem to have disrupted human experience, especially from that moment when the mediocre metal plates that were used in antiquity

8. Colonel Butler-Bowdon's remarks are quoted in the notice of publication of his translation of *The Book of Margery Kempe* in *The Times* (London), September 30, 1936, p. 13.

gave way at the end of the Middle Ages to silver-backed mirrors produced by Venetian technique. From that moment, the image in the mirror became a part of the scene of life. . . . "[9] The mirror image complemented Renaissance anthropology, stimulated the new art of self-portrait, and permitted people to see themselves as unique beings. In relation to autobiography it worked, on the one hand, to revitalize the Christian tradition of confession, exemplified at its most sublime in Augustine's *Confessions*. And on the other hand, by stimulating attention to the individual, the mirror image helped to turn autobiographers away from the "deforming" theological image in which every subject is first a creature—and a sinner. The medieval world view had to break down before "man could have any interest in seeing himself as he is without any taint of the transcendent."[10] For Gusdorf, Cellini and Montaigne were the first autobiographers. Certainly *The Book of Margery Kempe*, which was designed to reflect God's grace in the life of a sinner, was "tainted" by the transcendent.

Gusdorf's attention to the invention of the mirror is significant in relation to Margery Kempe, who was "ordained to be a mirror," but most critics assign the beginnings of "real" autobiography to a date later than the end of the Middle Ages. Generally it is claimed as a product of post-Enlightenment Western culture and associated with the rise of historical consciousness in the West after 1800.[11] Only when the individual personality was recognized, valued, and cultivated could autobiography become what it now is—"the literary form in which such an individuality could best account for itself."[12] When that "individuality" perceived itself in relation to the sweep of history, and to a particular historical moment, modern autobiography was born.

9. Georges Gusdorf, "Conditions and Limits of Autobiography," p. 32.
10. *Ibid.*, p. 34.
11. Karl J. Weintraub, "Autobiography and Historical Consciousness," 821.
12. *Ibid.*, 847.

Unlike other self-revealing literary forms (letters, journals, and the like), modern autobiography assumes the existence of a persistent conscious "self" interacting through a lifetime with the world outside. This "self" is the center of an individual universe; shaped by experience, it acts in turn to shape events and relationships. It is an agent, thus not (or not entirely) a creature of circumstance or of God's will. In medieval autobiography, however, the protagonist is not perceived or presented as the primary agent in the creation of a life: that role belongs to God.[13] In other words, the medieval "self" is not the modern "self": like the "family" or the "state," the "self" is a human construction subject to historical change.[14] Margery Kempe's sense of herself pervades every page of her book, but that "self," which she called a "creature," is of the fifteenth century, not of the twentieth.

An autobiographer has a story to tell; in service of the story, the author shapes the raw material of inner and outer experience (thoughts and feelings as well as events) into a coherent narrative. The writer must be convinced that his or her life is special and worth remembering, having value and significance for readers separated by time and distance from personal knowledge of the subject and the circumstance. But an autobiography is more than a portrait, more than an entity captured in a particular time and place and stage of development. Margery Kempe traveled here and there, changed from a fearful sinner (in her own estimation) to a favorite child of God. Her development, the interior changes that correspond to the exterior movement of the story, differentiates her book from conven-

13. A notorious exception among medieval autobiographies is Abelard's *Historia calamitatum*—which technically is not an autobiography at all, but a letter to a friend. Medieval historians (if not literary critics) treat this work as autobiography because they find in it evidence of a twelfth-century turn toward awareness of the "self."

14. For a recent and fascinating contribution to the discussion of the medieval "self," see Caroline W. Bynum, "Did the Twelfth Century Discover the Individual?" in *Jesus as Mother,* pp. 82–109.

tional hagiography and from much medieval autobiography. According to Roy Pascal, in Suso's *Life of the Servant*, for example, "the stages of the author's development are more exemplary than real."[15] Pascal believes that works in which the behavior of the subject, and its consequences, are more mythic and exemplary than individual and "real" are not autobiography but theology.

Certainly Margery Kempe had no intention of writing theology; she had enough trouble fending off accusations of preaching, which was not permitted to women. It is true that her interpretations are generally cautionary (for example, her business failed because God was calling her to a different life), but the episodes and anecdotes themselves are her own and not the conventional exempla of contemporary preaching and hagiography. Margery meant her book to be a witness, not a theological treatise. She was explicit about why she wrote, and for whom, and what she intended to write: "Here beginneth a short treatise and a comfortable, for sinful wretches, wherein they may have a great solace and comfort to themselves and understand the high and unspeakable mercy of our Sovereign Saviour . . . this little treatise shall treat somewhat in part of His wonderful works, how mercifully, how benignly and how charitably He moved and stirred a sinful caitiff unto His love" (p. 235). The book was written as a testimony and inspiration to other Christians, designed to comfort them by displaying God's gracious activity in the author's life. That intention was consistent with Margery's vocation to be a mirror, and with the calling of all Christians to comfort one another and to save souls. In her own estimation, and that of her scribes, she was singularly blessed by her "feelings," which arose from intimacy with God. She had been chosen for special favors; grateful witness was a natural response. Her book was supposed to reflect divine activity, but in her own (not a mythic or exemplary) life.

To recognize an author's stated intention is not to preclude

15. Roy Pascal, *Design and Truth in Autobiography*, pp. 24–25.

all the other motivations, conscious and unconscious, that impelled her to write. Medieval and modern authors share a universal passion for self-justification; behind the published agenda (whether this is to report a conversion or a political campaign) lies a hidden agenda—and the autobiographical form offers an irresistible opportunity to relive the past.[16] In her witness to God's love, Margery Kempe also justified her behavior, answered her critics, and explained apparent mistakes and inconsistencies. She took full advantage of the opportunity to remake her life as she would have liked it to be, and probably as she "re-membered" it in the act of "re-creation."

An author's memory is problematic even for readers of modern autobiography, whose dependence on subjective recollection is modified by ample documentation—by letters, newspapers, tapes, and photographs. Medieval people had no newspapers, tapes, or photographs, and Margery Kempe was illiterate. Her letters (if any) were written for her and read to her, and none of them survives. But medieval people did possess a powerful oral tradition, and they could use their memories in ways that are not possible in our society. From experience with nonliterate modern cultures, we know that people can (and do) preserve their laws, their romances, and their sacred revelations without benefit of paper or tape. Such communities often appoint and train specialists in memory, but even ordinary people develop powers of recall and recognition far beyond our present capacities, distracted as we are by the multiple stimuli of the learned and popular media.

Margery Kempe did not live in a nonliterate society; books (although she could not read them herself) were an important part of her world. But she did live without newspapers or

16. Peter Abelard, for example, wrote his "letter" to explain his mistakes and tragedies in a manner that would help him to go on with his life, to make sense of the troubles that plagued him, to find meaningful roots for present unhappiness, and to reorder his past in ways that satisfied his understanding of God, of the world, and of himself. See Mary M. McLaughlin, "Abelard as Autobiographer: The Motives and Meaning of His 'Story of Calamities.' "

television, and her book testifies to her ample recollection of
Scripture and devotional writings. In his valuable article on
the piety of Margery Kempe, Anthony Goodman referred to her
"shafts of recollection,"[17] her literal recall of what was read or
preached to her. Phrases from Scripture and images from devotional works learned "by heart" crop up everywhere in her
thoughts and conversation. When she was satisfied with her
spiritual progress, she remembered "the sentence of Saint Paul;
'To them that love God, all things turneth into goodness'. So it
fared with her" (p. 159).

Margery's recollection of words and phrases preached in
sermons or used in conversation, like her recollection of Scripture,
can reasonably be assumed to be very good. The more formal
speech in her book—the language used by Christ in the colloquies and by her spiritual advisers (as Goodman says, "the
grave but familiar tones of the Lynn elite")[18] is consistent with
the language of contemporary sermons and other writings. In
Margery's conversation with Julian of Norwich, reported in
some detail, the style as well as the content of their talk is
compatible with what we know of Julian.[19] The casual speech
of family and neighbors seems also to be authentic in vocabulary and imagery, although its accuracy cannot be tested.
Margery's account of her meeting with Julian can be compared
with the ideas and language of Julian's own writings, while the
character and words of John Kempe are known only through
his wife's book. But much of his talk, too, is reassuringly
"natural" and psychologically appropriate—for example, the
conversation in which Margery finally succeeded in persuad-
ing him to give up their sexual relationship. John opened that
discussion with this question: "Margery, if there came a man
with a sword, who would strike off my head, unless I should

17. Anthony Goodman, "The Piety of John Brunham's Daughter, of Lynn,"
p. 349.

18. *Ibid.*, p. 350.

19. Edmund Colledge, O. S.A., and James Walsh, S. J., eds., *A Book of
Showings to the Anchoress Julian of Norwich*, 1:35–36.

commune naturally with you as I have done before, tell me on your conscience—for ye say ye will not lie—whether ye would suffer my head to be smitten off, or whether ye would suffer me to meddle with you again, as I did at one time?" (p. 16). This is exactly the kind of gambit that might be attempted by a man trying to corner a tough adversary, a man who wanted an opportunity to say—as John did, when he heard his wife's answer—"Ye are no good wife" (p. 16). It has all the childish desperation of chronic marital argument.

Margery Kempe was not overly concerned with her memory, or with the chronology of her book, which she freely admitted was imperfect. She set forth her experiences "not written in order, each thing after another as it was done, but like as the matter came to the creature in mind when it should be written; for it was so long ere it was written that she had forgotten the time and the order when things befell" (p. 237). Despite the disclaimer, her book is impressive not only for its fullness and detail, but—where it can be checked—for its accuracy.[20] But of course it cannot always be checked, and we do depend on her recollection. Even more than most mental functions, memory is subject to the strains and stresses of psychic conflict; what we remember (and forget) is determined by our needs, defense mechanisms, and feelings of pain and pleasure. Psychologists have established by experiment what was long known by observation and intuition, that memory is profoundly affected by intense emotion. As David Rapaport explains in *Emotions and Memory*, more is involved than the recall of names and numbers: " 'emotional factors' may not only quantitatively facilitate or inhibit remembering, or result in forgetting. They were found to organize the emerging memories, condensing, distorting, and symbolically replacing them. They were found to lend persist-

20. Hope Emily Allen, who with Sanford Meech checked every verifiable statement in the *Book*, spoke of Margery's "instinctive and zealous honesty" and of her "superior realism and apparently exceptional desire for veracity" (Meech and Allen, *Margery Kempe*, pp. xv, 289).

ence to certain ideas, impelling them steadily into consciousness in an obsessive fashion."[21]

The memories of Margery Kempe were determined by "emotional factors," or strong feelings—feelings of love and shame, grief and joy. She remembered her colloquies with Christ, perhaps word for word as they came to her, because these touched the deep center of her spiritual life. She vividly recounted her first experience of childbirth, with its traumatic pain and fear. Quite apart from what she neglected to say, chose to ignore, or consciously distorted, inevitably there was much that she forgot. But what she did remember and recount was the story of a life—an inner as well as an outer life, the events of the outer life shaped in retrospect by the forces of memory and emotion. The manifestations of the inner life—the psychic center of a human being—are "truly", represented in the selective processes of memory, as in dream and fantasy, even if we are not always able to understand or interpret them.[22]

Unlike most autobiographers, Margery Kempe had a close check on her unaided memory. She dictated to scribes—men who knew her well, knew her circumstances, and presumably could intervene if they recognized distortion or inaccuracy. The first part of her autobiography, Book I, with eighty-nine chapters, was written down by one scribe; Book II, with ten chapters, by the other, who rewrote the first book before he brought the story up to date in the second. The two books are asymmetrical; Book I is not only many times longer, but fuller in detail and richer in mystical colloquies. The two parts were separated, not by logical or literary considerations, but by the death of the first scribe. Book I begins with Margery's marriage and illness, her early meditations and mystical experiences. It has a long central section (seventeen chapters) on her pilgrimages, and another (eleven chapters) concerning the various charges

21. David Rapaport, *Emotions and Memory*, p. 270.
22. See Christine Downing, "Re-Visioning Autobiography."

of heresy and troublemaking that she endured back in England. Meditations and colloquies are scattered throughout, especially densely in the latter part of Book I. Book II, in a more hurried and relatively terse style, tells of her son's visit and death, of Margery's journey to Prussia with her daughter-in-law, which became a pilgrimage to Wilsnak and Aachen, and of her return to England. It ends abruptly with her return to Lynn, and an "appendix" describes her method of saying her more formal prayers.

The first scribe was an Englishman living in Germany who knew Margery well; he lived with her when he came to England with his wife and child. This man did not write well in English or German; his spelling and handwriting were confused and illegible. Book II begins with the story of Margery's son, who had moved to Germany, married a German woman, and returned to England to visit his parents. He had spent a dissipated youth, but had reformed through his mother's efforts and prayers. He became ill the day after he returned home, and died at his parents' house after a month's illness.

The coincident circumstances of the son and the first scribe have inspired the natural suggestion that they were the same person.[23] They were both Englishmen, married and living in Germany, who knew Margery well and lived with her, and they died within a short time of one another, if not in the same year. The coincidence is striking but not conclusive. Many natives of Lynn lived and did business in Germany, and Margery would have been acquainted with those who shared her religious interests. Moreover, it is difficult to imagine why she would not have identified the scribe as her son, for she believed her book to be a holy work of spiritual benefit for those associated with it, and she liked to take credit for her son's reformation and good works. Moreover, if the account of his death is accurate, he was

23. The suggestion was first made to Hope Allen by Joan Wake in a letter of December 13, 1935 (in the Hope Emily Allen papers at the Bryn Mawr College Archives).

at home for only one month and was ill the entire time. Whoever the first scribe was, he played a significant part in the making of the book. Because the work was entirely rewritten by his successor, his influence has been discounted, but it is likely that this man—a layman who lived in Margery's house—was close enough to her to be important in the selection (and perhaps the recollection) of episodes. He probably was an encouraging listener, a source of support and confidence, and his enthusiasm may have nourished the full and lively character of Book I.

The second scribe (also unnamed) was a priest who began to rewrite Book I in 1436, four years after he first tried to read it and to think about working on it. During the period when he could not or would not read the text, Margery believed that he was afraid to be associated with her, for she was much criticized at that period. Convinced by his conscience, and by reading certain holy lives (see below), he finally did read and rewrite Book I. In 1438, when he began to write Book II at Margery's dictation, there were further difficulties: "his eyes failed so that he might not see to make his letters and could not see to mend his pen. Everything else he could see well enough" (p. 237). Persuaded by Margery to trust God and herself, he recovered his sight and wrote Book II. In its brevity, it seems rather an afterthought, as if the priest were not eager to persist much longer in his task. It may be, of course, that Margery herself was ill or worn out; she was about sixty-five years old in 1438, and had not had an easy life. She may also have been inhibited (as she was not with the first scribe) by the priest's authority, or by his anxiety.

Her second scribe was literate, if not learned, and had a substantial investment in Margery's behavior, reputation, and credibility. In flagrant opposition to accepted standards of pastoral theology (see discussion below, Chapter 4), he encouraged her to perform wonders: to predict the future, and to pronounce on the character of various strangers. Margery, described as "loath and unwilling to do such things" (p. 45), gave in to his requests because he threatened not to write unless she "proved" her inspiration. Apparently, neither Margery nor her scribe was sufficiently confident to "prove the spirits" as Lady Julian advised, by observing their fruits in the life of the visionary; they shared a rather crude interpretation of 1 John 4:1 ("Beloved, do not believe every spirit, but test the spirits to see whether they are of God; for many false prophets have gone out into the world"). In Chapters 24 and 25 of Book I, the priest becomes a character in Margery's trials and appears in an ambiguous light. He was not her confessor, thus not technically bound by rules for confessors, but his threats, indecisiveness, and encouragement of her more sensational abilities show him concerned less for her soul than for his own career and reputation. In these and other respects he differed from biographers of other medieval holy women, lacking their dignity as well as their distance. In fact, of course, he was not a biographer but a scribe—a difficult, and perhaps more compromising, role.

Chapter 62 of Book I describes one of Margery's severer trials. She was excluded from the sermons of a visiting Franciscan preacher on account of her loud crying, which disrupted the service and annoyed the friar. She became more than ever an object of public shame, and the preacher was obdurate; he would not relent even when Margery's clerical friends visited him with "wine to cheer him" (p. 137) and argued that her crying came from God and was not in her control. Rejecting their pleas, the friar not only excluded Margery but promised to "shame her maintainers" (p. 139) as well. Such a threat from so influential a person intimidated the half-hearted, including the second scribe, who turned against her.

According to Margery (and presumably also to the fickle scribe, who wrote the story), God then acted—through a book— to bring him back to her side. The central issue at that moment was Margery's tears—whether they were a mark of grace or of insanity, illness, or troublemaking. The priest was convinced in their favor by reading accounts of other holy tears, especially those of Marie d'Oignies, a thirteenth-century beguine whose

biography had been written by Jacques de Vitry.[24] De Vitry's
Life of Marie includes a chapter that describes her loud and
uncontrollable weeping at the thought of the Passion or at
images of the Cross. When she tried to restrain her tears they
kept increasing, until she was ordered by a priest of her church
to be quiet. She asked God to teach the priest that no one can
withstand holy tears, and on that very day, when he sang his
mass, he was nearly drowned by floods of tears which soaked
his book and his altar cloth. Then he learned to respect "Christ's
handmaiden" and to believe that the gift of tears could not be
resisted.[25]

Margery's scribe was given the story to read, or to reread and
consider, by a man described as a "worshipful clerk, a bachelor
of divinity" (p. 140). (The entire controversy must have been
interesting to pious people in Lynn; obviously the clergy took
sides.) The priest took the *Life* of Marie very seriously, and
pursued the subject of tears through other religious writings.
These works, which are named in Chapter 62 of Book I, reassured him of Margery's orthodoxy.[26] He may also have wished
to emulate de Vitry, who was a bishop and later a cardinal.

24. The *Life* of Marie is available in a Middle English translation of de
Vitry's text, edited by Carl Horstmann, "Prosalegenden: Die Legenden des ms.
Douce 114," *Anglia* 8: 102–196. The Latin version (quoted by Margery's
scribe) is available in *Acta sanctorum*, 25:547–572. For discussions of de
Vitry's writings and career, see Brenda M. Bolton, "Mulieres sanctae," and
idem., "Vitae Matrum."

25. Jacques de Vitry, "Vita Maria Oigniacensis," 551.

26. The priest read "in a tretys whech is clepyd 'Þe Prykke of Lofe,' þe ij
chapitulo þat Bone-auentur wrot of hym-selfe þes wordys folwyng, 'A, Lord,
what xal I mor noysen er cryen? Þu lettyst & þu comyst not, & I, wery &
ouyrcome thorw desyr, begynne for to maddyn, for lofe gouernyth me & not
reson. I renne wyth hasty cowrs wher- þat-euyr þu wylte. I bowe, Lord, þei þat
se me irkyn and rewyn, not knowyng me drunkyn wyth þi lofe. Lord, þei
seyn, "Lo, ȝen wood man cryeth in þe stretys," but how meche is þe desyr of
myn hert þei parceyue not.' & capitulo Stimulo Amoris & capitulo ut supra.
He red also of Richard Hampol, hermyte, in Incendio Amoris leche mater þat
meuyd hym to ȝeuyn credens to' þe sayd creatur. Also, Eliȝabeth of Hungry
cryed wyth lowde voys, as is wretyn in hir tretys" (Meech and Allen, *Margery
Kempe*, pp. 153–154).

Marie d'Oignies was only one of the European holy women whose stories were available in fifteenth-century England (their character and influence are discussed in Chapter 6 below). But the *Life* of Marie, like most of these works, is very unlike *The Book of Margery Kempe*. It is not an autobiography but a biography in the hagiographic mode, and it begins with the saintly infancy of the subject, who belonged to the Lord from her mother's womb, rarely played childish games, and exemplified from the beginning her eventual sanctity.[27] Margery's book, in contrast, relates the conversion of a sinner. Both works are divided into two parts, but are otherwise quite different in structure. Each section of the *Life* of Marie has thirteen chapters; the first section moves from her birth and childhood through her marriage and early trials to her graces (including tears) and ascetic practices. In the second section her virtues are discussed, then her coming to Oignies, her final sickness, and her holy death. The structure of the work is balanced, orderly, chronological, and consistent in voice and tone.

The *Life* of Marie was very important for both Margery and her scribe—particularly for the latter, since it convinced him that religious tears were irresistible and persuaded him to write. It also presented a model of a married lay woman of unimpeachable life, a woman whose habits and circumstances were quite similar to Margery's and whose sanctity was recorded by an eminent churchman. Of course, it may also have influenced, consciously or unconsciously, the selection of materials for the *Book*: for example, Margery's repeated efforts to wear white (at God's command) and the controversy surrounding that issue may have been reiterated to point up her likeness to Marie, who wore a white woolen coat and mantle.[28] It cannot have escaped anyone's attention that Marie lived in chastity with her husband, also named John.

Unlike most of the literary, religious, and social influences

27. De Vitry, "Vita Maria," 551.
28. *Ibid.*, p. 555.

on Margery Kempe and her book, that of the *Life* of Marie d'Oignies is clear, specific, and easy to document. It is much more difficult to measure the influence of the life and writings of Saint Birgitta of Sweden. The story of Birgitta and her legend and cult in fifteenth-century England, and its relation to the world of Margery Kempe, will be examined in the context of contemporary female sanctity in Chapter 6 below. But the "literary" influence of her *Revelations*, while it cannot be isolated from other factors, is relevant here in relation to the creation of Margery's book.

"Bride's book" was mentioned several times in Margery's; the two works were explicitly associated in veracity and divine origin. God said: "For I tell thee forsooth, right as I spoke to Saint Bride, right so I speak to thee, daughter, and I tell thee truly that it is true, every word that is written in Bride's book, and by thee it shall be known for very truth" (p. 38). Birgitta's visions were written down by the saint in Swedish and translated into Latin by one of her amanuenses. They were translated into English several times during the fifteenth century; seven such manuscripts survive, and undoubtedly there were others. The ones we have were abridged or abbreviated, some drastically, so that we do not know exactly what Margery meant by "Bride's book."[29] However, we do assume that all the English translations shared the subject, and to some extent the style, of the original. The visions, often expressed symbolically or allegorically, are grand in scale; many are concerned with international political and ecclesiastical questions remote from the simple scriptural stories and local happenings that interested Margery Kempe. They are presented in separate episodes without much connecting tissue; there is a good deal of repetition, and no overarching scheme. In this respect, at least, Margery's book resembles "Bride's."

Despite Birgitta's international reputation, she was not a

29. The Middle English translations of the *Revelations* are described in *The Revelations of Saint Birgitta*, ed. William Patterson Cumming, pp. xvi–xxi.

remote figure like the authors of other works read to Margery, but another woman as well as a great saint. When Margery went to Rome in 1414 (forty-one years after Birgitta's death), she looked for places and objects associated with the saint and spoke to Birgitta's maid and her landlord, who told her that Birgitta had been, "ever homely and kind to all creatures that would speak with her" (p. 82)—that is, approachable. Margery visited the saint's death chamber, where a German priest preached about her life and revelations. She could kneel "on the stone on which Our Lord appeared to Saint Bridget" (p. 82), an experience of numinous power for a medieval pilgrim.

It is not surprising that survivors of Birgitta's *famiglia* were busy keeping alive the saint's memory in Rome, because although she had been canonized in 1391, the process had to be confirmed in 1414 and again in 1419. The effects of the Schism, the politics of the Council of Constance, and the widespread concern over private relevations made it desirable to keep Birgitta's life and accomplishments before the pious public. Her followers, not content to press for canonization, were determined to win acceptance also for her rule and her order. When Margery returned to England from Prussia in 1434 she visited Syon Abbey, the first Birgittine convent in England. But the cult of Birgitta in England spread far beyond Syon; thanks to the political and ecclesiastical implications of certain of the *Revelations*, it was supported by the Lancastrian kings and by an enthusiastic coterie of English prelates.

Birgitta and her writings served as personal and religious as well as literary models for both Margery Kempe and her scribe. The official acceptance of the *Revelations*, as well as the popularity of the saint, were important factors in allowing Margery's book to be written at all. It has been suggested that Margery wanted to be England's Birgitta—an unlikely ambition, given the great differences in their social background, education, and personalities. It is more to the point that devout lay and clerical people in England had taken the Swedish saint to their hearts, and that Birgitta's writings made visionary women and their literary productions more than respectable. (Shared themes in the lives and writings of these very different women are discussed in Chapter 6.)

Despite the example of the *Life* of Marie, and the profound influence of the life and *Revelations* of Birgitta, *The Book of Margery Kempe* is an autobiography: the story of a life told by its subject. De Vitry's work was less a model than a proof-text; it reassured Margery's scribe, but his own undertaking was very different. He was not writing the life of a saint (or a would-be saint) from the outside, but writing down what Margery told him, more in the manner of Birgitta's amanuenses than of Marie's biographer. Margery (like Birgitta) was commanded by God to tell her story, and her scribes were necessary instruments, not leading spirits in the enterprise. The second scribe had to be cajoled and manipulated before he would write at all.

Margery's book was shaped by all kinds of influences and pressures on her memory and motivations, but it was essentially hers. However, the priest, who was always anxious to protect her reputation and enhance his own, undoubtedly introduced his concerns, and in some cases his learning and his opinions. For example, when Margery answered various accusations of heresy, she spoke in measured statements of careful orthodoxy. (Unlike Joan of Arc, she was never led into theological traps, but neither were her accusers as determined or unscrupulous as Joan's.) The scribe, who wanted her to appear perfectly orthodox, probably rephrased her accounts of these episodes. Such a shaping of the text can be assumed, particularly in doctrinal questions, without treating the book as the priest's creation. The relation of author and scribe in this work is complicated and uncertain, but it remains Margery's book, even if the shadowy scribal presence clouds the image in the mirror.

With all the questions that cannot finally be answered about *The Book of Margery Kempe*, the work nevertheless does provide a substantial basis for examination of the author's experience and environment. It reveals a great deal, not only about the inner life that is the first concern of spiritual autobiography, but about the people and events and institutions that filled and colored her world. Bearing in mind the unresolved issues of memory, influence, and motivation, I have accepted Margery's *Book* primarily as the product of her own experience and imagination. We discover the unique person, Margery Kempe, in its pages, and even more about the forces that shaped her piety, her relationships, and her way of life. The work is her own, but like any literary creation, it is also—unmistakably— a product of its particular historical context.

In the chapters that follow, I shall approach Margery Kempe and her book from a variety of perspectives. I shall begin where Margery began: with an attempt to establish the nature of her special vocation, her calling to be a mystic and a pilgrim, and of the ways in which she learned to know and love God. I shall turn next to her social and domestic environment: the family, class, and community that molded and educated her. Church and clergy played a central role in her experience of God and of this world, so a chapter is devoted to her relationship with the institution and its representatives. In Chapters 5 and 6 I shall examine the experience of Margery Kempe in relation to a tradition and a context: the tradition of affective piety and the context of late medieval female sanctity. And in conclusion, I shall review some of the ways in which *The Book of Margery Kempe* has been understood in the half-century since the manuscript was discovered and suggest some approaches that may help us to form our own interpretations of author and book.

1) Women not drunken, see Campbell's
    Masks of God :
    hunting — shamanic practice

2) _absorption_ into the One
      2
   until   ↳ climax with no
   only _like_   δατα ψυχη ἐνδυσιδιω̄σις?

              ↳ necessity of logical nature
                      (metaphysical)
              ↳ no removal of
                 subject and object

         if there is absorption, the (A)
   absorption ← there is no distinction
   of Plotinus   between subj. - object . (B)
         if not B, then not A

3). Sacred function versus profane(?)
      function — to oneself
         (primarily individualistic)

Chapter Two

"A HAIRCLOTH IN THY HEART"

Pilgrim and Mystic

MARGERY KEMPE was both a mystic and a pilgrim. She spoke directly with God and received the divine gift of tears, but she remained in the world and even traveled widely in the service of her vocation. As a "chosen soul" (p. 227), she was comforted and instructed through meditation and colloquy with divine beings. She had a clear sense of her calling and (much of the time) remarkable confidence as well as persistence in pursuing it. To appreciate her vocation and to understand her self-confidence, we must examine the ways in which she knew God's will and how she followed it.

Critics of Margery's book have differed: was she a "real" mystic, or simply a hysteric or a hypocrite? Obviously, the answer depends in part on what mysticism is believed to be. *The Oxford Dictionary of the Christian Church* defines it as "an immediate knowledge of God attained in this present life through personal religious experience. It is primarily a state of prayer, and as such admits of various degrees from short and rare divine 'touches' to a practically permanent union with God."[1] Margery "saw" events from Christ's life and took part in them. When she meditated on the Nativity or the Crucifixion, she did not "think about" Christ's birth or death but participated in them. She also received direct divine instruction about prayer and ascetic practices. She conversed at length with Jesus

---

1. *The Oxford Dictionary of the Christian Church* (London, 1974), p. 952.

and the Virgin; when she asked them questions, they answered. In lengthy colloquies, they described themselves and their relationship to her soul. The knowledge of God acquired by such means was an "immediate" one, "attained ... through personal religious experience." If we accept the definition above, Margery Kempe was a mystic.

The history of mysticism, and of Christian mysticism in particular, makes it easy to disagree about what a mystic is. To a great extent, Christian mysticism was based on ideas and experiences that arose in classical antiquity and were absorbed into early Christianity. Many Christian mystics have followed in the tradition known as "Dionysian," after the sixth-century Neoplatonist Pseudo-Dionysius. Their approach to knowledge of the divine and to mystical union is through the "*via negativa*," stripping away sense experience and the products of reason (thought, argument) until the bodily senses and mind of the believer are empty, and the soul is available to receive divine emanations. The theological focus is not on the divine attributes (for example, God is one), but on what God is not (for example, God is not material). Elements of Dionysian mysticism, particularly the effort to purge the self of the distractions of sense experience, are present in all forms of mysticism. But because of Christ's humanity, and because Christian beliefs about Creation and Incarnation do not permit either the world or human nature to be perceived as intrinsically evil or worthless, many Christian mystics have found different paths to union, using their senses, their emotions, and their reason to assist in the approach to God.

The emphasis on feeling in devotion, or "affective piety," will be discussed in Chapter 5 in relation to the tradition of piety to which Margery Kempe belonged. Some of the confusion over whether or not she was a "true" mystic derives from the existence of several traditions of Christian mysticism and from the tendency of church historians to regard Dionysian mysticism as "higher" or "purer" than other varieties (see Chapter 7 below). Margery Kempe was not a follower of the *via negativa.* Her intimate knowledge of God came primarily through meditation on the joys and sorrows of the human life and death of Jesus, in which her emotions helped her to participate in divine experience through the humanity she shared with Christ.

Most schemes used to describe the mystic's approach to God focus on the three "stages" of purgation, illumination, and union. (No scheme, of course, describes the experience of every mystic, neither is there a "typical" approach to God.) At the beginning—even before the purgative stage—the believer frequently experiences what Evelyn Underhill has called "the awakening of the transcendental consciousness"[2]—a vivid, well-defined, and joyful experience of a reality outside the self or the familiar world. In the language of mysticism the event is known as "conversion," although the subject may have been (and probably was) a faithful believer before it occurred. It is a conversion to a new state of consciousness, not to a system of belief.

Margery's first direct encounter with the divine took place when Christ visited her in her illness after childbirth. It was an intensely vivid and dramatic event; forty years later, when she wrote her book, she recounted his exact words, his expression, and the color of his mantle. The visit was accompanied by extraordinary visual phenomena which helped to fix it in her memory: "And anon, as He said these words, she saw verily how the air opened as bright as any lightning. And He rose up into the air, not right hastily and quickly, but fair and easily, so that she might well behold Him in the air till it was closed again" (p. 2). Margery was saved from madness by this experience, but she soon relapsed into worldliness. Her relapse was chastised by worldly failure, and she resolved to sin no more, but the resolution arose more from fear than from love of God: "Then this creature, seeing all these adversities coming on every side, thought they were the scourges of Our Lord that

2. Evelyn Underhill, *Mysticism*, p. 176.

would chastise her for her sin. Then she asked God's mercy, and forsook her pride, her covetousness, and the desire that she had for the worship of the world . . . " (p. 5).

Her true "conversion" began with a very different kind of experience, an event so profound that it altered her entire life:

> On a night, as this creature lay in her bed with her husband, she heard a sound of melody so sweet and delectable, that she thought she had been in Paradise, and therewith she started out of her bed and said:—
>
> "Alas, that ever I did sin! It is full merry in Heaven." [P. 5]

She suffered extraordinary trials and temptations afterward, but never turned again from her vocation to a special life. This was the critical experience of her conversion, and it is remarkable that it should have come to her in something as abstract as heavenly music. Although she was so closely attached to the human Jesus, and so dependent on his presence, this turning point (unlike every other religious experience she reports) was independent of "human" phenomena. Music and sound were familiar accompaniments of medieval mystical experience,[3] but it is surprising that melody alone, without words or reassurance or splendid scenes, precipitated her conversion.

After an initial experience of the divine, or at some early stage in their journey, most mystics undergo a period of purgation or purification. The "awakening," which reveals the enormous distance between human and divine, fills the mystic with consciousness of sin and finitude. She attempts to free herself from the worldly objects, feelings, and habits that impede progress toward the divine. Poverty, chastity, and obedience are valued because they permit and encourage detachment from the things of the world and the former self. Mortification, even great suffering, is welcomed because it burns away the physical, social, and intellectual trappings that burden the soul's ascent. Purgation is a deliberate attitude and

---

3. See, for example, Richard Rolle, *The Fire of Love*, pp. 147–154.

process, and it continues through the mystic's life, although it is most important and central to the beginner.

After Margery's conversion, her attitudes and behavior underwent radical and permanent change. First, her fear was more and more replaced by love of God and yearning for Heaven: "This melody was so sweet that it surpassed all melody that ever might be heard ... and caused her ... to have full plenteous and abundant tears of high devotion, with great sobbings and sighings after the bliss of Heaven.... Ever after this inspiration, she had in her mind the mirth and the melody that was in Heaven ... " (p. 5). (The word "inspiration" above is a weak translation of "drawt" in the text, for it fails to convey the sense of pulling, or call, implied in the original.)[4]

The event precipitated a period of strict penitence, of turning away from the world and the flesh, of mortification undertaken for love of Heaven: "And also, after this creature heard this heavenly melody, she did great bodily penance. She was shriven sometimes twice or thrice a day" (p. 6). At this time Margery began to despise the sexual relationship with her husband, to wear a haircloth, and to fast and pray as much as the circumstances of her life allowed.

In the Christian tradition, temptation, as well as penitence, is part of the purgative stage of mystical experience. There is an outstanding model in the life of Christ, who not only fasted and prayed in the wilderness after his baptism, but was tempted by the devil before he returned to his ministry. Margery, too, when she (mistakenly) felt she had defeated the pull of the world, was shocked and humbled by fierce new temptations: "The first two years when this creature was thus drawn to Our Lord, she had great quiet in spirit from any temptations.... Our Merciful Lord Jesus Christ, seeing this creature's presumption, sent her ... three years of great temptation ... " (pp. 7–8).

---

4. "& euyr aftyr þis drawt sche had in hir mende þe myrth & þe melodye þat was in Heuen" (Meech and Allen, *Margery Kempe*, p. 11).

Margery's particular temptation was to "lechery," with a man other than her husband. She struggled for two or three years despite all her efforts to overcome the sin by prayer and penitence. Humiliation added to her misery: the man rejected her, and she "went away all shamed and confused in herself at seeing his stability and her own instability" (p. 9). Her shame and sorrow were terrible, for she was "as far from feelings of grace, as they that never felt any, and that she could not bear, and so she gave way to despair" (p. 9). But although she despaired, she did not revert even temporarily to the person she had been before she heard the heavenly music. Even when she felt little except pain and failure, she remained "drawn" to God.

As the spiritual life progresses, the mystic is rewarded more frequently with "gleams of ecstatic vision,"[5] although periods of ecstasy or illumination may be mingled with bitter periods of despair and aridity (sometimes termed "the dark night of the senses"). More and more often, however, come the joys of illumination, marked by a consistent awareness of a reality beyond that of every day. There may be heightening of physical perceptions and a new intuitional energy expressed in hearing or seeing manifestations of the divine, which may be auditory or visual "signs and wonders." The self is not merged with God, but remains separate and self-conscious.

For Margery, the terrible period of purgation and trial ended when Christ came to her in church and promised her the bliss of Heaven. In this first extended colloquy, she was assured and reassured of her own goodness. She advanced from the harsh novitiate of the beginner, acted out primarily in external behavior, to the inner education of the more advanced. She was promised "a haircloth in thy heart" (p. 10) to replace the haircloth on her back and promoted to direct divine instruction in spiritual matters.

Despite the initial wonderful melody, Margery did not often

5. Underhill, *Mysticism*, p. 226.

dwell on "signs and wonders" received by the physical senses—generally, such manifestations frightened her. Once she saw the Host flutter at the Consecration, when God used that method to foretell an earthquake, but she made little of the matter (and there is no record of an earthquake). On another occasion she foretold by way of a sweet smell the return of a good prior to Lynn: "Our Lord said unto her:—'By this sweet smell, thou mayest well know that there shall, in a short time, be a new Prior in Lynne, and it shall be he who was last removed hence'" (p. 156). Occasionally she did hear sounds and melodies: "Sometimes she heard with her bodily ears such sounds and melodies that she could not well hear what a man said to her at that time, unless he spoke the louder. These sounds and melodies had she heard nearly every day for the term of twenty-five years, when this book was written, and especially when she was in devout prayer..." (p. 75). Her eyes, as well as her nose and ears, perceived wonders: "She saw with her bodily eyes many white things flying all about her on every side, as thick, in a manner, as specks in a sunbeam.... She saw them many divers times and in many divers places, both in church and in her chamber, at her meat, and at her prayers, in the fields, and in town, both going and sitting" (p. 75). Sweetness and sounds were fairly common mystical delights; the "white things" were unusual. They alarmed her until God reassured her that they were tokens "that there are many angels about thee" (p. 76).

Many mystics (including Margery's near-contemporary Richard Rolle) experienced feelings of supernatural warmth. For "about sixteen years" Margery felt "a flame of fire, wondrous hot and delectable, and right comfortable, ... she felt the heat burning in her breast and at her heart..." (p. 76). She was afraid of the heat too until God explained that "this heat is the heat of the Holy Ghost, which shall burn away all thy sins; for the fire of love quencheth all sins" (p. 76). Rolle had conceived of the fire not as consuming sin but as indicating that "the mind is truly ablaze with eternal love."[6] Margery mentioned heat again as part of the holy joy of writing her book, when "oftentimes there came a flame of fire about her breast, full hot and delectable" (p. 198).

These physical manifestations of "illumination" were not central to Margery's experience: her colloquies with God were much more important. She knew that supernatural sights and sounds were only aids to draw her closer to God, but she appreciated them when they did not frighten her. Once she was much comforted by touching Christ in a dream, and "she thought she took His toes in her hand and felt them, and to her feeling, it was as if they had been very flesh and bone" (p. 190). She thanked God, realizing that such experiences helped her to approach the divine through the sacred humanity. Unlike mystics in the Dionysian tradition, Margery was glad and grateful for any link to God, whether physical, emotional, or "ghostly" (spiritual).

The essential aspect of Margery's experience of the divine was her direct communication with God, in meditation and in what she usually called "teaching," when God spoke to her. Much of what she learned was ineffable—so powerful, so far above her understanding that she could never repeat it. If she spoke to her confessor right after a contemplation she could tell him about it, but very soon she "forgot" what she had learned. (The same phenomenon is true of dreams, which often are forgotten unless they are told or written down immediately.) Like dream-experience and dream-metaphor, Margery's ways of learning and knowing God were not entirely available to the analytic processes of reason.

In descriptive schemes of the mystic's progress through the purgative, illuminative, and unitive "stages" of ascent to God, the illuminative period of joy, growth, and increasing mastery of the self is followed by the condition known to Saint John of the Cross as "the Dark Night of the Soul." The Dark Night is

6. Rolle, *Fire of Love*, p. 89.

characterized by fatigue, despair, and consciousness of God's absence. The illuminative gifts are withdrawn, and the soul suffers alone through cold and silence. The Night precedes and makes possible the final surrender to the will of God which marks the death of the self, and the true union which may be symbolized in mystical marriage—the passionate and permanent love affair and merging of God and the soul. The most vivid allegorical expression of the mystical marriage, in the Middle Ages, was the *Song of Songs*, an enormously popular subject of sermon and commentary.[7] Its erotic language and marriage metaphor were familiar and comfortable ways for medieval people to think about intense religious experience.

There is no evidence in Margery's book of any experience comparable to Saint John's "Dark Night of the Soul." After her conversion, she was never very far from God, but neither was her soul "merged" with the divine. She always retained a separate, commenting self with an active will, and with powerful emotions with which to love God and seek Heaven. Her "wedding to the Godhead," which took place while she prayed in one of the great Roman churches, was thoroughly characteristic of Margery's individual style of piety and not at all typical of a mystical marriage. In the first place, she resisted the proposal, "for she was full sore afraid of the Godhead; and she had no knowledge of the dalliance of the Godhead, for all her love and all her affection were set in the manhood of Christ . . . and she would not for anything be parted therefrom" (p. 74). Christ had to apologize to his Father for Margery's reluctance. The wedding took place, despite her fears, among an assembly of saints and angels, and Margery thanked God for "His ghostly comfort, holding herself, in her own feeling, right unworthy to any such grace as she felt" (p. 75). In this episode, the language of a contemporary English wedding service was combined with

7. For a discussion of interpretations of the *Song of Songs* in medieval English mysticism, see Wolfgang Riehle, *The Middle English Mystics*, pp. 34–55.

the common visual imagery of a mystical wedding (frequently portrayed in paint and glass)[8] to denote the spiritual reality of union with God in terms available to the imagination of Margery Kempe. Margery was a unique individual, and while the conventional "stages" of the mystic's progress toward God illuminate her story, they do not describe the totality of her experience.

Every mystic, and indeed every medieval Christian with aspirations to holiness, respected and tried to observe the ascetic practices modeled for them by monks and nuns. Fasting, regular prayer, and celibacy were minimum requirements of the religious life; moderate forms of these were expected of devout lay persons, and a more rigorous mortification of the flesh was required of saints. Ascetic practices nourished Margery's faith while they distinguished her from "worldly" persons. She regarded such observances as privilege, not deprivation, never questioning their value.

After her conversion, Margery longed so much for the "bliss" of Heaven that she adopted as strict a way of life as possible. "She gave herself up to great fasting and great watching; she rose at two or three of the clock, and went to church, and was there at her prayers unto the time of noon and also all the afternoon" (p. 6). Obviously this regime conflicted directly with her old way of life and her social role: as her contemporary, the "Goodman of Paris," pointed out to his wife, married women were not supposed to rise for matins.[9] A woman who identifies herself primarily as the mother of fourteen children cannot spend every morning and afternoon in church. Margery's vocation was not compatible with (active) marriage or motherhood, and she

8. Margery was in Italy during the "Venetian Process" of the canonization of St. Catherine of Siena, who had experienced a mystical wedding to Christ. For a study of the canonization, see Robert Fawtier, *Sainte Catherine de Sienne*. For a brief discussion of some medieval descriptions and paintings of the mystical weddings of Catherine of Siena and Katherine of Alexandria, see Paul Carus, *The Bride of Christ*, pp. 53–107.

9. *The Goodman of Paris*, p. 47.

put on her new life in concrete ways to deal with the concrete realities of her situation. When she wore a haircloth, she "laid it in her kirtle as secretly and privily as she might, so that her husband should not espy it. Nor did he, and she lay by him every night in his bed and wore the hair-cloth every day, and bore children in the time" (p. 6). Not yet permitted to live apart, she made herself—and her husband—as different (and uncomfortable) as possible. All her ascetic practices (fasting, spending the day in church and the night in prayer, wearing the haircloth) separated her physically from John Kempe's bed and board. Release from his bed was more important than from his board: before John agreed to chastity, he made her promise not only to pay his debts but to "eat and drink with [him] on the Friday as ye were wont to do" (p. 17). Margery took that dilemma to God, who agreed that breaking the Friday fast was less important than winning her freedom from the marital bond.

Despite her close attention to external signs, Christ's instruction to Margery Kempe was consistently directed inward, toward the true religion of the heart. Outward signs had great value in the establishment of her new life, but Christ's teaching placed obedience, and communion with himself, over formal acts: "Fasting, daughter, is good for young beginners, and discreet penance. . . . And to bid many beads is good for those that can do no better, yet it is not perfect. . . . I have oftentimes told thee, daughter, that thinking, weeping, and high contemplation is the best life on earth, and thou shalt have more merit in Heaven for one year of thinking in thy mind than for a hundred years of praying with thy mouth. . . . " (pp. 76–77).

Weekly Communion was a special privilege for a lay person in the fifteenth century, and Margery worked very hard to make good her claim to it. Frequent Communion was not only a source of grace but also, like celibacy, a mark of religious distinction. She received the permission of the archbishop of Canterbury to "choose her confessor and to be houselled every Sunday" (p. 38), and she managed weekly Communion even in foreign cities and under difficult circumstances.

Margery Kempe's religion was not one of works-righteousness; good deeds and pious practices were subordinated to contemplation and to love of God. But the message of the Gospel was not neglected. In Rome, her confessor ordered her to serve a poor old woman, and she did so for six weeks "as she would have done Our Lady; . . . and when the poor woman's wine was sour, this creature herself drank that sour wine, and gave the poor woman good wine that she had brought for her own self" (p. 74). When she demurred at going home to care for her sick husband, Christ said: "Thou shalt have as much reward for keeping him and helping him in his need at home, as if thou wert in church, making thy prayers. Thou hast said many times thou wouldst fain keep Me. I pray thee now keep him for the love of Me . . . " (p. 165).

Inner and outer habits and practices worked together in Margery's religious life. Before she went to Jerusalem she was ordered by Jesus to wear white clothes, and she did so, although she was afraid of the scorn and ridicule they provoked: "They will say I am a hypocrite and wonder at me" (p. 24). She tried to persuade Bishop Repington of Lincoln to clothe her in white, and Repington argued that she should wait until after her pilgrimage. At that point Jesus intervened, telling Margery to "say to the Bishop that he dreadeth more the shames of the world than the perfect love of God" (p. 27). The bishop was ambivalent, for although he did not agree to her request, he did give her money to buy her clothes and ask her to pray for him.[10]

The issue of the white clothes, which obviously had great

10. Hope Allen mentioned that in 1399, by order of Richard II and Parliament, a white-robed sect was forbidden to enter the country. These probably were the Flagellant "Bianchi," or "Albi," who traveled from France to Italy in the wake of an outbreak of plague in the 1390s, creating confusion and antagonizing orthodox churchmen wherever they went. That the group was known and feared in England is clear from the prohibition, but as Allen suggests, it is unlikely that Margery Kempe was involved with them. She was not a Flagellant, and she was not part of any group. See Meech and Allen, *Margery Kempe*, p. 314. (For a vivid description of the "Bianchi," see Iris Origo, *The Merchant of Prato*, pp. 319–325.)

symbolic significance for Margery and for her acquaintances, was never finally settled. When she was alone and afraid (and had recently been persecuted for her eccentricity), she bargained with God about the clothes, promising to wear them "if Thou bringest me to Rome in safety" (p. 64). The clothes made her conspicuous; she was, after all, a married woman, and the archbishop of York (for one) asked the obvious question: "Why goest thou in white? Art thou a maiden?" (p. 111). It was one of the practices that made Margery's life difficult, tried her self-confidence, and set her apart as peculiar or unique.

Whiteness had (and still has) a specific meaning and value in Christian symbolism. In colloquy Jesus told Margery: "Moreover, thou thinkest that the Holy Ghost sitteth on a white cushion, for thou thinkest that He is full of love and purity, and therefore it beseemeth Him to sit on a white cushion, for He is the giver of all holy thoughts and chastity" (p. 192). White was a symbol of purity, particularly of sexual purity, as well as of holiness. The question was not about the meaning of the color, but about whether Margery was entitled to wear it. Symbolic rites and costumes are reserved, in any society, for those who have gone through the stipulated training, discipline, and initiation. Margery was a married woman, not a nun: her insistence on the clothes, and the resentment they aroused, were outward expressions of the singularity of her calling.

Margery Kempe was a pilgrim: indeed, pilgrimage was an essential aspect of her vocation. She was a typical medieval pilgrim in that she traveled to greater and lesser shrines to venerate relics, to commemorate the lives and deaths of Christ and the saints, and to expiate her sins. Pilgrimage reflected her devotion to the sacred humanity of Christ and her desire to share in his Passion. She also went to visit experts in the spiritual life—to seek assurance, holy conversation, and special opportunities for religious experience. And pilgrimage permitted her to exist, when she first left home, within what Victor and Edith Turner have described as "liminal" space in which customary social, domestic, and even geographic restrictions are suspended.[11] Her great pilgrimage made an excellent transition from the old life to the new.

In the late Middle Ages, pilgrimage became increasingly popular and accessible to new groups of people. More middle-class people traveled, and there were more female pilgrims than there had been since the time of Paula and Egeria a thousand years before. The growing number of women pilgrims attracted attention and some criticism. Their motives were scrutinized, and opponents of women's pilgrimage fell into two predictable groups: those who felt that most women were not serious pilgrims, and those who "worried" that they would be crushed or stampeded in the crowds around the relics.[12] The most famous female pilgrim in medieval literature, Chaucer's Wife of Bath, obviously fell into the first group; she was not much edified by her travels:

> And thries hadde she been at Jerusalem;
> She hadde passed many a straunge strem;
> At Rome she hadde been, and at Boloigne,
> In Galice at Seint Jame, and at Coloigne.
> She koude muchel of wandrynge by the weye.
> Gat-tothed was she, soothly for to seye.[13]

By the fifteenth century, the ancient tradition of visiting the relics of the saints and the places where Jesus lived and died

11. Victor Turner and Edith Turner, *Image and Pilgrimage in Christian Culture*, p. 7; see esp. chap. 1.

12. In *Pilgrimage*, pp. 261–262, Jonathan Sumption describes the increase in the number of female pilgrims in the later Middle Ages. He states that the "fickle tastes of women seem to have been partly responsible for the abrupt rise of obscure shrines" and reports that women were excluded from certain shrines attached to monastic churches (which may explain their interest in "obscure" shrines!). Sumption says it was feared that "the weaker sex," especially those who were pregnant, would be trampled by the crowds. This rationale resembles the antisuffragist theory that frail or pregnant women might be "trampled" at the polls.

13. *The Complete Works of Geoffrey Chaucer*, p. 24.

had been reinvigorated by a burgeoning interest in travel and in foreign places. The popularity of *Mandeville's Travels* from its first appearance in 1357 reflected a growing fascination with the strange. Curiosity, repeatedly condemned by preachers, played a large part in the wanderings that occurred in the fifteenth century and by the end of the century was a major factor in the beginning of the great age of European exploration and discovery. In Margery Kempe's time, however, the major outlets for the curious remained the beaten tracks of Christian history. But pilgrims as well as other travelers were more and more interested in what they saw and heard along the way, and as literacy increased (still more after the invention and spread of printing), they began to write about their experiences.[14] Margery Kempe, however, was no John Mandeville; she wrote about places and people only as they touched her own concerns. When she mentioned "the great town of Zierikzee," for example, it was to report that she cried "abundant tears of contrition" (p. 50) there.

Margery Kempe was a part of this new movement insofar as her opportunity to travel arose from circumstances she shared with other middle-class people of her time. But her motivation was not at all "modern": a true medieval pilgrim, she longed to see and to touch the relics and reminders of Christ's life on earth. Devoted to the human Jesus, she wanted to stand where he had stood. Unlike many of her contemporaries, she was not much interested in foreign places for themselves. She hated and feared sea travel and in fact was never very happy or secure outside of England. But that was of little account: discomfort was part of the imitation of Christ, and spiritual health much more important than a good bed free of lice and fleas.

Soon after her first "contemplations," Margery "was urged in her soul to go and visit certain places for ghostly health" (p. 15). She and her husband visited local shrines, including

---

14. A number of late medieval pilgrims left diaries, guidebooks, phrase books, and manuals of advice for their successors. For a full bibliography of these see Sumption, *Pilgrimage*, pp. 355–378.

York and Bridlington, where Margery spoke with local clergy and holy anchorites and recluses. In nearby Norwich, she visited the saintly vicar of the cathedral, Richard Caister, and talked with Dame Julian. At this stage Margery was not a pilgrim so much as a novice learning her vocation. She went in search of living people, authorities in the world she was entering, rather than shrines and relics.

Inevitably, she was soon drawn to the three great pilgrimages: Rome, Jerusalem, and Saint James. Of these the greatest, and her first destination, was the Holy Land, for "this creature ... had a desire to see those places where He was born, and where He suffered His Passion, and where He died, with other holy places where He was in His life, and also after His resurrection" (p. 24). Her longest journey began in fall, 1413. Traveling by way of Constance and Venice, then by ship to the Holy Land, she arrived in the spring or summer of 1414. In that same summer she returned to Italy to visit Rome, stopping at Assisi en route. She spent the following winter in Rome and returned to England in the spring of 1415.[15]

It was unthinkable in the fifteenth century for a pilgrim (especially a woman) to travel alone. Margery waited at Yarmouth for a ship and a company, and the group sailed together to Zierikzee, then continued overland to Constance. Her troubles multiplied with the miles. Her fasting annoyed her companions, as did her weeping and constant conversation about God, and the pilgrims were consistently rude and unkind. At Constance, for example, they "made her sit at the table's end, below all the others, so that she ill durst speak a word" (p. 52). But not everyone was hostile; certain people—usually men in authority— took Margery's side. The papal legate in Constance listened to her story, observed the way she was treated, and sharply reproved the company. They retaliated by leaving her in his charge, taking her maidservant with them. The legate looked

15. See the chronology in Meech and Allen, *Margery Kempe*, pp. xlix, 284–285.

after her until an old Englishman named William Wever volunteered to be her guide. Helped by friendly people along the way, Margery and William reached Bologna before the others, which so impressed the pilgrims that they took her back, on the agreement that she would not "speak of the Gospel where we are, but shall sit still and make merry, as we do, both at meat and at supper" (p. 55).

Mutual dislike and acrimony persisted during the sea voyage from Venice to the Holy Land, with hostilities ranging from general disapproval to petty persecution: a priest in the group even stole one of Margery's sheets. But the Church had ruled that quarrels as well as debts must be settled before a pilgrim could receive the spiritual benefits of the Holy Places, and Margery asked her companions' forgiveness and gave them hers. In Jerusalem, as might have been expected, she could not refrain from a passionate response that was bound to exasperate the pilgrims. On Mount Calvary, in fact, she first experienced the violent "cries" that she distinguished from the incessant weeping to which she was accustomed. Sobbing and roaring, she visited the famous sites: the Holy Sepulchre, Mount Sion, Bethlehem, the room of the Last Supper, where she took Communion and received the plenary indulgence attached to that place, even though Jesus assured her that her sins were forgiven before she came. She visited the Jordan and "Mount Quarentyne" (the mountain where Jesus spent forty days in the wilderness), where a handsome Saracen helped her when her companions would not. Most of the Franciscan guides, as well as the Saracens, befriended her; as before, "she found all people good to her and gentle, save only her own countrymen" (p. 64).

The pilgrims proceeded toward Rome from the Holy Land, and Margery was abandoned again when they reached Venice. This time she was rescued by a hunchbacked man named Richard, whose help had been predicted by a holy anchorite in England. She visited the Portiuncula in Assisi on Lammas Day (August 1), 1414, and was reassured about her special gifts by an English friar. She went on to Rome in the company of an

Italian woman (Margaret Florentyne) and was accepted at the Hospital of Saint Thomas of Canterbury, which provided spiritual as well as physical services for English pilgrims. But enemies prevailed again, and she was put out of the Hospital, greatly upset because she could not find an English-speaking confessor. Jesus sent Saint John the Evangelist to hear her confession until she found a sympathetic German priest and they learned (through prayer) to understand one another. Neither poverty nor outcast status prevented Margery from finding everything a pilgrim to Rome might hope to discover.

Despite a frightening crossing to England from Middelburg in Zealand, Margery maintained her determination to make the third great pilgrimage to Saint James of Compostela, in Galicia.[16] In the summer of 1417 she sailed to Saint James from Bristol, where she met Richard the hunchback and returned money she had borrowed from him in Rome. She spent two weeks in Spain (about which she says nothing in the *Book*), and when she returned, went immediately to visit the Holy Blood at Hayles without stopping to rest after the voyage.[17]

Margery's last recorded journey, which took place in 1433–1434, was a much more dismal and disorderly affair than her great pilgrimages. After a horrifying crossing with her daughter-in-law from Ipswich to Danzig, she was afraid to go anywhere by sea. The Lord told her to leave Danzig, but she had no companion until a stranger invited her to go with him to see the Precious Blood at Wilsnak. They took ship, and Margery was pleased by the absence of wind until the calm began to irritate her companions; then she prayed for a wind and was terrified. God "bade her lay down her head so that she would not see the

16. Judging by a contemporary humorous lament, that journey had an especially bad reputation for seasickness and other miseries among English pilgrims. See *The Stacions of Rome and the Pilgrims Sea-Voyage*, p. 37.

17. The Holy Blood was brought to Hayles in 1270, and the relic and the shrine were especially popular during the Lollard crisis of the early fifteenth century (at his trial, Sir John Oldcastle denied the significance of the Blood). In 1417, a visit to Hayles was a statement of orthodoxy.

waves" (p. 212), but she was still afraid. (Perhaps even the Lord was annoyed with her by this time, since the advice seems either futile or short-tempered.)

The travelers arrived in Stralsund and began a strenuous overland journey through lands hostile to England and to English people.[18] Margery cried much of the time, annoying her companion, who revenged himself by walking too fast for her to keep up. They saw the Precious Blood but did not rest long before starting home by way of Aachen, where they visited the great relics of that city.[19] Her escort then abandoned her, leaving her in a strange country to a series of unpleasant experiences. She suffered terribly from vermin, but was unwilling to strip to remove them as the people around her did, and she feared continually for her chastity. All the long way home, Margery joined whatever people or groups would have her, but "was too aged and too weak to hold foot with them. She ran and leapt as fast as she might till her might failed" (p. 218).

This was the last journey recorded in Margery's book, which ends abruptly with her return to Lynn. The place of pilgrimage in her story, and in her religious life, is complex, but represents at the simplest her reaching for an opportunity to participate in Christ's life and death. Medieval people went on pilgrimage for all kinds of reasons—to satisfy their curiosity, to "experience an alternative mode of social being"[20] (or to get away from home), and, most of all, to establish contact with the numinous quality of holy places and holy objects. Margery went because God told her to go, and her departure for Jerusalem was also her departure from home. But above all, she traveled to extend her experience of the sacred—as she put it, "to visit

18. In the 1430s there was open hostility between the English Crown, English merchants, and several cities of the Hanseatic League. See Meech and Allen, *Margery Kempe*, p. 345.

19. Aachen was a popular shrine especially for German pilgrims in the later Middle Ages: Saint Birgitta of Sweden and Blessed Dorothea of Montau visited the city and its relics.

20. Turner, *Image and Pilgrimage*, p. 39.

those holy places where Our Lord was quick and dead" (p. 50).
Victor and Edith Turner have said that "if mysticism is an interior
pilgrimage, pilgrimage is exteriorized mysticism."[21] The mystic
and the pilgrim are not separate or separable in Margery Kempe.

Of all the aspects of Margery's vocation, the most conspicuous was her habit of tears. Her crying, more than anything else,
made trouble among her contemporaries and has been inexpli-
cable (or unacceptable) to readers of her book. And yet Margery's
tears were essential to her vocation. She was called to inspire
sorrow, by her "great sorrow," in her fellow Christians.

A tradition of holy tears had long existed in medieval
Christianity. The tears of the Virgin, which are not mentioned
in the Gospels, were invented by medieval Christians who
created a Mother of Sorrows to weep for the Man of Sorrows.
The Magdalene—lover and weeper, redeemed by her tears—
and the Virgin—the old woman crying at the foot of the Cross
or holding in her lap her crucified Son—were powerful figures
in medieval spirituality. Margery perceived these two weeping
women as closest of all to Christ. From earliest times, tears were
connected to prayer: John Cassian was one of the first to define
compunction as a necessary part of effective prayer.[22] The
Gregorian Sacramentary included a prayer for tears, and the
Benedictine Rule established the relationship of tears and prayer
within the very heart of Western monastic spirituality.[23] Tears
were actively sought; they were welcome to God. A votive mass
for tears in the Sarum Missal begins with the following prayer:

> All-powerful and merciful God, who brought forth a spring of
> living water from the ᴄᴀrth for the thirsting people, draw forth

21. *Ibid.*, p. 7.

22. See Jean Cassien, *Conférences*, p. 63.

23. "And let us be assured that it is not in saying a great deal that we shall be
heard, but in purity of heart and in tears of compunction" (Leonard J. Doyle, ed.
and tr., *St. Benedict's Rule for Monasteries* [Collegeville, Minn., 1948], p. 41).

tears of compunction from the hardness of our hearts, so that we may be able to grieve for our sins and merit receiving their remission from your pity.[24]

The prayer above, with the Secret and the Postcommunion in that mass, introduces the imagery of tears that pervades Margery's book.

English preachers and religious writers accepted tears as a means to loosen the hold of sin. The *Speculum christiani*, a fourteenth-century treatise for religious instruction, lists seven methods of "relaxing" sin: the fourth is tears, authorized by Christ's promise to mourners in the Beatitudes. Saint Jerome is also quoted as an authority on tears, saying "Prayer quemeʒ god, bot the tere constreyneʒ; prayer softeʒ, the tere commpelleʒ."[25] When Margery visited Jerome's tomb in Rome, the saint himself appeared to speak to her of tears: "Blessed art thou, daughter, in the weeping that thou weepest for the people's sins, for many shall be saved thereby. And daughter, dread thee nothing, for it is a singular and special gift that God hath given thee—a well of tears which man shall never take from thee" (p. 86).

Margery adopted the image of the "well of tears," saying, "Therefore, Lord, I would I had a well of tears to constrain Thee with, so that Thou shouldst not take utter vengeance on man's soul, to part him from Thee without end" (p. 129). The image of the well is instructive, quite different from the common image of a fountain or a river of tears, which washes away sin but does not accumulate. Margery's tears were, among other things, her religious capital, wealth that she could and did share with other people. She frequently bargained with the Lord, and on one occasion made God the "executor of all the good works that Thou workest in me" (p. 13). Reminding God that her own sins had been forgiven, she suggested that her

24. *The Sarum Missal Edited from Three Early Manuscripts*, p. 402.

25. *Speculum christiani*, p. 214.

tears and prayers might be used for the sins of others. She
wished she could "give the people contrition and weeping
. . . as well as I could give a penny out of my purse" (p. 129).
The "executor" and the "purse," like the well, were familiar
and natural images, for buying and selling and lending and
saving were important activities among the merchants of Lynn
in the fifteenth century. The late medieval system of indulgences
assumed a "treasury" of merit, a significant metaphor in an increasingly commercial society. Unlike the feudal lord of Ansel-
mian theology, Margery's God, who controlled the economy of
salvation, functioned as a great banker or a merchant prince.

Margery's weeping went through several changes in style
and significance during the course of her life. In the first
place, her tears did not begin at all until after her conversion.
Despite her violence and despair after the birth of her child,
when "she would have destroyed herself many a time" (p. 2),
there is no mention of tears. Nor did she weep when she failed
in business and was scorned by her neighbors. Her crying
began when she heard the heavenly melody, which "caused
her, when she heard any mirth or melody afterwards, to have
full plenteous and abundant tears of high devotion, with
great sobbings and sighings" (p. 5). At that time she began
to weep for joy at the bliss of Heaven, to weep with remorse
for her sins, and to weep with compassion for the sorrows of
Jesus and his Mother.

In the Holy Land a new kind of crying began:

> And when they came up on to the Mount of Calvary, she
> fell down because she could not stand or kneel, and rolled
> and wrested with her body, spreading her arms abroad, and
> cried with a loud voice as though her heart would have
> burst asunder; for, in the city of her soul, she saw verily
> and clearly how Our Lord was crucified. [P. 57]

Margery called that experience "the first cry that ever she cried
in any contemplation" (p. 57), distinguishing it from the weeping that went before. This violent, physically active, and un-

controllable crying was unlike the quieter tears to which she was accustomed; when she returned to England she mentioned that people in Lynn "had never heard her cry before . . . for she had her first cry at Jerusalem, as is written before" (p. 92).[26]

The new cries arose in certain special circumstances: when she was reminded of the Passion, when a person or an animal was hurt or wounded, and sometimes at the sight of a crucifix. They occurred very frequently in the Holy Land and in Rome, less often when she first returned to England, and then they increased again: "Once she had fourteen in one day, and another day she had seven, and so on, as God would visit her" (p. 58). On one Corpus Christi Day she cried " 'I die, I die,' and roared so wonderfully, that people wondered upon her, having great marvel of what she ailed" (p. 95). By her "cries," she apparently meant what might be called an "outcry"—a sudden, loud scream or groan, sometimes accompanied by interjections, such as "I die."[27]

The new cries attracted even more unfavorable attention than had Margery's earlier fits of weeping. She was suspected of hypocrisy, of drunkenness, of demonic possession. Almost always she accepted slander and reproof—even welcomed it—as a necessary and valuable access to the Cross. Even though religious tears were known and respected within the devotional tradition, Margery's cries were seen as extreme; "many said there was never saint in Heaven who cried as she did, wherefore they would conclude that she had a devil within her" (p. 92). Her cries frightened even her friends:

26. Hope Allen suggested that the cries began at Calvary because there Margery heard in recollection "the dying cry of the Saviour." Allen reviewed the tradition of tears at the vision of the Passion and in the Holy Land, particularly the tears of St. Birgitta (Meech and Allen, *Margery Kempe*, p. 290).

27. Good Friday as well as Corpus Christi was a day of special tears. Margery's fourth-century predecessor, Egeria, said of Christians in the Holy Land that "there is no one, young or old, who on this day does not sob more than can be imagined for the three whole hours, because the Lord suffered all this for us" (*Egeria: Diary of a Pilgrimage*, p. 112).

Some said she had the falling evil, for she . . . wrested her body,
turning from the one side to the other, and waxed all blue and
livid, like the colour of lead. Then folk spat at her for horror of
the sickness, and some scorned her and said that she howled as
if she were a dog, and banned her and cursed her. . . . Then they
that beforetime had given her both meat and drink for God's
love, now they put her away, and bade her that she should not
come in their places, because of the cruel tales that they heard of
her. [P. 92]

The accusation of hypocrisy was often repeated, but Margery
passed various tests devised to discover whether she cried in
order to impress the crowd. A sympathetic priest in Rome took
her to an empty church and gave her Communion, but "she
wept so plenteously and sobbed and cried so loud that he was
astonished himself" (p. 72). Much later, two priests who doubted
her sincerity took her to a lonely church in the country where
she "cried as loud, or louder, than she did when she was
amongst the people at home" (p. 183). She knew herself that the
crying was not under her control, for "she might not weep but
when God gave it her," neither could she resist it, for "the more
she tried to withstand it or put it away, the more strongly it
wrought in her soul" (p. 85).

The people of King's Lynn, even those who were sometimes
angry or contemptuous of Margery's tears, recognized their
power. When a great fire burned the Guildhall and threatened
Saint Margaret's Church and the town itself, Margery prayed
and wept all day, and her fellow parishioners begged her to
continue, "fully trusting and believing that through her crying
and weeping, Our Lord would take them to mercy" (p. 148).
She begged God to put out the fire, and when snow fell out of a
sky that had been perfectly clear all day, the fire was quenched
and all were grateful. But when the danger was over, her
services were forgotten, and she was slandered again for her
tears.

Even though Margery welcomed tears as a gift, she suffered
terribly from the more violent cries and "would rather have

wept softly and privily, than openly, if it had been in her power" (p. 141). Early in her experience of cries, she asked Jesus why she had to have such noticeable and awkward tears. She begged him to take them away, at least at sermons, since more than anything else she feared exclusion from preaching. Christ was very firm with her and explained once more that Margery's cries were a token of his love, of his desire that the Virgin's suffering be appreciated, of the bliss that comes with compassion, of the redemption available to sinners, and a sign to Margery that the pains she might have had in dying, and in the next world, were being exchanged for present suffering. She was assured, besides, that she was no more an occasion of sin for others (as she had been told) than Christ himself had been an occasion for sin. Convinced and content, she returned enthusiastically to her trials.

The cries that began in Jerusalem lasted more than ten years.[28] Eventually, however, the Lord did take them away, apparently so that she could go into the church again during services. God did not dry up her tears entirely, but stopped the cries so that she "cried no more afterwards so loudly, nor in that manner as she had done before, but she sobbed wonderfully afterwards, and wept as sore as ever she did before, sometimes loudly and sometimes quietly, as God would measure it Himself" (p. 142). No cries are reported during the part of her life covered in Book II; presumably she continued to sob and weep, but without cries, until she died.

28. Margery's "cries" began in the Holy Land in 1414 and continued through the rest of her stay abroad, through her trials in Leicester and York and Beverly, and at home in Lynn during the long period of her various illnesses. These illnesses were first "the flux," then a long sickness "which was set in her right side, lasting the time of eight years, less eight weeks, at divers times" (p. 125); it may have been chronic appendicitis or gall bladder inflammation. She is precise about the duration of her illnesses, but less so about her cries, which she says lasted "ten years" (p. 128). They must have lasted longer, because the period between her visit to the Holy Land and the end of that eight-year illness was at least twelve years (see Meech and Allen, *Margery Kempe*, pp. 318–320).

With the exception of the Franciscan preacher who banished her from his sermons, those to whom Margery turned as spiritual authorities understood and appreciated her tears. Dame Julian assured her that "when God visiteth a creature with tears of contrition, devotion, and compassion, he may and ought to believe that the Holy Ghost is in his soul" (p. 34). Julian quoted Saint Paul and Saint Jerome on religious tears and encouraged Margery not to fear the world's contempt. The anchorite who was Margery's principal confessor told her that "tears with love are the greatest gift which God may give on earth" (p. 37). In Constance, when the pilgrims tormented her, the papal legate told them, "As for her weeping, it is not in my power to restrain it, for it is the gift of the Holy Ghost" (p. 53). Margery frequently was reassured about her tears by the Virgin, who urged her to feel no shame about crying for the pain of Christ, any more than she herself was ashamed to cry "when I saw Him hanging on the Cross—my sweet Son, Jesus" (p. 61).

Tears were an essential feature of Margery's vocation. Soon after her conversion, Jesus called her to a special responsibility for her fellow Christians. The language in which he spoke to her about her duties and authority granted extraordinary powers and responsibilities: "I am in thee and thou in Me, and they that hear thee, hear the voice of God. Daughter, there is no sinful man living on earth, that, if he will forsake his sin and live after thy counsel, such grace as thou promisest him, I will confirm for thy love" (pp. 15–16). Margery was not told that she could "forgive" sins, like a priest, but she was told to use her tears to mediate between God and repentant sinners. A sinful monk, believing that she knew God's will, begged her to tell him whether he would be saved. She said: "If I may weep for you, I hope to have grace for you" (p. 19). She did weep, whereupon Jesus advised her how the monk had sinned and how he might be saved, and she counseled him and helped him to repent. Her tears were so powerful and so pleasing to God that she could make them available to other sinners.

Sometimes her ability to perceive the fate of souls was

troublesome. One woman, learning that her husband was in purgatory, became so angry that she tried to turn Margery's confessor against her. Foreknowledge was often painful; Margery feared demonic suggestion, and harsh truths provoked anger. When there was good news, on the other hand—for example, when the good prior came back to Lynn—her information was welcome and her reputation enhanced. As with other kinds of publicity she received, she profited directly from the positive aspects of fame and spiritually from slander or mistreatment that brought her closer to God.

Margery acquired a following among people who desired her tears and prayers, especially when they were dying, "for, though they loved not her weeping or her crying in their lifetime, they desired that she should both weep and cry when they should die, and so she did" (p. 158). She wept for the dying as if they were Christ or his Mother. On one occasion, she was asked to visit a woman who had gone insane after childbirth. The poor woman could not speak to anyone, and her behavior was so frightening that she was isolated and manacled. Margery visited her once or twice a day and prayed for her, and the woman spoke to her reasonably and before long was cured. The cure was perceived as a miracle, at least by the scribe, "for he that wrote this book had never, before that time, seen man or woman . . . so far out of herself as this woman was, nor so evil to rule or to manage" (p. 164). If Margery recognized her former self in the madwoman, she did not say so, but it seems likely that she knew she had functioned in this recovery as had Christ in her own, saving her from insanity by kindness and prayer.

Unlike some of her famous contemporaries (Joan of Arc, Catherine of Siena, Birgitta of Sweden), Margery Kempe had no public vocation, no political or ecclesiastical mission to make peace or to reform the Church. Her vocation was with individual souls, and possibly with great numbers of them. Christ said: "I have ordained thee to kneel before the Trinity, to pray for all the world, for many hundred thousand souls

shall be saved by thy prayers" (p. 13).[29] Early in her ministry
Margery asked Jesus: "What shall I do for the people?" and he
answered: "It is enough to thee to do as thou dost" (p. 39).

The vocation that required Margery Kempe to leave husband
and children, to dress in white, to go on pilgrimage, to receive
special attention from Church and clergy, was no ordinary or
insignificant calling. Chosen for divine favor, she was turned
to God through a mystical conversion, conducted through the
elementary stages of the mystic's education, and visited with
the gifts and wonders of divine illumination. Her ascetic habits
and practices, including participation in the great pilgrimages
of medieval Christianity, made it clear that she was dedicated
to the spirit and not to the world. Her tears—painful, conspicuous, troublesome—were given by God to make her a mirror of penitence, compassion, and God's saving love for sinners.
With the help of repeated assurance from Christ and from her
advisers, Margery was convinced of her calling and accepted
her afflictions as necessary, even desirable. Her life was very
difficult, but an easy life was never one of the rewards given to
God's special friends. Her vocation was unique, shaped to her
soul by the individual teaching of Christ and to her circumstances by the environment that made her who she was. The
singular qualities of her calling can best be appreciated in
relation to the city, the family, and the education that formed
her character and provided the setting for the beginning of her
spiritual journey.

29. Mechthild of Magdeburg also saved "thousands" of souls from purgatory.
For a full and fascinating discussion of the vocations and roles of some of
Margery's Continental predecessors (including Mechthild), see Caroline W.
Bynum's essay on the nuns of Helfta in *Jesus as Mother*, pp. 170–262.

Chapter Three

"SHE WAS COME OF WORTHY KINDRED"

The Burnham Family of King's Lynn

W HEN Margery Kempe moved out from her household and her birthplace onto the wider stage required by her vocation, she entered an international company of pilgrims and holy persons. Her travels extended east to Jerusalem, north to Prussia and Scandinavia, and south to Italy and Spain. But she remained an English woman, formed in a specific time and place and by a particular family, church, and society. She grew up in late fourteenth-century King's Lynn, in Norfolk—a vital, prosperous place whose civic, commercial, and religious activities and institutions were thoroughly interwoven, in the manner of medieval towns.

King's Lynn was not a very old city. Until the end of the eleventh century, "Lin" was an obscure village lost in the salt marshes of the Wash. Throughout the early Middle Ages, the fenland of coastal East Anglia was a thinly populated land of swamps and marshes, subject to floods, difficult of access, and probably malarial. Settled agriculture was possible only on the islands that rose above the flood and vast stretches of peat, and the economy of the region depended on its harvest of fish, eels, and salt, for local use and limited trade.

The fens were lonely, unhealthy, and frightening. They were

described in the eighth-century *Life of St. Guthlac* as a place of "manifold horrors and fears, and the loneliness of the wild wilderness."[1] For those very characteristics, however, they were attractive to those who sought hardship and solitude, including Saint Guthlac himself and many other hermits and congregations of monks and nuns. East Anglia is still famous for its convents and churches, and its very early foundations include not only Guthlac's Crowland, but Peterborough (founded in 655), Thorney (662), and a convent founded at Ely by Saint Aethelthryth in 673.

The last is interesting in relation to the story of Margery Kempe. Aethelthryth was an East Anglian princess married to a king of Northumbria, and Bede says: "Though she lived with him for twelve years she still preserved the glory of perfect virginity."[2] Bede tells of the discovery of the saint's body long after her death, uncorrupted in the grave—"token and proof that she had remained uncorrupted by contact with any man."[3] Like Margery Kempe, Aethelthryth argued for years with her husband, who tried to bribe the bishop to persuade the queen to consummate the marriage. Eventually she prevailed, and retired to Ely to found a convent, where she remained for seven years as an abbess with a reputation for amazing sanctity. When her successor decided to have Aethelthryth's body exhumed and placed in the church, she looked for a stone coffin for the remains. Bede's description of that endeavor illuminates the historical geography of East Anglia: "So they got into a boat (for the district of Ely is surrounded on all sides by waters and marshes and has no large stones) and came to a small deserted fortress not far away [Grantchester, where they found a marble coffin].... Ely ... derives

---

1. Felix, *Life of St. Guthlac*, ed. and tr. C. W. Goodwin (1848), quoted in H. C. Darby, *The Medieval Fenland*, p. 8.

2. *Bede's Ecclesiastical History of the English People*, p. 391.

3. *Ibid.*, p. 393.

its name from the large number of eels which are caught in the marshes."[4]

The monasteries of the fens were looted and burned by the Danes in the eighth century, but the invaders were as disinclined as their predecessors to settle in that country. The landscape remained lonely and desolate, warmed by religious passion but almost unaffected by the advances in agricultural technology that gradually altered the face and extended the civilization of Western Europe between the ninth and the twelfth centuries. The Anglo-Saxon monastic revival of the tenth century did reach East Anglia, however, causing new monasteries to be built and old ones restored: Peterborough in 963, Ramsey in 969, Ely in 970, Thorney in 972, and Chatteris in 980. A twelfth-century monk of Peterborough described the country-side and its apparent destiny: "From the flooding of the rivers, or from their overflow, the water, standing on unlevel ground, makes a deep marsh, and so renders the land uninhabitable, save on some raised spots of ground, which I think that God set up for the special purpose that they should be the habitations of His servants. . . . "[5]

Such was the backcountry of Lynn, and it is not surprising that the town faced outward toward the Continent when it gathered strength in the twelfth century. But even though the rise of Lynn was mercantile and commercial, the spark that ignited its explosion was in part religious—the achievement of a Norman bishop, Herbert de Lozinga, who built priories and churches throughout his see of Norwich. Margery Kempe's parish church of Saint Margaret's, Lynn, was founded by de Lozinga in 1101. The city grew under the protection and in the shadow of the bishops of Norwich, who were the feudal lords of Lynn and the surrounding countryside throughout the medieval centuries.

4. *Ibid..*, pp. 395, 397.

5. "Historiae coenobii Burgensis," p. 2, in *Historiae Anglicanae Scriptores Varii*, ed. J. Sparke (1723), tr. and quoted in Darby, *Fenland*, p. 21.

Brass rubbing: "Robert Braunche and his wives Letitia and Margaret."
Fourteenth-century brass from St. Margaret's (8'10" × 5'2"). Courtesy of
the Reverend G. W. F. Lang.

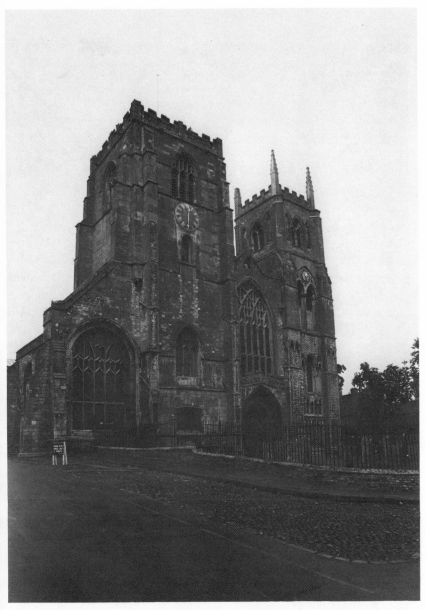

St. Margaret's West Front. The foundation deed of St. Margaret's, sealed by Bishop Herbert de Lozinga in 1101, refers to the building of a church in honor of "St. Mary Magdalen, St. Margaret, and all holy virgins." Its present-day parishioners worship where Margery Kempe wept, prayed, and listened to sermons.

St. Nicholas Chapel: South Elevation Looking West. In Margery's time, St. Nicholas was a "chapel-at-ease" attached to St. Margaret's.

Norman wealth, energy, and interest in church building brought people and activity to Lynn at the end of the eleventh century, but the economic and commercial expansion of the North Sea basin transformed the village into a great city in the twelfth. As population increased, the pressure on land and food supplies inspired the development of unlikely and inaccessible places. The fens were natural sites for attempts at farming, and although large-scale drainage was not achieved until the seventeenth century, small operations greatly increased the extent of arable and inhabitable land. Matthew Paris wrote in the thirteenth century: "Concerning this marsh a wonder has happened in our time; for in the years past, beyond living memory, these places were accessible neither for man nor for beast, affording only deep mud with sedge and reeds, and inhabited by birds, indeed more likely by devils as appears from the life of St. Guthlac. . . . This is now changed into delightful meadows and also arable ground."[6]

Not only did the people of the fenland begin to grow their own agricultural products, but Lynn became an outlet for the farms and pastures of Cambridgeshire and the Midlands. By the middle of the thirteenth century, the silting of the Wisbech estuary had diverted the major streams of the region (the Great and Little Ouse and the Nene) until they entered the ocean near Lynn.[7] Quantities of corn, malt, and ale were shipped to the Continent; after the twelfth century, the export of corn was exceeded only by that of wool. Sheep were raised around the Wash, and in that the monastic revival and reform played an important part, for it was the newer orders (Cistercians, Gilbertines, and Premonstratensians) who specialized in sheep farming and kept abreast of Continental developments in animal husbandry. Throughout the medieval period, wool and

6. Matthew Paris, *Chronica Maiora*, ed. H. R. Luard (1872), under the year 1256, tr. and quoted in Darby, *Fenland*, p. 52.

7. See Eleanora Carus-Wilson, "The Medieval Trade of the Ports of the Wash," 185.

corn were the major exports of Lynn, along with Derbyshire lead and salt from the local salt pans. Lynn and the neighboring port of Boston were for more than a century the primary exporters of English raw materials, feeding not only the people of northern Europe, but the voracious mills of Flanders. Wool went to Flemish weavers to be made into fine cloth, much of which came back to England (again through Lynn and Boston) to dress the rising middle and upper classes.

Flemish cloth was the major import, but there were many others: luxuries, such as furs, spices, and French wine, along with timber and fish for a growing (and frequently fasting) population. The height of Lynn's prosperity came in the late thirteenth century, before the Hundred Years' War and the Black Death diminished the supply of wealth available for purchases abroad. The English Crown, struggling to pay for its dynastic wars, placed so many duties and embargoes on the export of wool that trade declined. Simultaneously, the wealth and strength of the Hanseatic cities made them successful competitors. Increasingly, German merchants dominated all the Northern ports. Entrenched in Norway and Iceland, they refused or restricted the trading rights of other foreigners. German economic power created German influence (cultural and religious) in Lynn, where as Eleanora Carus-Wilson reports, "mayors of Lynn even chose to be remembered in their parish churches by memorials in the German style."[8]

The merchants of Lynn were an enterprising company, and they maintained a large measure of their former prosperity by fighting their own battles overseas without much help from their rulers. In Stralsund, in 1391, they were arrested for infringing trading rules, and in 1402 the Hanseatic League reenforced an old edict against English merchants settling in the Hansa cities to trade with the Prussian interior. In the early fifteenth century, the fishermen of Lynn mounted a major effort to challenge the German monopoly of the North. The

8. *Ibid.*, 196

stockfish (a form of cod) caught off Iceland was highly prized in England, for it could be dried and preserved successfully. The boats of Lynn fished off Iceland against German orders for several years; ultimately, however, German influence on the Danish overlords of Iceland prevailed, and the English ships were excluded.

The trade in stockfish was sufficiently active to leave traces in contemporary imagery. When Margery Kempe reported God's praise of her obedience, she used a vivid simile from the harbor and the kitchen: "Daughter, thou art obedient to My will, [God said] and cleavest as sore to Me as the skin of a stockfish cleaveth to a man's hands when it is seethed . . . " (p. 78). The citizens of medieval Lynn, whether or not they were traders, were much affected by the commercial connections that gave color and variety to their cultural and domestic life.

The politics of Lynn were also dominated by trade and by a merchant oligarchy whose money came from trade. The bishops of Norwich were the lords of Lynn, and de Lozinga its first benefactor. However, when the city grew, its richer families became ever more powerful and more eager to control their own fate. Very early, there was conflict between the bishops of Norwich and the rich men of Lynn, with the bishops summoning the lower classes of the town to their support, and the oligarchy turning to the kings. The town's first charter, granted by King John in 1205,[9] gave the burgesses the right to hold courts, to fine offenders, and to establish various tolls and tariffs. They

---

9. Norfolk was generally sympathetic to John, who had substantial connections with Lynn. He granted the city its charter in 1205 and received (according to legend) "three beautiful palfreys as a slight token of grateful appreciation." (H. J. Hillen, *History of the Borough of King's Lynn*, 1:48. John retreated to Lynn during his war with the barons in 1216. When he left the city, the royal treasure was lost in the Wash in "a dark stagnant pool of water known as 'King John's Hole' " (Hillen, 1:56). "King John's Cup"—a much later work—supposedly rescued from the Hole, can be seen in the Guildhall today. The king did not long survive the disaster; perhaps the story that his death was caused by a "surfeit of lampreys" appeared because lampreys were a staple of the diet of the fens.

were relieved of the Danegeld and permitted to form a self-governing merchant guild. Throughout the medieval period the Guild of the Holy Trinity played a major part in the affairs of Lynn. Women were admitted to membership, and the last public record of Margery Kempe is the note of her admission in 1438.[10]

The richest merchants—those who inherited membership in the Guild of the Holy Trinity or could pay its large initiation fees—not only controlled the mercantile fortunes of the city, but shared its municipal offices among themselves. The names of a few families appear and reappear on the lists of officeholders, and prominent among them is the name of Burnham. Margery's father was mayor of Lynn in 1370, 1377, 1378, 1385, and 1391; he was one of its two Members of Parliament in 1364–1365, 1368, 1376, 1379–1380, 1382–1383, and 1384.[11] His son Robert was a Member of Parliament in 1402 and 1417. When Margery boasted to her husband that "she was come of worthy kindred," she was correct, if ungenerous.

Conflict between the bishops of Norwich and the wealthy citizens of Lynn was endemic, and as the city grew more prosperous, the stakes rose on both sides, until even "symbolic" struggles were waged in deadly earnest. In 1377, for example (when John Burnham was mayor), the burgesses were forced to concede a victory to the bishop in a battle over precedence. Bishop Despenser demanded that the wand carried before the mayor in processions be carried before him too, and in the

10. "Women were also admitted as members by paying the usual fee. Absolute equality prevailed between the men and women; yet the 'sisters' more especially participated in the spiritual benefits of the association." (Hillen, *King's Lynn*, 2:744) I do not know why Margery's admission to the Guild, to which she certainly was entitled by family connections, was so long delayed—perhaps she had "settled down" by 1438 and was accepted more comfortably in Lynn. She may have made a special effort to win acceptance during the year her scribe was beginning to write Book II.

11. Meech and Allen, *Margery Kempe*, p. 360. See also May McKisack, "The Parliamentary Representation of King's Lynn before 1500."

St. Margaret's Place and Queen Street. The fifteenth-century Guildhall stands across from St. Margaret's at the corner of Queen Street. Once the Hall of the Trinity Guild (to which Margery Kempe belonged), the Guildhall now houses the archives and "Regalia" of the city.

ensuing riot, two of the bishop's servants were injured. Under
royal pressure, that score was settled in favor of the bishop. The
burgesses paid a hundred pounds in compensation for the
injuries and provided a "huge wax candle"[12] to be offered in
the Church of the Holy Trinity in Norwich. In many instances
the burgesses were victorious, but obviously there were limits
to their encroachments upon feudal-episcopal power.

Whatever their troubles with the Germans or the bishops,
the ruling families had their way within the town. Medieval
Lynn had a reputation for extended and violent class conflict,
but its middle and lower classes never were able to break the
grip of the oligarchy. Riots were ineffective, for disorder was
firmly resisted by all authority—civic, royal, and ecclesiastical—
and the municipal system was too firmly established to admit
unruly outsiders. Self-perpetuation was the rule: in choosing
a mayor, for instance, the aldermen of the Guild of the Holy
Trinity named four electors, who chose four more, who chose
eight, who chose the remaining four, and these "jurats" appointed
the mayor. Offices rotated among established families.

No evidence exists of John Burnham's attitude toward his
unusual daughter, but the position of the family was as solidly
entrenched as any in Lynn, which may help to explain Margery's
attitude toward authority and her immunity from actual bodily harm. There is an instance of such protection in an account
of her appearance before the bishop of Worcester. Unintimi-
dated, she challenged the bishop to explain her arrest, and
he apologized and asked her to dinner: "Margery, I have not
summoned thee, for I know well enough that thou art John
of Brunam's daughter, of Lynne. I pray thee be not wroth, but
fare fair with me, and I shall fare fair with thee, for thou shalt
eat with me this day" (p. 96). There may have been more of
such protection, direct and indirect, than Margery reported or
even recognized. Her manners and style, eccentric as they were,
displayed a confidence which may have come as much from the

12. Hillen, *King's Lynn*, 1:131.

security of family and class as from assurance of divine favor. Despite social and commercial conflict at home and overseas, prominent citizens of Lynn lived very well. In the later Middle Ages, the mansions of rich English merchants were stocked with the luxuries they imported. Aristocratic standards of taste prevailed, along with aristocratic separation from the poor. The great merchants were "gentlemen" with capital, wholesalers and foreign traders, with enormous local influence and political power. Sylvia Thrupp called them proud people who "kept themselves, at least in the larger towns, very much aloof from the retail traders, artisans, and workers."[13] The men of such families were supposed to live like "gentlemen," and to acquire at least the rudiments of a bookish education—in short, to separate themselves from the sources of their wealth. Their large stone houses, which still can be seen in Lynn, stood apart from the poorer streets, and their sons went to school and learned at least a little Latin. It is never safe to assume that the "daughters of educated men"[14] share the experiences of their brothers, but Margery's illiteracy is still somewhat surprising. By the late fourteenth century, the women of such households usually learned at least how to read and write. Margery Kempe may have been a rebel even in youth.

It would be wrong, however, to exaggerate the "aristocratic" tone of the Burnham household. Thrupp's description was written of the late fifteenth century, and Margery grew up a hundred years earlier. Certainly there is no hint in the *Book* of the notion of the "lady" as ornament, neither did its author suggest that there was any social stigma attached to her participation in trade. One can speculate, however, that some meas-

13. Sylvia Thrupp, "The Problem of Conservatism in Fifteenth-Century England," 365.

14. The phrase was coined by Virginia Woolf in *Three Guineas* (New York, 1966), p. 5. She explained (p. 146) that "our ideology is still so inveterately anthropocentric that it has been necessary to coin this clumsy term—educated man's daughter—to describe the class whose fathers have been educated at public schools and universities."

ure of her intense anxiety about worldly activity (her attempts at brewing and milling) reflected a suspicion that these were not appropriate activities for her father's daughter. The assumed disapproval of the Father in Heaven may have been connected to the rising status of the father in Lynn.

Of all her family relationships, Margery wrote most about her father and her husband; we infer from her comments that whatever she felt about John Burnham, she derived self-confidence, a sense of importance, and real protection from his status. Her behavior must have been difficult for her parents, but apparently they did not disown her entirely, for it is likely that she would have mentioned such a rejection as one of her trials. She said almost nothing about her children, making no mention of arrangements for their care when she left home. She did describe her earnest endeavors to turn one of her sons away from worldliness and her joy at his conversion and marriage, but she does not speak of loving or missing any of her children. The birth of the first was such a hideous experience that it would be surprising if later pregnancies brought her much joy, particularly after she found her vocation. Once she had established her need and wish to be celibate and had entered into conflict with her husband over that issue, children may have represented defeat, frustration, and distraction from her relationship to God.

As for John Kempe, despite their early differences, she learned to appreciate his goodness, not only his eventual agreement to chastity, but his support "when all others failed" (p. 25). And yet, when she was asked by the Virgin whom she would have with her in Heaven, Margery asked only for her confessor. The Virgin responded: "Why asketh thou more for him than thine own father or thine husband?" (p. 13). Margery answered that she owed the priest a great deal for working for her spiritual welfare, and the Virgin tactfully added (unasked): "yet shall thy father be saved and thy husband also, and all thy children" (p. 13). Margery took care of John Kempe, at Christ's command, when he was old and sick, but she looked back at their married life, and seemed to look at him, not with affection but with disgust at her former "delectable thoughts, fleshly lusts, and inordinate loves to his person" (p. 166). After her conversion she "never desired to commune fleshly with her husband, for the debt of matrimony was so abominable to her that she would rather, she thought, have eaten or drunk the ooze and the muck in the gutter" (p. 6).

Margery never spelled out her ideas about what human relationships should be, neither was she explicit or analytical about her own. But we learn something about her perceptions of ideal relationships from her colloquies with Christ, who told her how to behave with him:

> For it is fitting for the wife to be homely with her husband. Be he ever so great a lord, and she ever so poor a woman when he weddeth her, yet they must lie together and rest together in joy and peace. . . . [15]
>
> Daughter, thou desirest greatly to see Me, and thou mayest boldly, when thou art in thy bed, take Me to thee as thy wedded husband, as thy dearworthy darling, and as thy sweet son, for I will be loved as a son should be loved by the mother, and I will that thou lovest Me, daughter, as a good wife ought to love her husband. Therefore thou mayest boldly take Me in the arms of thy soul and kiss My mouth, My head, and My feet, as sweetly as thou wilt. [P. 77]

She was told to love Jesus as a mother and wife ought to love her son and her husband, and the passion and intimacy of that relationship far exceeded her earthly relationships as those appear in her book.

Margery Kempe loved God best in the human Jesus, who appeared to her most often as a beautiful young man or a boy baby. But God existed in many kinds of connection to chosen souls:

15. This passage echoes the story of "Patient Griselda," the poor woman married to a great lord, which has sometimes been interpreted as a metaphor of the relation of the soul to God. It was a popular story in the Middle Ages: Chaucer used it as his Clerk's tale.

> Therefore I prove that thou art a very daughter to Me, and a
> mother also, a sister, a wife and a spouse. . . . When thou studyest
> to please Me, then thou art a very daughter. When thou weepest
> and mournest for My pain and My Passion, then thou art a very
> mother having compassion on her child. When thou weepest for
> other men's sins and adversities, then thou art a very sister. And
> when thou sorrowest that thou art so long from the bliss of
> Heaven, then art thou a very spouse and a wife, for it belongeth
> to the wife to be with her husband, and to have no very joy till
> she cometh into his presence. [P. 23]

In this passage, human relationships illustrate aspects of the
relationship of the believer to God. As theological analogies,
their power and usefulness depend on a shared understanding
of what certain human ties are, or should be, and thus give
evidence of social ideals. The verbs are revealing: in modern
idiom, the daughter tries to *please* the father, the mother
sorrows over the child, the sister *sympathizes* with the brother,
the wife *longs* for the husband. These were feelings and activities expected of women in relation to their families, and they
were not exemplified in the domestic experience of Margery
Kempe. It seems unlikely that she pleased John Burnham very
much or very often. She may have sorrowed over her son, but
she reports that she chastised him for his evil behavior and
asked God to punish him. We know nothing about her feelings
for her brother either in childhood or later, but we do know
that she never (after her conversion) longed for the company of
John Kempe.

Jesus was not the only figure in Margery's spiritual family.
She identified closely with the Virgin as woman, mother, and
mediatrix. Early in her religious life, Jesus told her to "think of
My Mother, for she is the cause of all the grace that thou hast"
(p. 11). She followed that suggestion faithfully, choosing in
meditation to become the Virgin's handmaiden in caring for
the Child and to comfort the sorrowful Mother after the
Crucifixion. In a recital of Margery's graces and services, the
Lord said: "And also, daughter, I thank thee for all the times

that thou hast harboured Me and My blessed Mother in thy bed" (p. 194). Margery's attitude toward the Virgin was that of a loving, respectful daughter-in-law—much more loving and respectful than her own daughter-in-law, who was cold and rejecting when Margery accompanied her home to Germany. As usual, human ties did not approach the warmth, constancy, and splendor of spiritual experience.

In meditation, Margery was present at the Virgin's death, when she received loving assurance that her sins were forgiven. Her loud tears—first hushed by the apostles—were graciously accepted by Mary, who responded (from her deathbed) with a substantial speech about tears and pardon. Here the apostles appear as unsympathetic men who do not appreciate Margery's sensitivity, while the Virgin (the most elevated being present) rewards her compassion. Shedding the role of servant and handmaiden, Margery became a beloved daughter. Margery never mentioned her own mother, who may have been distressed—perhaps more than John Burnham—by the outlandish behavior of her daughter, which flagrantly departed from the norms of the "good woman." In God's Mother, Margery found a mother to appreciate her.

Misunderstood and tormented by neighbors, fellow pilgrims, and strangers, Margery Kempe looked to Heaven for comfort, companionship, and conversation about holy things: "Sometimes Our Lady spake to her and comforted her in her sickness. Sometimes Saint Peter, or Saint Paul, sometimes Saint Mary Magdalene, Saint Katherine, Saint Margaret. . . . They spoke to the understanding of her soul, and informed her how she should love God, and how she should best please Him, and answered to what she would ask of them . . . " (p. 195). Among the saints, Margery found brothers and sisters as well as triumphant exempla of problems she faced and solutions she hoped for. Believing herself to be a sinner, she turned to reformed sinners for comfort; lacking feminine sympathy and companionship, she turned to saintly women. She felt a special devotion to Mary Magdalene, whose place in Heaven was close to Christ.

Saint Peter, one of her favorite "sinners," was comforted in language almost identical to that with which Christ comforted Margery during her first illness. Ashamed to face the Virgin after the Crucifixion, Peter was urged to come into her presence: " 'Ah! Peter,' said Our Lady, 'dread thee not, for, though thou hast forsaken my sweet Son, He forsook never thee, Peter, and He shall come again and comfort us all right well . . . ' " (p. 179). Margery's despair and alienation after childbirth had been a great sin—analogous to Peter's abandoning Jesus—but her sin, like his, was forgivable and forgiven by a loving Father.

Certain women saints always appeared in Margery's visions of the intimate courts of Heaven. Among them were Margaret of Antioch and Katherine of Alexandria, two legendary virgins whose cults flourished in the High and late Middle Ages. (The influence of the legends of these saints is discussed in Chapter 6 below.) Many English churches were dedicated to Saint Margaret during the late Middle Ages, including Margery's parish church. Saint Margaret was also the patroness of the borough of Lynn; her symbols decorate its arms. She was the special advocate of women in labor, and it would be surprising if Margery did not call on her during the births of her children.[16]

Next only to Jesus and his Mother, Margery was devoted to Saint Mary Magdalene, whose medieval cult and legend were

16. See Francis Bond, *Dedications and Patron Saints of English Churches*, p. 17. For the legend and iconography of St. Margaret in Lynn see Hillen, *King's Lynn*, 1:30–34. The saint's legend always included some version of her narrow escape from the jaws of a dragon, and despite her own virginity, her victory over the dragon made her the help and protector of women in labor. Martin Luther attacked the practice of calling on her, telling women not to repeat "St. Margaret legends and other silly old wives' tales" but to labor (and to die, if necessary) secure in the knowledge that labor and childbirth were pleasing to God (Martin Luther, "The Estate of Marriage," in *Luther's Works*, Vol. 45 [Philadelphia, 1959], p. 40).

based on the fusion of several biblical characters.[17] She was always included among God's favorites and among the re-formed sinners with whom Margery identified. Like almost all female wickedness, the Magdalene's sins were presumed to be sexual, although Saint Luke (7:37) calls her only "a woman of the city, who was a sinner." Margery, who believed herself to have been a "lecherous" woman, had a special compassion for those suffering from sexual sin and temptation. But her feeling for Mary Magdalene was more intimate, more human, and therefore more ambivalent than her devotion to any other saint. She and the Magdalene were like sisters, with the com-petitiveness as well as the love that exists in that relationship: " 'Ah! Blissful Lord,' said she, 'I would I were as worthy to be secure of Thy love, as Mary Magdalene was.' Then said our Lord:—'Truly, daughter, I love thee as well, and the same peace that I gave to her, the same peace I give to thee. For, daughter, there is no saint in Heaven displeased, though I love a creature on earth as much as I do them. Therefore they will not other-wise than I will' " (p. 161). Apparently Margery was anxious about provoking Mary Magdalene's displeasure; she identified so closely with her that she feared the saint might feel the jealousy that she experienced herself. In meditation, Margery saw Mary Magdalene receive the Virgin's permission to handle and kiss the feet of Christ after the Crucifixion. Perhaps she was jealous as well as distracted by love and grief, for "the said creature thought that she ran ever to and fro, as if she had been a woman without reason, greatly desiring to have had the Precious Body by herself alone . . . " (p. 177).

Like the Virgin, Mary Magdalene was a model of the mourner—the weeping woman. Her tears, mentioned in Scrip-ture as acceptable to Jesus (Luke 7:44), both inspired and legitimated Margery's tears. At certain times, the gift of tears

17. The Magdalene cult and legend in the Middle Ages are described by Victor Saxer in *Le culte de Marie Madeleine en Occident*, vol. 2.

caused Margery great trouble and anguish, and her identification with the woman that Christ loved must have helped to
sustain her vision and self-confidence. Heavenly relationships
compensated for the limitations of inadequate and insensitive
human beings. Margery found in Heaven a family and a circle
of loving friends and brought them down to earth to comfort
and protect her in her earthly trials.

We may speculate about the domestic environment of Margery
Kempe from the few direct comments in her book and from
external evidence of her father's status and position. We may
also infer attitudes toward real and ideal family relationships
from her account of the divine beings with whom she lived in
harmony and joy. She left no account of her early education,
either religious or practical, and for that it is helpful to turn
to contemporary documents that illustrate the values and daily
lives of women in middle-class households. Margery held very
strong views about her own vocation—what her work should
be—and medieval writings about and for married lay women
reveal significant discrepancies between her behavior and
contemporary expectations.

The letters of the Paston family, Norfolk neighbors of Margery
Kempe, show the lives of the Paston women as busy and
responsible. Most of the Paston letters date from the latter part
of the fifteenth century; the family belonged to the rural gentry
rather than the urban bourgeoisie and was involved in the
Lancastrian (and their own) cause instead of municipal politics.
However, their letters—particularly those of Margaret Paston to
her husband—offer authentic glimpses of fifteenth-century domestic life. Remarks like the following demonstrate the concerns that occupy most people in any century: "As for hering,
I have bowt an horslode for iiijs vjd. I can gett none ell
[eels] yett. . . ."[18]

Religious concerns held a substantial place in the consciousness of these very practical people; when John Paston was ill,

18. *The Paston Letters A.D. 1422–1509*, 2:229.

his mother ordered a wax image of his weight for the shrine of the Virgin at Walsingham, and his wife went there to pray for him.[19] Loving husbands and wives and careful parents are revealed in the *Letters*, and women who could not only read and write but act as stewards for large estates, managing many retainers and complicated households. Despite the social position of the Pastons, which was closer than that of Margery Kempe to the world of the nobility, there is no evidence of aristocratic scorn of hard work.

Contemporary books of advice contribute mixed impressions of the fourteenth-century "lady," although such works are notoriously difficult to interpret, since they tend to be prescriptive rather than descriptive. Two books of advice, both French, are enlightening: that of the Knight of La Tour-Landry, who wrote a book for his motherless daughters in the 1370s, and of the "Goodman of Paris," who wrote for his young bride in the 1390s.

The Knight's book was translated into German and English (by William Caxton in 1484), and widely read in England.[20] It set forth the conventional feminine virtues of piety and chastity: the young women were to serve the poor, to attend church regularly and devoutly, and to avoid both interest in fashion and occasions of scandal, which apparently were related in their father's mind. The Knight's book was somewhat influenced by courtly attitudes, but his daughters were instructed much as Margery Kempe must have been instructed. In their common religious tradition, the image of the "good woman" was based on the Old Testament wife of Proverbs 31. It is a pious, thrifty, and hard-working image, very different from both the aristocratic lady and the Christian female saint or virgin martyr. Presumably the "good woman" was the predominant female model in the prosperous bourgeois society in which Margery Kempe was raised, making her departure from the ideal all the more interesting.

19. *Ibid.*, p. 5. See also David Knowles, "The Religion of the Pastons."
20. *The Book of the Knight of La Tour-Landry*, p. xiii.

The background of the "Goodman of Paris" was closer to the world of Margery Kempe than was that of the Knight. The Goodman wrote a book of counsel for his young wife (about fifteen years old, to his sixty) to aid her in the two necessary achievements of a married woman: "namely the salvation of your soul and the comfort of your husband."[21] (Margery Kempe obviously found these two objectives incompatible and chose the first.) Like John Kempe, the Goodman was of lower social status than his wife; he assured her, however, that if he did not correct her errors, the women of her family would quickly do so. Most of the book is taken up with religious behavior, including attendance and behavior at mass, and the sins and virtues pertaining to a young matron. "Proper" (social) behavior and "godly" behavior were inextricably related, as they would remain for centuries in women's lives.

The Goodman's book is an archive of social history. As well as a manual of piety and etiquette, it is a cookbook, a gardening book, and a treatise of household management—for example, it offers six ways to get rid of fleas in the bed and bedroom. With its many servants and guests, the household must have resembled that of John Burnham or John Kempe, and it is difficult to imagine Margery devoting herself to the infinite detail required of a housewife in such an establishment. Indeed, the expectation of incessant and demanding labor and attention make it easy to understand why she had to leave home to take up her vocation. Piety was encouraged, but the necessities of husband and home came first, and religion was expected to enhance, not to interfere with, domestic life. The Goodman explained the meaning of matins, but "not because I mean that you, dear sister, nor married women, should rise at this hour."[22]

Margery Kempe, who wrote about what interested her and not about domestic details, told almost nothing of her life at home as an unmarried girl, wife, or mother. Nor did she write

21. *The Goodman of Paris*, p. 43.
22. *Ibid.*, p. 47.

Queen Street. Old houses along Queen Street, once known as "Wingate" and inhabited by prosperous bourgeois families in medieval times.

Warehouse off Queen Street. The houses of merchants such as John Burnham and John Kempe were not separated from their shops and warehouses.

about her surroundings, social or physical, except as they affected her spiritual life. Her education is not described; we
assume that she had none from books, except what she heard
in church, until she found a priest to read to her in later life. As
a girl, she must have learned much from conversations at her
father's table about events and ideas from overseas. The Bible
was read in church, where she also heard stories about the
saints. Of course she was taught to say her prayers.

In the decree *Omnis utriusque sexus*, the Fourth Lateran
Council of 1215 stipulated annual confession and Communion
for all Christians. In some respects, this stipulation was the latest
and most successful stage of a process of Christianization and reform which had been carried on throughout Europe since the
time of Charlemagne. It required a clergy capable of hearing confessions—that is, with a working knowledge of moral
theology—and a laity instructed in the rudiments of the faith.
Thirteenth-century English bishops, like their colleagues on the
Continent, struggled to implement the decrees of the Council,
and they emphasized penance in particular. W. A. Pantin pointed
out that cross-examination of penitents made the confessional
"as important as the pulpit as a potential means of religious instruction."[23] Among the more important episcopal writings were
Robert Grosseteste's treatises on confession and his *Templum
domini* (a handbook for parish priests) and Archbishop Pecham's
De informatione simplicium, issued in 1281. Pantin described
this work as "a programme of religious instruction: the fourteen
articles of faith, the ten commandments of the Law and the two
commandments of the Gospel, the seven works of mercy, the
seven virtues, the seven vices, and the seven sacraments."[24] These
basic tenets of the faith were to be expounded at least once a year
to the Christian people, and we can assume that Margery
Kempe participated in this regular instruction.

By the later fourteenth century, a substantial number of

23. W. A. Pantin, *The English Church in the Fourteenth Century*, p. 192.
24. *Ibid.*, pp. 193–194.

manuals, both in Latin and in the vernacular, enabled hard-working and half-educated priests to respond to the bishops' demands. These treatises generally contained the same elements as Pecham's *De informatione* and also gave advice on how to hear confessions, on appropriate questions for different penitents, and on penances suitable for various sins and faults. Many of the works emphasized sexual sins, marital problems, and the duties of the laity, such as emergency baptism. The frequent mention of that topic and the emphasis on the religious responsibilities of midwives serve as reminders of the pervasive fear of death and horror of sin and damnation that surrounded childbirth in the Middle Ages. Certainly this was an important aspect of the experience of Margery Kempe, who had fourteen children.

The *Speculum christiani*, an elementary handbook of theology written in a mixture of Latin and English, was one of the most popular religious works of fourteenth-century England. A large number of manuscript copies survive, and it was one of the first books printed in English (between 1478 and 1480). For the convenience of parish priests, it brought together various authorities (the Bible and the Church Fathers) on all kinds of subjects from "conscience" to "tribulation." Much of Margery Kempe's early religious education must have come from catechetics based on such works, through which she was taught the alphabet of faith. After her conversion she educated herself by talking to holy and learned persons, by listening to sermons, and by hearing books read aloud, but the process of Christian education began in early childhood.

Apart from what was learned at home and at church, various sources of education existed for people without formal schooling. The physical environment in which Margery was raised supplied her with vivid pictorial representations of Christ, the saints, and Old and New Testament stories. God was glorified, and the people of God edified, by artistic creations; divine beings and divine activity were everywhere represented in stone and glass. In a world in which most people could not read, Christians learned their faith and history through images as well as letters. The doors and windows of churches, the pictures and statues within, made textbooks of biblical theology out of buildings erected for the worship of God. Worship was both stimulated and carried out in tangible, concrete materials as well as in the words and liturgical actions of clergy and people. In the late Middle Ages, artists and prelates joined to make the churches effective as well as beautiful environments for religious education.

The imagery of Margery's meditations was colored by what she saw as well as what she heard. On her journeys to the Holy Land and to Rome her visual education was obviously much expanded, but even as a child, she encountered in local churches pictures of the lives of the Holy Family and the saints, with all the detail characteristic of medieval religious art. She did not write about what she saw, although it is reflected in her meditations, but on one occasion she did report her response to an "image": "this creature saw a fair image of Our Lady called a 'pieta', and, through beholding that sorrow, her mind was all wholly occupied in the Passion of Our Lord Jesus Christ, and in the compassion of Our Lady, Saint Mary, by which she was compelled to cry full loud and to weep full sore . . . " (p. 135). A seventeenth-century account of one East Anglian pietà reveals the character and emotional impact of such images: "in the tabernacle at the South End (of Long Melford Church in Suffolk) . . . there was a fair image of our Blessed Lady having the afflicted body of her dear Son, as he was taken down off the Cross, lying along her lap, the tears as it were running down pitifully upon her beautiful cheeks, as it seemed bedewing the said sweet body of her Son, and therefore named the Image of our Lady of Pity."[25]

Margery's meditations on the Passion (Chapters 79–81, Book I) have many sources—in preaching, in the liturgy for Holy

---

25. Christopher Woodforde, *The Norwich School of Glass Painting in the Fifteenth Century*, p. 90.

Week, in devotional writings—but they also were inspired by works of art. For example, there is today in Saint Luke's Chapel in Norwich Cathedral a retable which illustrates in brilliant glass the scourging, crucifixion, burial, and ascension of Christ —all much as they appear in Margery's meditation. (The retable was given to the church by Bishop Despenser and local leaders in 1381.) The physical environment of Margery Kempe was saturated with the lessons of faith.

By the late fourteenth century, the citizens of many English towns could also observe the Christian story as it was presented annually in cycles of plays. In *The Play Called Corpus Christi*, V. A. Kolve says that for the education of the people, "the medieval Church relied on confessional teachings, sermons, wall paintings, stained glass, and in certain parts of England, a drama that showed the history of the world."[26] Like sermons, religious art, and religious literature, the plays were designed to teach and inspire as well as to delight and entertain. They presented Christian history (which is, as Kolve says, almost identical with Christian theology)[27] to the people of God. Medieval Christians were expected to respond emotionally as well as intellectually to their history, and the plays were intended to pull them into the narrative. The scenes, characters, and events of the Bible were portrayed as present, tangible realities.

In the later Middle Ages, religious passions tended to focus on the concrete, the specific, the "here and now"; that focus nourished the cult of relics and the devotion to the Holy Places, where the sites of Christ's earthly life could be seen, touched, and even measured. The plays satisfied the taste for the concrete, mixing miraculous with ordinary events and the actions of God with those of human beings. Kolve points out that "Mary

26. V. A. Kolve, *The Play Called Corpus Christi*, p. 3.

27. "Christianity as a religious system has traditionally made its ultimate claims not in terms of philosophical truth but in terms of history: its authentication resides in what has happened or will happen. At its center is a story superior to all the theological refinements erected upon it in its power to save men's souls" (*ibid.*).

rides on an ass into Egypt, and she is physically 'assumpt' into heaven; in this drama, both actions *happen*, and they happen in equally literal ways."[28] In its historical, literal aspect and its symbolic, figurative aspect, the Christian story was simultaneously shown and experienced. Participants and audience were expected to respond with the widest range of emotional expression, from ribald laughter to deepest grief.

The earliest recorded performance of a cycle of plays was at York in 1376, and scholars believe that by the middle of the fifteenth century, a full cycle may have been regularly performed in various cities.[29] Those that survive originated in Chester, Wakefield, York, and Lincoln, but there were many others. And besides the cycles, or "Corpus Christi" plays, there were Passion plays, miracles, saints' plays, and more. In the twelve or so cities of the cycles, it is believed that the entire community was involved, and not only as spectators. Individual plays were the responsibility of the various guilds, but the enterprise as a whole belonged to the town. The plays were performed outdoors, and we assume that not only the citizens of the town attended, but also people from neighboring cities, villages, and farms.

Margery Kempe does not mention plays in her *Book*, but at least twelve were regularly performed by various guilds in Norwich in the late fourteenth century, including "The Creation of the World," by the Mercers and Drapers, and "The Resurrection," by the Butchers and Fishmongers.[30] There were plays in Lynn, too: in 1385, when Margery was about twelve years old, the town chamberlains paid 3s.4d. to players for an "interlude" on the feast of Corpus Christi, and the same amount for an "interlude" of Saint Thomas.[31] There must have been others, probably with Margery in the audience; these were the sort of civic and guild functions that occupied the attention

28. *Ibid.*, p. 26.

29. Eleanor Prosser, *Drama and Religion in the English Mystery Plays*, p. 4.

30. *The Victoria History of the County of Norfolk*, 2:250.

31. Alan H. Nelson, *The Medieval English Stage*, p. 190.

and received the support of her family. It is likely that she attended plays in childhood and youth, but apparently they were not important to her (as were sermons) after her marriage and conversion.

But whether or not Margery Kempe ever saw a play, and whether she liked or disliked or was indifferent to them, they provide important evidence about her world. They also shed light on aspects of her *Book*; for example, her easy familiarity with the Holy Family and the saints is entirely characteristic of the style and attitudes of medieval playwrights. Of course the plays, although their subject is Christian history, reflect medieval attitudes about all kinds of topics, including contemporary ideas about women and marriage. Such information contributes to our understanding of Margery Kempe herself, and even more to our understanding of the reactions she evoked in those around her.

The character and situation of Noah's wife, who is barely mentioned in the Bible but was a major comic figure in the plays, are particularly revealing. In medieval drama and legend, according to Kolve, Mrs. Noah became "the root-form of the shrewish wife, and her relationship with Noah became the archetype of everyday marital infelicity."[32] Like the nagging wives of the fabliaux or the misericords in English churches,[33] Mrs. Noah belonged to the thriving comic tradition of the "woman on top"[34]—the woman who attempts to rule a man. In artistic and literary expression, the disorder thus provoked created ugliness, and the shrew herself was hideous as well as ridiculous. In theological terms, Mrs. Noah represented Christians slow or unwilling to enter the Ark (the Church) of their

32. Kolve, *Corpus Christi*, p. 146.

33. M. D. Anderson, *Drama and Imagery in English Medieval Churches.* See esp. pl. 36 (n.p.), a photograph of a "horned" woman in a Ludlow misericord.

34. For a brilliant discussion of this theme in popular art and festival, see Natalie Zemon Davis, "Women on Top," in *Society and Culture in Early Modern France*, pp. 124–151.

salvation, but her dramatic function was to provide the raucous comedy of relief. In the Chester and Towneley plays, the Noahs staged a rousing physical battle before Mrs. Noah was persuaded and dragged on board the Ark. It was a funny, slapstick scene, and the playwright could depend on an enthusiastic response provoked by conflict between its disorder and the general belief in divine and "natural" order. Interruptions or rebellions within the universal hierarchy (in which God ruled men, and men women) produced sin and chaos, which were ultimately tragic—as in the Fall and the Crucifixion— but might be experienced, for relief, as wildly comic. In such scenes, the reaction of the audience arose in part from the gulf between their belief in order and the chaos of the play, and perhaps from related discrepancies in their own lives.

In the middle classes of late medieval English towns, certain women ran businesses, belonged to guilds, and enjoyed legal independence and substantial financial resources. In a situation like that of Margery Kempe, in which a wife's family was richer and more prominent than her husband's, a woman might have real social and economic authority outside the family as well as within. In respect to the equality of the sexes, the later Middle Ages was an unusual period. In earlier times, when wealth was derived entirely from the possession, inheritance, and exploitation of land, women had no access to power or autonomy outside the family. With the exception of great heiresses (Eleanor of Aquitaine is the supreme example), and particularly in lands influenced primarily by customary law, lay women had little autonomy and almost no legal existence as individuals.[35] After the end of the Middle Ages, when the first stirrings of protocapitalism and industrialization began to separate the home from the workplace, men controlled not only public power but women's legal, social, and economic existence.

35. For a helpful summary of the position in early medieval Europe, see Jo Ann McNamara and Suzanne Wemple, "The Power of Women through the Family in Medieval Europe: 500–1100," in M. Hartman and L. W. Banner, eds., *Clio's Consciousness Raised* (New York, 1974), pp. 103–118.

(This situation was reflected and advanced, in Protestant countries, by the teaching of the reformers, who made a vocation of homemaking and destroyed women's only institution: the convent.)[36] But in the thirteenth through the fifteenth centuries, although theoretical categories of dominance and authority were not altered, there was a degree of real equality and a surprising flexibility in individual circumstances and local arrangements.[37]

Historians have been puzzled by the discrepancy between life and literature in the matter of attitudes toward women. Eileen Power argued that most theories about women were created by small and circumscribed groups (in particular, by clergymen). Although these groups, with their near monopoly of formal education, were influential, their theories did not necessarily describe the reality of most people's lives. Working women, in and out of families, played an active and dignified part in medieval society. John Leyerle pointed out that neither the sagas nor the Paston letters reflect antifeminism, for "these texts reflect the actuality of family life where women were constantly present and vitally important to the family's continuity and well-being."[38] He added that antifeminism flourished in places where women were not present and had little economic significance—among the celibate clergy—and is reflected in their writings. The Wife of Bath would have agreed with him:

---

36. An account of this process is given by Jane Dempsey Douglass, "Women and the Continental Reformation," in Rosemary Ruether, ed., *Religion and Sexism* (New York, 1974), pp. 292–318. On p. 295, Dempsey Douglass quotes Luther (*Enarrationes in 1 Mose*, WA 43, 20, pp. 31–36): " 'If a mother of a family wishes to please and serve God, let her not do what the papists are accustomed to doing: running to churches, fasting, counting prayers, etc. But let her care for the family, let her educate and teach her children, let her do her task in the kitchen . . . if she does these things in faith in the Son of God, and hopes that she pleases God on account of Christ, she is holy and blessed.' " Such an attitude would have made Margery Kempe's vocation impossible.

37. Eileen Power summarizes some of these arrangements in *Medieval Women*, pp. 53–75.

38. John Leyerle, "Marriage in the Middle Ages," 415.

For trusteth wel, it is an impossible
That any clerk wol speke good of wyves . . .
By God! if wommen hadde writen stories,
As clerkes han withinne hire oratories,
They wolde han writen of men more wikkednesse
Than al the mark of Adam may redresse.[39]

Literary critics and historians have made an important distinction between theoretical antifeminism and the "facts" of real life, but they tend to overlook another set of "facts"—that is, the psychological disturbance created by discrepancies of ideology and actuality. Confusion over equality and dominance made sexual strife a natural subject for comic treatment in literature and drama, for it was an area in which comic relief was especially welcome. The theme of husband beating, or the "woman on top," was popular in many literary genres.[40] In the example of Mrs. Noah, it took place in the midst of solemn, sacred history, where the defeat and surrender of the "shrew" carried all the majestic sanction of the history of salvation.

But Mrs. Noah is only one representative of the defiant woman (the shrew, the hag) in medieval literature. The argument over "mastery" is the theme of Chaucer's "Marriage Group" of Canterbury Tales, of the "Querelle de la Rose," and of that permanent figure of fun, the talkative old woman, made ridiculous by her pretensions to authority, sexuality, and autonomy.[41]

---

39. *The Complete Works of Geoffrey Chaucer*, p. 99.

40. Despite the popularity of the image, wife beating was much more common than husband beating in the Middle Ages (as in all other periods), and in fact was specifically permitted by canon law. See Power, *Medieval Women*, p. 16.

41. For a bibliography of the medieval argument about women, see Francis Lee Utley, *The Crooked Rib*. The subject has been discussed in several recent articles, including Michael W. Kaufman, "Spare Ribs"; William Matthews, "The Wife of Bath and All Her Sect"; and Hope P. Weissman, "Antifeminism and Chaucer's Characterization of Women."

The core image of the garrulous dame came from the Latin classics, and most of the supporting arguments against her from the Church Fathers, who branded with their fears Christian attitudes toward women (that is, toward women who were sexually active). By the fourteenth century, the ancient arguments and stereotypes had become less exclusively religious, more secular and bourgeois like their society. The fabliaux were profoundly misogynistic; Joseph Bédier, who recognized the underlying rage and hatred in the tales, called their image and conception of women "the dishonor of a literature."[42] Dishonor is serious enough, but more serious was the part played by the image of the "hag" in the witch hunts of early modern times.[43]

We need not be surprised at the coincidence of a forceful antifeminism, with its caricatures of foolish, vicious, or ridiculous women, with a period of marked autonomy for women in the "real" world. Backlash is not a new invention, and ridicule was (and is) an effective weapon against the threat of being "beaten" by a woman. It was uséd against Margery Kempe, whose fellow pilgrims did not like her. They expressed their dislike in several ways, one of which was to make a comic spectacle of the woman who attracted attention, who won the favor of powerful persons, and who claimed a privileged relationship with God: "for they did her much shame and much reproof as they went, in divers places. They cut her gown so short that it came but little beneath her knee, and made her put on a white canvas, in the manner of a sacken apron, so that she should be held a fool and the people should not make much of her or hold her in repute" (pp. 51–52).

Margery Kempe was not humble or deferential; she came

42. Joseph Bédier, *Les fabliaux*, p. 285.

43. The literature of the witch hunters contains evidence to support the theory that notions about the "nature" of women inspired and fueled the witch hunts. For example: "All witchcraft comes from carnal lust, which is in women insatiable" (Heinrich Kramer and Jakob Sprenger, *The Malleus Maleficarum*, ed. and tr. Montague Summers [New York, 1971], p. 47).

from a powerful family, and she addressed her fellow Christians (even priests and bishops) in direct and straightforward language. Her domestic and social background gave her the necessary confidence to persist in her strange vocation and unpopular way of life in spite of contemporary norms concerning the behavior of married women. She found in Heaven not only parents and lover, but companionship for her journey and comfort for her trials. The lay religious education and the artistic creations of late medieval English culture fed her imagination and helped to shape her vision of the divine. She met scorn and disfavor from many people, probably including most of her earthly relations, but she traveled her lonely path with substantial protection and support. She found safety and encouragement in the existence (if not the approval) of her "worthy kindred," in the friendship of Christ and the saints, and most significantly in her "ghostly Mother"—the Church—and its representatives.

Chapter Four

"HER GHOSTLY MOTHER"

Church and Clergy

EVEN when she was most isolated or troubled, Margery Kempe never perceived her singular calling to be in conflict with her Church, or with the clergy who were her best friends as well as her teachers and advisers. Mystics in any period are vulnerable to charges of heresy and disobedience, because their direct communication with God tends to bypass the services and sacraments of the Church. Margery was especially vulnerable, not only because she was an outspoken woman and a lay person without formal education, but because she lived at a time of serious disruption in the Church at home and on the Continent. The agitation over Lollardy in the English Church reflected the greater agony of Schism in the Church Universal. The ecclesiastical disturbances of the early fifteenth century made it necessary for Margery to define and pursue her peculiar vocation against a background of both heresy and repression.

In Margery's lifetime, and in her neighborhood, there were several outbreaks of heresy and of persecution. In 1401 the statute *De haeretico comburendo* was passed by Parliament and the first Lollard went to the stake. That first victim was William Sawtrey, parish priest of Saint Margaret's, Lynn. Margery was something more than a regular communicant of Saint Margaret's in 1401, and she must have known Sawtrey, although his name does not appear in her book (possibly an instance of scribal editing). Norwich was a center of Lollardy and of persecution in the early fifteenth century; at least sixty men and women were tried for heresy by the episcopal court between 1428 and 1431.[1]

Lollardy was never a well-organized movement with a consistent set of teachings. Its beginnings are generally traced to John Wycliffe and his circle at Oxford in the 1370s, but there were enormous differences (and only tenuous connections) between the scholarly Wycliffe, who wrote academic treatises in Latin, and the tradesmen and apprentices who were tried in Norwich in the time of Margery Kempe. Very early (after the Peasant's Revolt of 1381 and the official condemnation of Lollardy in 1382), the movement lost its academic and aristocratic supporters. By the 1430s the heart of the heresy belonged to artisans and small tradesmen and servants—working people who did not read Latin, if they could read at all.[2] The spread of the movement was assisted by the growth of a class of devout, literate lay people, but many of its enthusiastic adherents lacked any formal education beyond what they learned in the Lollard "schools."[3]

The consistent agenda of Lollardy, from Wycliffe onward, had less to do with doctrine than with religious disposition and moral attitude. The movement represented a continuing protest against the greed, avarice, and wealth of the Church and its upper clergy. With all the differences among its various adherents, it retained a disposition toward scriptural simplicity and away from sacerdotalism and elaboration. Lollards tended to regard certain beliefs and practices as idolatrous, or worse. These varied over time and among individuals, but they generally included transubstantiation, clerical celibacy, Friday fasts, images, pilgrimage, special prayers for the dead, and the belief

1. See Norman P. Tanner's edition of Westminster Diocesan Archives MS. B.2, *Heresy Trials in the Diocese of Norwich, 1428–31.*

2. For an insightful discussion of this question, see Margaret Aston, "Lollards and Literacy"; see also Claire Cross, " 'Great Reasoners in Scripture.' "

3. Aston, "Literacy," 352.

that confession to a priest was necessary for salvation. These practices, lacking scriptural origin, were regarded as human fabrications, excuses for priests to make money from the Christian people they were called to serve.

Obviously, Margery Kempe was no Lollard. The vocation that she struggled so hard to follow was characterized by practices abhorred by Lollards, including fasting, pilgrimage, and frequent confession. She admired and responded to holy images, and she was perfectly orthodox in her understanding of the Eucharist. Margery Kempe went to Walsingham to "offer in worship of Our Lady" (p. 207); her Lollard neighbor Margery Baxter (tried at Norwich in 1429) called the place "Falsyngham" to express her scorn of shrine and pilgrimage.[4] The enormous religious and temperamental differences between the two women are nicely pointed up in the testimony of Margery Baxter, who claimed "that it was more economical to eat on Friday the scraps of meat left over from the preceding day than to go to the market and buy fish!"[5] Such an argument would never have occurred to Margery Kempe, who was called a Lollard; the charge had little to do with her beliefs or practices.

The English Church and its royal protectors responded to Lollardy on the one hand with burning and repression, and on the other with efforts not only at reform (such attempts were endemic) but at revival. One response, according to E. F. Jacob, was to "increase the emotional artistic appeal of churches, encourage books of piety, and generally to fan the flame of faith."[6] This is the response which Hope Allen called a "Fifteenth-century Counter-Reformation"[7] and believed to be responsible in part for the attention paid to Margery Kempe. Female visionaries and their writings had had small place in

4. Tanner, *Heresy Trials*, p. 47.

5. *Ibid.*, p. 15.

6. E. F. Jacob, *The Fifteenth Century*, p. 299.

7. Letter from Hope Allen to J. A. Herbert, July 10, 1946 (Allen papers, Bryn Mawr College archives). The idea and the phrase ("Fifteenth-century Counter-Reformation") appear frequently in Allen's writings.

traditional English piety; the threat of Lollardy apparently made them more acceptable. Paradoxically, the efforts of Crown, Church, and civil authority to combat the Lollards may have allowed Margery Kempe to be heard even while they kept her defending and defining her own orthodoxy.

From the very beginning, and despite all trials, Margery's devotion to the Church never wavered. Immediately after her conversion "she, considering this wonderful changing, seeking succour under the wings of her Ghostly Mother Holy Church, went and offered obedience to her ghostly father" (p. 235). Her experience was personal and extraordinary, but she took it immediately to the Church for acceptance and sanction. Christ called her "a pillar of Holy Church" (p. 22),[8] and this she remained, although neither Christ nor Margery perceived God as embodied entirely, or necessarily, in the institution. In the Holy Land, Christ spoke to her about authority and obedience:

> I am well pleased with thee, daughter, for thou standest under obedience to Holy Church, and because thou wilt obey thy confessor and follow his counsel who, through authority of Holy Church, hath absolved thee of thy sins and dispensed thee so that thou shouldst not go to Rome and Saint James unless thou wilt thine own self. Notwithstanding all this, I command thee in the Name of Jesus, daughter, that thou go visit these holy places and do as I bid thee, for I am above Holy Church, and I shall go with thee and keep thee right well. [P. 61]

Fortunately, conflicts between God's will and that of the Church did not often occur, and when they did, they concerned matters of behavior rather than doctrine. Sometimes Margery was divinely directed to do things that were misunderstood (for example, to wear white clothes), but when God spoke of doctrine, it was the doctrine taught by the Church. In her several exami-

---

8. In the margin next to this phrase, the manuscript is decorated with a drawing of a pillar (Meech and Allen, *Margery Kemp*, p. 29).

nations for heresy, Margery's answers (whether or not they were shaped by her scribe) were perfectly orthodox, and she reiterated her intention to be obedient. She told the examiners at York: "If there be any clerk amongst you all who can prove that I have said any word other than I ought to do, I am ready to amend it with good will. I will neither maintain error nor heresy, for it is my full will to hold as Holy Church holdeth, and fully to please God" (p. 109). The scribe may have rephrased her answers and even her intention, but she did not have his help when she faced the examiners, and she never was convicted of heresy.

Irrespective of her beliefs, Margery's conspicuous position and unusual vocation provoked all kinds of charges. Like most heterodox, evangelical, or fringe groups, the Lollards were accused of permitting women to play a public role.[9] Female prominence may have been exaggerated—"excessive" participation by women is always a useful charge[10]—but the danger was real. Margery Baxter and other Lollard women were active and outspoken, and they were arrested (and burned) along with men.

Margery Kempe was specifically called a Lollard for the first time at Canterbury, where her weeping attracted unfavorable attention. She told the monks a Bible story (a dangerous action in itself, given the Lollards' fondness for Scripture), and one of them said to her: "I would thou wert enclosed in a house of

9. The Lollards were accused not only of allowing women to preach but of making women priests and allowing them to celebrate mass. I suspect that this fearful possibility was based on misunderstanding of the erratic behavior of one person, reported in the *St. Alban's Chronicle*: "Non multo post captus est quidam Lollardus, vocabulo Willelmus Cleydone: qui in tantum demenciam ruerat, ut eciam filiam sacerdotem constitueret et missam celebrare faceret in domo sua die quo coniunx eius a puerperio surgens purgenda ad ecclesiam processisset. Hic ergo captus, examinatus et convictus de heresi London est combustus" (V. H. Galbraith, ed., *The St. Alban's Chronicle 1406–1420*, p. 89). It seems probable that *filiam* is a scribal error for *filium*, and that Cleydon made his *son* a priest and permitted him to celebrate mass on the day that his son's wife went to church to be "purified" after childbirth. If Cleydon's daughter, and not his son, became a priest, then her husband must have "risen from childbirth," which is unlikely.

10. See Eleanor C. McLaughlin, "Women and Medieval Heresy."

stone, so that, there, no man should speak with thee" (p. 20).
She answered him boldly and thanked the monks for their
scorn and reproof. When she left the monastery they followed
her, crying: "Thou shalt be burnt, false Lollard. Here is a
cartful of thorns ready for thee, and a tun to burn thee
with" (p. 21). She was rescued by two young men who asked
whether she was a heretic; when she said she was not, they
escorted her home and asked her to pray for them. Again
Margery had found people to believe in her, but the episode
illustrates not only the Lollard scare but an ancient suspicion of religious women who were not safely enclosed.
Much later, during a lengthy contest with the mayor of Leicester,
Margery was called "a false strumpet, a false Lollard, and
a false deceiver of the people" (p. 98). The basic theme of
this triple accusation is not Lollardy but hypocrisy, and the
underlying question concerns a "religious" woman living in
the world.

There are ancient and effective sanctions against women
who preach and teach men. The archbishop of York tried to
make Margery promise not to teach in his diocese, but she
refused and dared to back up her refusal with Scripture: "I
shall speak of God . . . unto the time that the Pope and Holy
Church hath ordained that no man shall be so bold as to speak
of God. . . . And also the Gospel maketh mention that, when
the woman had heard Our Lord preach, she came before Him
with a loud voice and said:—'Blessed be the womb that bore
Thee, and the teats that gave thee suck.' . . . And therefore, sir,
methinketh that the Gospel giveth me leave to speak of God"
(p. 113). Not surprisingly, the clerks said she must be possessed
to speak of Scripture, calling upon their natural ally, Saint
Paul, for reinforcement. Margery made a quick distinction
between preaching and "speaking of God": "As quickly as
possible, a great clerk brought forth a book and laid Saint
Paul, for his part, against her, that no woman should preach.
She answering thereto said:—'I preach not, sir; I come into

no pulpit. I use but communication and good words, and that I will do while I live' (p. 113).[11] Saint Paul's authority must have been used against Margery more than once, for Jesus spoke to her later about the apostle, who made amends by promising her "as much grace . . . as ever thou hadst shame and reproof for his love" (p. 146).

Margery was always under suspicion of sexual misconduct, perhaps because her way of life puzzled and infuriated those who could not imagine a chaste woman outside the walls of home or convent. Apparently, evidence of sexual misbehavior (or of any sexual activity, once she had exchanged the vow of chastity with her husband) would have discredited her "feelings." When she returned from the Holy Land, she visited an anchorite who had once been her friend but had listened to gossip while she was away. He asked what she had done with the child she had borne overseas and refused to believe her when she told him she was chaste. In Leicester, when she had answered questions on the Eucharist, the mayor followed the clerks' theological questions with sexual innuendo, and again she had to defend her way of life: " 'Sir,' she said, 'I take witness of My Lord Jesus Christ . . . that I never had part of man's body in this world in actual deed by way of sin, but of my husband's body, to whom I am bounden by the law of matrimony, and by whom I have borne fourteen children' " (p. 102).

Margery's isolated and unusual circumstances made her espe-

---

11. The *Speculum christiani* makes this distinction between preaching and teaching: "Prechynge es in a place where es clepynge to-gedyr or foluynge of pepyl in holy days in chyrches or other certeyn places and tymes ordeyned ther-to. And it longeth to hem that been ordeynede ther-to, the whych haue iurediccion and auctorite, and to noon othyr. Techynge es that eche body may enforme and teche hys brothyr in eurey place and in conable tyme, os he seet that it be spedful. For this es a gostly almesdede, to whych euery man es bounde that hath cunnynge" (p. 2). It is difficult to say whether "he," "his," and "every man" in the passage above are instances of the "generic man"; presumably they are, and women were included in the general permission to teach.

cially vulnerable to abuse as well as innuendo, as she was well aware. Imprisoned at Leicester, she begged the mayor to "put me not among men, that I may keep my chastity, and my bond of wedlock to my husband" (p. 99). Questioned by the steward, she answered correctly but provoked his anger, so "the steward took her by the hand, and led her into his chamber and spoke many foul bawdy words unto her, purposing and desiring, as it seemed to her, to oppress her and ravish her" (p. 100). Margery used the most effective defense available, saying: "Sir, for the reverence of Almighty God, spare me, for I am a man's wife" (p. 100). In a patriarchal society, in which women are protected against violence by the existence and status of male friends and relatives, a woman who lacks (or appears to lack) a protector is vulnerable. John Kempe was not present in Leicester, and the mention of his name did not deter the steward, who grew angrier when Margery defied him. She then appealed to a more powerful protector, for "he scared her so much that she told him how she had her speech and her dalliance of the Holy Ghost . . . " (p. 100). The steward feared God more than an absent husband, for he ceased to threaten her and returned her to jail.

A woman who was neither married nor unmarried, housewife nor nun, threatened those who lived by ordinary rules. When Margery was arrested as a Lollard by the duke of Bedford's men, they took her to the town of Hessle, where her appearance touched off a reaction that reveals the anxiety about her way of life which lay beneath the charge of heresy: "Then they brought her again into Hessle, and there men called her 'Lollard,' and women came running out of their houses with their distaffs, crying to the people: — 'Burn this false heretic!' (p. 117) They proceeded toward Beverley, where they met other people who told her: "Damsel, forsake this life that thou hast, and go spin and card, as other women do, and suffer not so much shame and so much woe. We would not suffer so much for any money on earth" (p. 117). Margery was imprisoned in Beverley, but she continued to talk to people who stood outside her window.

She won their sympathy so that "women wept sore, and said with great grief in their hearts:—'Alas! woman, why shalt thou be burnt?' " (p. 118). The last paragraph of that chapter is so realistic, and its details seem so authentic, that it is impossible to say whether its overtones of the Passion are deliberate or are simply the unconscious echo of a lifetime of hearing and meditating on the Gospel:

> Then she prayed the good wife of the house to give her drink, for she was sick with thirst, and the good wife said her husband had borne away the key, wherefore she could not come to her, nor give her drink. Then the women took a ladder and set it up to the window, and gave her a pint of wine in a pot, and took her a cup, beseeching her to set away the pot privily, and the cup, so that, when the good man came, he might not espy it. [P. 118]

At Beverley, Margery appeared again before the archbishop of York—much to his annoyance, as he had hoped to be rid of her. The men who arrested her called her "Cobham's daughter" (p. 119)[12] and a Lollard messenger and denied that she had been to Jerusalem (Lollards did not make pilgrimages). As before, Margery insisted that she not be put among men, and the archbishop agreed. Soon she was summoned to listen to a new charge: that she had persuaded Lady Westmoreland's daughter (the duke of Bedford's cousin) to leave her husband. This Margery denied, saying that she had not seen Lady Westmoreland—or her daughter—for over two years, and that she had never suggested such a thing. The matter is not mentioned again, neither is there enough evidence to determine what lay behind the accusation, apart from the general suspicion of a married woman who left her own husband and household.

Suspected Lollards were always questioned about the Eucharist, for Wycliffe had denied transubstantiation, and Wycliffe's ideas, in various forms and degrees of confusion, spread to some of his

12. The notorious Lollard Sir John Oldcastle was also known as "Lord Cobham."

followers. In this matter Margery's orthodoxy was attested to by God, who said to her: "Daughter, I am well pleased with thee, inasmuch as thou believest in all the Sacraments of the Holy Church and in all faith that belongeth thereto" (p. 74). At her trial in Leicester, Margery answered the abbot as follows:

> Sirs, I believe in the Sacrament of the Altar in this wise; that whatever man hath taken the order of priesthood, be he ever so vicious a man in his living, if he say duly those words over the bread, that Our Lord Jesus Christ said when He made His Maundy among His disciples, where He sat at the Supper, I believe that it is His very Flesh and His Blood, and no material bread; and never may it be unsaid, be it once said. [P. 102]

This succint statement covered (and disavowed) the major points of the Wycliffe heresy: it affirmed transubstantiation and contradicted the Lollard form of Donatism, which denied sacramental powers to a bad priest and thus denied grace *ex opere operato*. Its precise language is not Margery's usual "homely" style, and it seems likely that this answer was phrased very carefully by her scribe.

Through all her trials, Margery never was questioned about the one aspect of her faith which may in fact have been heterodox— that is, her assurance of her own salvation. Christian doctrine does not admit that anyone can be perfectly certain of being saved; even if one is confident of a state of grace, through the signs of grace, one cannot be sure that death in a state of grace is foreknown by God. Margery, however, was frequently assured of salvation. God's promise was explicit: "Ah! Daughter, how often have I told thee that thy sins are forgiven thee, and that we are united (in love) together without end. Thou art to Me a singular love, daughter, and I promise thee that I shall come to thine end at thy dying. . . . And I have promised thee that thou shouldst have no other Purgatory than the slander and speech of the world" (p. 41). This was more than the promise of grace through Christ made to every Christian; it was a personal, private, and singular promise to

Margery Kempe, which more than compensated for all the slights she suffered.

Not only for its role in faith and salvation, but for its central place within the fabric of ordinary life, the Church shaped the underlying structures of social as well as religious experience for medieval Christians. Fast and feast days organized the calendar. On Corpus Christi Day, Margery followed the sacrament in procession; the liturgical rituals of Holy Week provided the basis for private visionary moments. The sights and sounds of the Church shaped her spiritual experience: "For many years, on Palm Sunday, as this creature was at the Passion with other good people in the church-yard, and beheld how the priests did their observance, how they knelt to the Sacrament, and the people also, it seemed to her ghostly sight as if she had been then in Jerusalem, and seen Our Lord in His Manhood received by the people, as He was whilst He went here on earth" (p. 168).

Like her neighbors, Margery was throughly involved in the affairs of the Church as a social and political institution. In the episode of the chapels, for example, she appears not as an ecstatic outsider, set apart and at odds with other Christians, but as an active citizen and church member with special gifts to contribute to local affairs. In 1432 a group of rich and powerful parishioners attempted to acquire for the Chapel of Saint Nicholas (attached to Saint Margaret's) the sacramental privileges of baptism, matrimony, and purification. (An earlier attempt to accomplish this had occured in 1378, when John Burnham was mayor of Lynn; both he and Margery's father-in-law are on record as opposed to the change.) In 1432 the bishop of Norwich suggested a compromise favorable to those who wanted privileges for the chapel, and Margery was consulted about her "feelings" in the matter—meaning neither her opinions nor her emotions, but her ghostly intimations: "This creature prayed to God that His will might be fulfilled, and, forasmuch as she had the revelation that they would not have it, she was the more bold to pray Our Lord to withstand their intent and slacken their boasting" (p. 49). "They would not have it" means that the opposition party would not accept the compromise. On the issues at stake, Margery agreed with her father's defense of the position of Saint Margaret's, which is not surprising. What is significant is her participation in the controversy and the way in which her private "feelings" were involved in the affairs of the local church and community. Margery described the event as "a right notable matter of the creature's feeling" (p. 48), implying that it attracted considerable attention. The episode testifies to the objective (almost "factual") manner in which divine inspiration was taken as normal by others as well as herself. Such "feelings" were perceived as neither subjective nor ephemeral.

Throughout the Middle Ages, dramatic and significant events were expected to occur in church—parish church as well as shrine. On a Friday before Whitsunday[13] Margery was nearly killed by a stone and timber that fell from under the church roof onto her back. Her Carmelite friend Master Aleyn weighed the stone and timber and pronounced her survival a miracle; characteristically, the material nature (in this case, the exact weight) of the objects was of supernatural interest. As with many such incidents, the interpretation was left to the beholder: was she punished for sin by being struck or preserved for virtue by miraculous intervention? "This worshipful doctor said it was a great miracle, and Our Lord was highly to be magnified for preserving this creature against the malice of her enemy, and told it to many people and many people magnified God much in this creature. Many also would not believe it, and thought it more a token of wrath and vengeance, rather than believe it was any token of mercy and kindness" (p. 15).

For Margery Kempe, however, the greatest attraction to church

13. Most of the important events in Margery's book are reported as occurring on Fridays—trials as well as happy events. Fridays, as fast days, were set aside by the Church to mark the memory of Christ's Passion, and Margery's "Fridays" enhanced the significance of her experiences.

was the sermon. In this she was truly a creature of her time: for Lollard and orthodox alike, the sermon was the center and substance of intellectual, spiritual, and social life, and effective preachers were popular heroes. Saint Bernardino of Siena said: "If of these two things you can only do one—either hear the mass or hear the sermon—you should let the mass go rather than the sermon."[14] The Franciscan saint's ideas about the importance of sermons were exactly like those of the Lollards, suggesting that Luther's *fides ex auditu* had deep and varied roots in late medieval piety. By the fourteenth century the sermon had become the central dramatic participatory event in Christian corporate life. The friars preached penitence rather than dogma; their sermons—on which their popularity rested— were designed more to convert sinners than to teach doctrine.[15] Congregations depended on sermons to bring to life the routines and rituals of their faith as well as to convey its substance, and Margery's book provides substantial evidence for the appreciation of fine preaching among devout lay people.

Margery's love of sermons increased as she advanced in her vocation. During her early struggles, her spiritual education was most often conducted in private colloquy and meditation. By the time she reached Rome, however, she could not be content without an English-speaking preacher: "Sometimes when the aforesaid creature was at sermons, where Duchemen and other men preached, teaching the laws of God, sudden sorrow and grief occupying her heart caused her to complain with mourning face for lack of understanding, desiring to be refreshed with some crumb of ghostly understanding . . . " (p. 85). The Church and its preaching stood at the center of social and spiritual life for most medieval Christians; for one such as Margery Kempe, it became her world.

14. St. Bernardino is quoted by A. G. Little in *Studies in English Franciscan History*, p. 133.

15. See Etienne Delaruelle et al., *L'église au temps du Grand Schisme et de la crise conciliare*, p. 638.

The numerous clerks of Margery's acquaintance, with whom she existed in states ranging from intimate friendship to violent animosity, illustrate in cross-section the English clergy of the late Middle Ages. Her book exposes their strengths and weaknesses, their several roles in the community, the image of the Church they reflected, and the service they provided at least to one devoted parishioner. *The Book of Margery Kempe* offers lavish testimony to the spiritual and social state of English churchmen in the fifteenth century.[16]

Like any devout Christian, Margery relied on the clergy for her basic spiritual needs of sermon and sacrament, but her special way of life and mystical experience made her dependent also on their social and emotional support. In *Sin and Confession on the Eve of the Reformation*, Thomas Tentler remarked that "social control was a function of sacramental confession."[17] For Margery, however, the control was less social than emotional: the styles and attitudes of her confessors were crucial to her psychic as well as spiritual welfare. In anguished fear of death and damnation after childbirth, she tried to relieve her conscience of an unconfessed sin. She called her confessor, but he "was a little too hasty and began sharply to reprove her, before she had fully said her intent, and so she would no more say for aught he might do" (p. 1). His ineptitude and her fear precipitated her breakdown.[18]

---

16. E.g., *The Book of Margery Kempe* is used as evidence of Arundel's sincerity and pastoral competence in (among others) Richard G. Davies, "Thomas Arundel as Archbishop of Canterbury, 1396–1414," and K. B. McFarlane, *Lancastrian Kings and Lollard Knights*, p. 65.

17. Thomas N. Tentler, *Sin and Confession on the Eve of the Reformation*, p. xvii.

18. See the comment by Eleanor Prosser in *Drama and Religion in the English Mystery Plays*, p. 115: "People were constantly warned from the pulpit concerning contrition without auricular confession and penance, and medieval playwrights presented dramatically the same warning." Prosser's discussion of guilt, confession, and penance (pp. 118–125) illuminates Margery's terror of dying without full confession.

Much later, Margery complained to her regular confessor: "He that is my confessor in your absence is right sharp with me; he will not believe my feelings; he setteth naught by them; he holdeth them but trifles and japes, and that is great pain to me, for I love him well and would fain follow his counsel" (p. 35). The anchorite explained that severity was important as well as comfort: "God, for your merit, hath ordained him to be your scourge, and he fareth with you as a smith with a file maketh the iron bright and clean. . . . The more sharp it is to you the more clearly shineth your soul in the sight of God, and God hath ordained me to be your nurse and your comfort" (pp. 35–36).

Margery knew many good priests, but also had to suffer bad ones—notably, the hateful priest in her company of pilgrims. He tormented her, but she had God's support in confronting him: "Daughter, dread thee not whatever he saith to thee, for though he run every year to Jerusalem, I have no liking for him, for as long as he speaketh against thee, he speaketh against me, for I am in thee, and thou art in Me. . . . As for this priest that is thine enemy, he is but a hypocrite" (p. 74). When Margery was banned from the sermons of the Franciscan preacher in Lynn, God renewed his assurance that no priest could be her enemy without being God's enemy: "There is no clerk that can speak against the life that I teach thee; and, if he does, he is not God's clerk: he is the devil's clerk" (p. 144). When she protested that the good life revealed to her should be shown to priests, God said they were too proud: "For daughter, I tell thee, he that dreadeth the shames of the world, may not perfectly love God. And, daughter, under the habit of holiness is hidden much wickedness" (pp. 144–145). Priestly office was no guarantee of God's favor, nor were sacramental powers sure tokens of sanctity.

Margery was not in the least diffident about criticizing priests, even those of the highest rank, and even when she was in hostile company. When she visited Thomas Arundel at Lambeth, she first rebuked his servingmen for swearing, then complained of them to the archbishop. She threatened the men with damnation and spoke more politely, but no less directly, to the primate: "My lord, Our Lord of all, Almighty God has not given you your benefice and great worldly wealth to keep His traitors and them that slay Him every day by great oaths swearing. Ye shall answer for them, unless ye correct them, or else put them out of your service" (p. 29).

Margery had a respectful view of what the archbishop's position was, or should be, but she also had a horror of cursing. She chided the English people in Middelburg for swearing and rebuked "religious men" at Hayles for the same fault: "some were right well pleased" (p. 97), she said. At York she was not afraid to say to those who threatened to burn her: "Sirs, I dread ye shall be burnt in Hell without end, unless ye amend in your swearing of oaths, for ye keep not the Commandments of God. I would not swear as ye do for all the money in this world" (p. 111). Her passionate dislike of swearing may have increased the risk that she might be accused of heresy, for in this period "abhorrence of oaths was a clue to: Lollardy."[19] There was, however, ample provocation and orthodox precedent for her attitude: G. R. Owst said that denunciations of swearing were "conspicuous pulpit commonplaces."[20] Poets as well as preachers complained that clerks, who should be more careful than other people, were among the worst offenders. The blasphemous habit of swearing by "Christ's blood," "Christ's nails," and so forth, shocked the devout, including Chaucer's Parson:

> For Cristes sake, ne swereth nat so synfully in dismembrynge of Crist by soule, herte, bones, and body. For certes, it semeth that ye thynke that the cursede Jewes ne dismembred nat ynough the preciouse persone of Crist, but ye dismembre hym moore.[21]

The Pardoner gave examples of the current fashion in oaths:

19. John McKenna, "Piety and Propaganda: The Cult of King Henry VI," in Beryl Rowland, ed., *Chaucer and Middle English Studies*, p. 78.

20. G. R. Owst, *Literature and Pulpit in Medieval England*, p. 415.

21. *The Complete Works of Geoffrey Chaucer*, p. 293.

"By Goddes precious herte," and "By his nayles,"
And, "By the blood of Crist that is in Hayles. . . ."[22]

Swearing was not the only vice of high churchmen and their attendants to provoke Margery's wrath and comment. When she appeared before the bishop of Worcester, "she saw many of the Bishop's men, all slashed and pointed in their clothes" (p. 96), and told them they were more like devil's men than bishop's men. "Slashing and pointing" and other extreme fashions in men's as well as women's clothes were castigated by preachers, who saw such fashions as extravagant, "foreign" in influence, and symptomatic of dangerous worldliness.[23]

Neither clerical rank nor her own perilous situation deterred Margery from speaking up. When the archbishop of York said he had heard bad reports of her, she answered: "I also hear it said that ye are a wicked man. And if ye be as wicked as men say, ye shall never come to Heaven, unless ye amend whilst ye be here" (p. 112). This surely is an extraordinary speech from a woman on trial for heresy in a time of burning.

Despite her bluntness, Margery generally got on very well with important clerics; with some exceptions, she was more popular with higher than with lower clergy. In Constance, when she was friendless and at odds with her fellow pilgrims, she sought out the papal legate. He listened to her confession and her troubles, believed her, and took time to visit the pilgrims. He defended Margery to them, and when they still rejected her, he "made arrangements for this creature and made her his charge as if she had been his mother" (p. 54). Margery visited Constance in 1413, when preparations for the Council must have been under way, but the legate took the trouble to pay attention to her problems.

Richard Caister, the saintly vicar of Norwich, answered her

22. *Ibid.*, p. 183.

23. Compare Owst, *Literature and Pulpit*, pp. 404–411. In his *Instructions for Parish Priests*, John Mirk ordered clerks, in particular, to avoid "cuttede clothes and pyked schone" (p. 2).

request for an hour of his time by saying: "Benedicite. How could a woman occupy an hour or two hours in the love of Our Lord? I shall never eat meat till I learn what ye can say of Our Lord God in the time of an hour" (p. 30). He became her friend and confessor and supported her against detractors. Thomas Arundel took time and care with her too; even after she scolded him for the behavior of his household, "their dalliance continued till stars appeared in the firmament" (p. 29). The archbishop of York would have liked the troublesome woman to vanish, but he was just and careful in his dealings with her. *The Book of Margery Kempe* shows the English clergy possessed of more sensitivity and attention to pastoral responsibilities than has generally been believed. (It is true, of course, that the clergy of Norwich in particular may have been especially careful with the daughter of a mayor of Lynn.)

Acceptance and support from clerical authorities were essential to Margery's inner and outer peace. Even with God's private assurance, she could not have maintained her eccentric existence without the sanction of the Church. At first she needed the archbishop's permission to live apart from her husband; later, clerical authorization was necessary for her to wear white clothes, to go on pilgrimage, to receive Communion weekly—in other words, to live the life God commanded and she wanted for herself. Besides, her life on the boundary of Church and society was psychically and physically dangerous and exhausting, and she needed the support and reassurance of respected persons in order to maintain her determination and self-confidence.

Margery Kempe was much more terrified of demonic suggestion than of arrest or ostracism. Her vocation as well as her psychic health depended on the conviction that her "feelings" came from God, but she could not be perfectly sure—for long— that the devil might not interfere. In her own mind, and in the teaching of the Church, her feelings required "proving" by persons recognized as authorities in the discernment of spirits.

From its earliest days, the Church was concerned with questions about the discernment of good and evil spirits, and this became a matter of profound concern in the later Middle Ages. Paul's first letter to the Corinthians mentioned *diakriseis,* or "the ability to distinguish between spirits" (1 Cor. 12:20) as a gift of the Holy Spirit—a charism granted to certain people for the good of the community. False confessors made the question complicated, and the second letter to the Corinthians warned of "false apostles, deceitful workmen" and added that "even Satan disguises himself as an agent of light" (2 Cor. 11:13–14). Saint Matthew provided a warning and a rule for distinguishing between good and bad spirits: "Beware of false prophets, who come to you in sheep's clothing but inwardly are ravenous wolves. You will know them by their fruits" (Matt. 7:15–16). The biblical warning that looks and words may deceive, and the emphasis on fruits (solid evidence of goodness in the life and works of the visionary), provided the basis for an extensive medieval literature of discernment.

A distinction was made between discernment itself, which was a divine gift, and "discretion," a broader term implying the virtue of prudence or care in almost any pastoral work requiring judgment. All writers insisted on humility and obedience as essential attributes of confessor as well as "prophet," and all emphasized "fruits" as the major criteria of spiritual soundness. In the English tradition, discernment was closely tied to pastoral responsibility: in the *Ancrene Riwle,* to frequent confession, and in *The Cloud of Unknowing,* to the arts of teaching and counseling.

The visions and prophecies of Saint Birgitta of Sweden provoked an outburst of concern over questions surrounding private revelations and discernment of spirits. Her *Revelations* were extensive, very widely known, and concerned with matters of national, international, and ecclesiastical politics. Like Saint Catherine of Siena, Birgitta worked and spoke publicly for the return of the pope to Rome. English churchmen participated actively in the discussion of the *Revelations,* which touched off a lively debate over the writings of women vision-aries.[24] Margery visited Constance just before the Council, when the argument was at its height. While the discussion was conducted on the highest ecclesiastical level, it raised questions that were reflected in pulpits and confessionals all over Europe.

The most important participant in the debate over discernment was Jean Gerson—mystic, theologian, and chancellor of the University of Paris. Gerson was a rare figure: a contemplative and visionary who was thoroughly involved with contemporary political and ecclesiastical affairs. In 1400–1401 he wrote "De distinctione verarum visionum a falsis"; during the Council of Constance, at which he led the anti-Birgittine forces, he wrote the definitive treatise, "De probatione spirituum." In that work he summarized the traditional teaching on discernment and acknowledged the danger of either approving or disapproving Saint Birgitta's *Revelations*. For the Council to approve of false or foolish revelations would be scandalous, but Saint Birgitta's writings were so well known and widely accepted that to disapprove them would threaten the devotion of many faithful people.[25]

Gerson neither accepted nor denounced Birgitta's *Revelations*, but he set forth the rules of discernment so that the danger of too numerous or inauthentic visionary writings might be avoided

24. The most complete account of the development of the cult of Birgitta in England is F. R. Johnston, "The Cult of St. Bridget of Sweden in Fifteenth-Century England." For a succinct description of one of Birgitta's English supporters, see W. A. Pantin, *The English Church in the Fourteenth Century*, pp. 175–181, on the career of Adam Easton, monk of Norwich and later cardinal.

25. Gerson was sympathetic to the Armagnac cause, and to Joan of Arc, in spite of his attitude toward conspicuous visionary women. In a treatise circulated under his name, but probably not authentic, he (or the author, who may have been associated with him) said: "Let us add, besides, that the Maid seems to have had no recourse to sorceries forbidden by the Church, nor to damnable superstitions, nor to the deceptions of crafty folk. Nor does she pursue her self-interest, since she exposes her body to the supreme peril to bear witness to her mission" (*Traité de Jean Gerson sur la Pucelle*, p. 19).

in the future. He listed the standard questions a confessor or other authority must ask: "To whom is the revelation made? What does the revelation itself mean and what does it say? Why is it said to have occurred? To whom was it disclosed for advice? How and whence did it originate?"[26] Satisfactory answers had to be received before a revelation could be regarded as divine in origin.

Acceptable revelations had to conform to Scripture, to Church doctrine, to good morals, and to reason; the tests of humility, discretion, patience, truth, and charity must be applied. The visionary must be of virtuous character—humble, truthful, chaste, and obedient. Negative signs such as pride, lust, or impatience reflected poorly on the vision and the visionary. The spiritual director must be especially careful about young persons and about women, "whose enthusiasm is excessive, greedy, changeable, unruly, and thus is suspect."[27] And furthermore: "if the visionary is a woman, you must consider how she talks with her confessors and instructors, whether she draws out continual conversations, under the pretext of frequent confessions, or in telling lengthy accounts of her visions, or by some other kind of discussions."[28]

Eric Colledge argued that Gerson's treatise was based on a clever rearrangement of Alphonse of Pecha's treatise *Epistola solitarii ad reges*, which was written in defense of (and to introduce) Birgitta's *Revelations*. Colledge said that Gerson would not "directly impute heresy to a canonized saint, but he may remind his readers of the many heretical visionaries there have been. . . . [Birgitta] was not a religious, lived in a constant blaze of publicity, and was much given to the public utterance of her views."[29] In her lesser sphere, the same might be said of Margery Kempe. There were two schools of thought about such

26. Jean Gerson, "De probatione spirituum," 180.

27. *Ibid.*

28. *Ibid.*, 184.

29. Eric Colledge, "*Epistola solitarii ad reges*," 46.

women, and although Margery was not a political, aristocratic saint with an international reputation, she certainly was caught up in the crosscurrents of the debate, and she and her advisers were conscious of the issues. Thanks to the widespread contemporary interest in visions and revelations, even humble preachers and confessors were aware of the requirements for discernment. Margery herself was fully alert to the danger of diabolical suggestion, and her concern was not discouraged by her clerical friends. As a woman, she may have been inspired by Saint Birgitta, but she also was subject to the suspicion that surrounded women's mystical experiences.

Particularly at the beginning of her religious life, Margery was "charged and commanded in her soul" (p. 32) to visit persons who were known to be gifted in discernment. At the end of her first colloquy, God sent her to the Dominican anchorite who became her long-time friend and confessor. He received her with reverence and promised her the benefits of his skill: "Daughter, ye suck even on Christ's breast, and ye have an earnest-penny of Heaven. I charge you to receive such thoughts as God gives, as meekly and devoutly as ye can, and to come to me and tell me what they are, and I shall . . . tell you whether they are of the Holy Ghost or of your enemy the devil" (p. 10).[30]

Bishop Repington not only encouraged Margery but urged her to write down her revelations, for he thought "they were high matters and full devout matters, and inspired by the Holy Ghost" (p. 26). Richard Caister "trustfully believed that she was well learned in the law of God, and endued with the grace of the Holy Ghost" (p. 32). The Carmelite William Sowthfeld urged her to be meek and humble, and assured her: "I believe not that Our Lord suffereth them to be deceived endlessly, that set all their trust in Him" (p. 33). Dame Julian, who was

30. The anchorite, like Julian of Norwich, used maternal imagery for Christ; Margery herself always perceived God as male and used masculine God-language.

recognized as an authority in distinguishing true from false spirits, emphasized "fruits" and advised Margery to accept what God sent: "if it were not against the worship of God, and profit of her fellow Christians, for if it were, then it were not the moving of a good spirit, but rather of an evil spirit. 'The Holy Ghost moveth ne'er a thing against charity.... Also He moveth a soul to all chasteness.... Any creature that hath these tokens may steadfastly believe that the Holy Ghost dwelleth in his soul' (pp. 33–34).

Despite the assurance of God's love and favor, which she did not seriously doubt, Margery was never completely confident about her own "feelings." She persisted throughout her life in efforts to have her visions as well as her way of life approved and confirmed: "This creature shewed her manner of living to many a worthy clerk, and worshipful doctors of divinity, both religious men and others of secular habit, and they said that God wrought great grace with her, and bade her she should not be afraid" (p. 34). Frequent discussion of her "feelings" relieved her anxiety, particularly when her confessor took responsibility on himself, as did the anchorite who "took it on charge of his soul that her feelings were good and sure" (p. 35). She did not mention that any of these men objected to her loquacity, despite Gerson's concern about that tendency in female visionaries.

Neither the anchorite, the scribe, nor her other directors seemed to follow the chancellor's advice for those who dealt with women: "Meanwhile, you who will hear and counsel such a one, beware that you do not applaud her or praise her, or admire her as a saint worthy of revelations and miracles. Rather, resist her, rebuke her harshly, reject her as one whose heart is exalted, whose eyes are raised up and who is engaged in great and wonderful matters that are beyond her."[31] Gerson urged priests to encourage penitents "not to seek the flavor of

31. Gerson, "De probatione," 181.

the sublime,"[32] but to practice their faith in the ordinary ways, "through the doctrine of the Scriptures and the saints, with the teachings of natural reason, lest she assume that she has the counsel not only of the angels but of God, and not only occasionally but almost constantly, or by daily conversation."[33] "Almost constantly" describes Margery's situation accurately.

The papal legate at Constance listened to Margery and pronounced her "feelings" to be "the work of the Holy Ghost" (p. 53). He probably was a member of the pro-Birgittine party, but he must also have been aware of the conservative attitude of many ecclesiastics toward private revelations. ("De probatione spirituum," with its norms for confessors, was not written until just after Margery's visit to Constance in 1413.) In general, she was more confident about her feelings after her pilgrimages. Her self-confidence in dealings with those who accused her of Lollardy indicates that although she may have feared the insinuations of the devil, she knew she was no heretic.

Margery did, however, suffer a recurrence of anxiety around the writing of her book—an activity that also inspired various "signs and wonders." She heard ineffable sounds and melodies while she was writing; she was frequently ill, and on each occasion was suddenly made well and told to return to her work. These miraculous phenomena worried her, even though Jesus and the Virgin both assured her of their approval of the project. It seems likely that writing a book was itself cause for anxiety; Dame Julian was a spectacular exception, but it was still true that English women in general did not write books. For whatever reason, Margery reflected seriously on her "feelings" during this stage in her life: "And sometimes those that men think were revelations, are deceits and illusions, and therefore it is not expedient to give readily credence to every stirring, but soberly abide, and pray if it be sent of God ... " (p. 199). That passage reflects advice given in almost all contemporary writ-

32. *Ibid.*
33. *Ibid.*

ings for visionaries and their confessors. In her book, Margery did not report discouragement from her advisers, but there must have been warnings, and she must have heeded them, for she certainly was bothered by her feelings:

> Sometimes she was in great gloom for her feelings, when she knew not how they should be understood . . . for dread that she had of deceits and illusions. . . . For sometimes, what she understood bodily was to be understood ghostly, and the dread that she had of her feelings was the greatest scourge that she had on earth; and especially when she had her first feelings; and that dread made her full meek, for she had no joy in the feeling till she knew by experience whether it was true or not. [P. 199]

Here she displayed the humility described by every authority as one essential mark of the divine origin of "ghostly feelings."

Anxiety over the related questions of discernment of spirits, religious enthusiasm, spiritual direction, and female visionaries was intense during Margery's lifetime. She was most directly affected, perhaps, by the contemporary and local form of "enthusiasm"—Lollardy—and by the response to it in the English Church. However, the reverberations of Saint Birgitta's *Revelations* are also apparent in Margery's book, as is her own intense fear of false "feelings," or as she put it herself, "the dread that she had of illusions." Such intense anxiety reflects, in addition to contemporary issues, her utter dependence on the "truth" of her feelings and on the men and the institution responsible for judging them—and for judging her. Cut off from family, neighborhood ties, and conventional social roles, Margery Kempe was understandably anxious about the validity of her calling and the sanction of her Church.

Not only Margery herself but the men with whom she discussed religious matters were influenced and worried by contemporary events and arguments that helped to mold their attitudes toward women in general and Margery in particular. In turn, of course, her attitudes toward the Church, and the shape of her vocation, were profoundly affected by the behavior and responses of the clergy. For Margery Kempe, the Church was a primary source of lifelong teaching and comfort, a basic constituent of her worldly as well as "ghostly" life, and an essential framework for her calling. Her "Ghostly Mother Holy Church," beset by heresy in its branches and Schism at its center, remained the body of Christ and the parent of the Christian people.

Chapter Five

"IN THE LIKENESS
OF A MAN"

*The Tradition of
Affective Piety*

ALTHOUGH the piety of Margery Kempe has seemed eccentric or "hysterical" to certain readers of her book, what bothered her contemporaries was not her devotional style but her behavior. It is true that aspects of her religious expression offended some people and frightened others. The clergy, however, generally supported her, and they did so partly because the forms and intentions of her prayers and practices belonged to an established and respected tradition of piety. Margery Kempe's way of life was highly unusual, especially in England, as the troubled response of her neighbors makes clear. To understand the sources of her support (as well as the nature of her vocation), she must be seen not simply as an eccentric but as a participant in a religious tradition four centuries old.

In the tradition of "affective piety,"[1] in which Margery Kempe's religious emotions and expression can be located, the aim was not so much to teach doctrine or offer formal worship as to move the heart of the believer. Generally this was accomplished through a personal, passionate attachment to the hu-

1. For a summary of the development of the affective tradition in prayer and meditation, see Elizabeth Salter, "Nicholas Love's 'Myrrour of the Blessed Lyf of Jesu Christ.'" See also Susan Dickman, "Margery Kempe and the English Devotional Tradition."

man Jesus, and particularly to the aspects of Christ's life which belong to the universal experience: birth and death, Nativity and Passion. Emotions were stirred to wonder and joy, bitter grief and sadness, and tears were actively sought as natural accompaniments to participation in the Christian story. The Gospels became more than ever the bases of pious writings, but the authors of affective meditations expanded on Scripture. They used their imaginations to invent conversations, incidents, and relationships in the lives of Jesus, Mary, and the saints— anything to touch the hearts and capture the attention of the devout. Their aim was conversion, and beyond that, salvation.

Margery Kempe's first direct encounter with the divine was a vision of Jesus "in the likeness of a man" (p. 2); later, Christ asked her to love him as a son, brother, husband, and father. Writers in the affective tradition used the many varieties of human love to talk about divine love and to stimulate the love of God in human beings. The God of affective piety was less Judge or Creator than Love, Lover, and Loved. Jesus the Comforter, who rescued Margery from desperate illness, was perceived by her at other moments as child and husband and father. In his humanity he satisfied human as well as "ghostly" needs—indeed, as we have seen, Margery herself made slight distinction between the two.

In summarizing the affective tradition as it contributes to the understanding of Margery Kempe, we will be looking very briefly at a broad and deep strain in Christian history. Most of the relevant writings are devotional works rather than speculative theology. Affective piety does not imply any particular theological stance, except the primacy of love over reason in the knowledge of God, nor does it mandate a special way of life, although most of its authors were monks or friars. Many of these works were written for female friends and relatives, and as literacy increased and lay piety blossomed in the later Middle Ages, they were written for lay people as well as those in religious life. Higher education and ecclesiastical position neither prescribed nor precluded affective piety, a mood and form of expression which advanced over all of Europe between the eleventh and the sixteenth centuries. There are many examples of such writings but very few surviving examples of the uses made of them, or the response to them, by lay people. Margery's book serves as evidence of the influence of the tradition among "ordinary" Christians. Her habits of prayer and meditation, strange as they may seem, were faithful responses to several centuries of instruction.

The first stirrings of affective piety—the earliest prayers and meditations consciously designed to use the emotions to move the believer toward God—are generally traced to Anselm of Canterbury and his circle in the late eleventh century.[2] R. W. Southern described the shift in emphasis in private prayer at this period as a "revolution,"[3] for the piety created by Anselm and his friends and imitators was quite unlike the inherited tradition of Carolingian piety, in which the private devotions of monks and lay people alike were centered almost entirely on the psalms.[4]

Anselm and his circle emphasized new subjects: episodes in Christian history, in the Gospels and the lives of the saints and the Virgin. They also created new forms in a more personal, complex, and elaborate language than that of the Psalter or the monastic office. Such prayers were intended for personal devotion and suited to the private cell. Anselm's introduction to a group of prayers clarifies his purpose:

> The prayers and meditations written below were written to inspire the reader's mind to the love and fear of God; they are not to be read in the midst of an uproar, but in quiet, not

2. Anselm carried to England a style of thought and writing which originated in northern Italy with Anselm himself and his master, Lanfranc, as well as Peter Damian and John of Fécamp (see Salter, "Love's Myrrour").

3. R. W. Southern, *St. Anselm and His Biographer*, p. 42.

4. See, for example, Ernst Duemmler, ed., *Alcuini Epistolae*, Ep. 243, p. 390, *Bibliotheca rerum germanicarum*, Vol. VI (Berlin, 1895).

quickly or rapidly, but gradually, attentively and painstakingly meditated. Neither, however, should the reader read through any of them at once, but with God helping, how much he feels will be effective in inflaming his desire to pray, or how much may please him. Neither must he necessarily begin at the beginning, but rather wherever it pleases him.[5]

The meditations were not ends in themselves, but springboards to personal experience, to be used privately and apart from the formal worship in which all Christians were expected to participate.

Anselm's focus was on the concrete and the tangible, and his concern was not speculation, but the believer's hopes and fears. The writer's own wishes, fears, and experience provided the motives for prayer; he was gripped by his fears and horrified by his sins.[6] His language was powerful, and his mood, intense: "Oh virginity, now not my delight, but my loss; now not my joy, but my despair: where have you departed, in what stench, in what bitter filth you abandoned me! Oh fornication, degrader of my mind, destroyer of my soul: whence did you steal unawares on your wretched [victim], from what a bright, what a joyous state you expelled me! . . . This is loss inconsolable, this is torment intolerable!"[7]

Anselm's *Oratio XVI*, addressed to Mary Magdalene, exemplifies the kind of prayer that was widely imitated and helped to shape the piety of Margery Kempe and her contemporaries. Emphasizing the love and tears of the saint, Anselm made clear the connection between her great love for Jesus and his love for her. She was the model of the weeping lover: "Saint Mary Magdalene, who came with a spring of tears to the spring of Christ's mercy, from which, thirsting greatly, you were refreshed abundantly, through which the sinner is justified, through which she grieving most bitterly is most sweetly

5. Anselm, *Orationes sive meditationes*, p. 3.

6. *Ibid.*, p. 76: "My life terrifies me."

7. *Ibid.*, p. 80.

consoled. ... "[8] The scene at the empty tomb is presented like a scene from a play, with characters, setting, and dialogue. It resembles the "Quem queritis," the trope in the Holy Saturday liturgy to which is credited the beginning of medieval (and modern) theater.[9] The "audience" of the prayer is caught up in the drama, weeping with Mary Magdalene and then sharing with her the ecstasy of the first witness to the Resurrection. Emotions range from overwhelming sadness to overpowering joy, and these emotions are to be experienced again by every Christian soul in meditation: "Oh how unlike are 'They have taken my Master, and I do not know where they have placed him,' and this: 'Because I have seen my Master and he has spoken to me'!"[10] This is not an allegorical or symbolic meditation but is designed to happen in the present to every participant.

Saint Anselm made vivid use of bisexual and multifunctional language about God. Not only Jesus but even Saint Paul was perceived as mother and nurse as well as father: "Oh Saint Paul, where is she who is called nurse of the faithful, cherishing her sons? Who is that loving mother, the one everywhere proclaimed to be in labor with her children? Sweet nurse, sweet mother, who are those children you bring forth and nurse, other than those you bear and educate, bringing them up in the faith of Christ?"[11] The roles of mother and father are conventional, but Christian teachers (and Christ himself) were expected to fill both roles: "You are both mothers therefore. And yet fathers too, as well as mothers. ... You are fathers by deed, mothers by disposition. You are fathers by authority,

---

8. *Ibid.*, p. 64.

9. For a description of the *quem queritis* and its place in the origins of medieval theater, see Rosemary Woolf, *The English Mystery Plays*, pp. 4–11.

10. Anselm, *Orationes*, p. 67.

11. *Ibid.*, p. 39. For a perceptive discussion of the use of maternal imagery by Cistercian writers, see Caroline W. Bynum, "Jesus as Mother and Abbot as Mother," in *Jesus as Mother*, pp. 110–169. See also the discussion of Anselm and Ailred in John Boswell, *Christianity, Social Tolerance, and Homosexuality*, pp. 218–226.

mothers by kindness. You are fathers through teaching, mothers through compassion. Therefore you are both mothers."[12] Through his teaching, Paul gives life—like a mother. "Do, mother of my soul, what the mother of my flesh would do."[13] Apparently there was nothing shocking or disruptive about ascribing to male saints (or to God) any attribute perceived as valuable. For the theologian whose God was that-than-which-nothing-greater-can-be-conceived, to neglect the essential attribute of maternity would have been to diminish God.

Seven of Anselm's prayers and meditations were sent to Adelaide, a daughter of William the Conquerer, in 1071. The impulse to write, collect, and send prayers, rules, and instructions to pious women goes back at least to Saint Jerome in the Christian tradition, and it flourished throughout the Middle Ages and beyond. Aristocratic women, lay women as well as nuns, frequently requested from their spiritual advisers and other admired churchmen directions for study and reading and prayer. The churchmen's need to fill such requests, and perhaps to see themselves reflected as spiritual giants in the eyes of devout women, produced much of the devotional literature of Christianity.[14]

The English Cistercian Ailred of Rievaulx (d. 1166) followed in the meditative tradition of Saint Anselm and corresponded with Saint Bernard. Even more fervently than his predecessor, Ailred attempted to enter into the events and emotions of the Gospels. One of his most interesting affective works is the "Triple Meditation," part of a rule for recluses written for his sister. In mood and content, it marks a significant step in the development of affective piety. When Margery Kempe placed herself in meditation among the holy persons at the manger or the Cross, she was obeying the instructions of Ailred as well as later writers.

12. Anselm, *Orationes*, p. 40.

13. *Ibid.*, p. 41.

14. Virginia Woolf said: "Women have served all these centuries as looking-glasses possessing the magic and delicious power of reflecting the figure of man at twice its natural size" (*A Room of One's Own* [New York, 1957], p. 35).

The "Triple Meditation" begins with the Annunciation and proceeds to the Visitation, a favorite subject of affective writers. Addressing his sister (and through her, other celibate women), Ailred described in touching terms the meeting of Elizabeth and Mary ("the barren wife and the virgin").[15] Then he spoke directly to his sister: "What are you doing, virgin? Run, I beg, run and take part in such joy, prostrate yourself at the feet of both, in the womb of one embrace your Bridegroom, in the womb of the other do honor to his friend."[16] Ailred, who so much appreciated human friendship, called attention to the "friendship" of the infants in their mothers' wombs. In Margery Kempe's account of the Visitation, the emphasis was on the friendship of the women, who "each worshipped the other, and so they dwelt together, with great grace and gladness twelve weeks" (p. 11). At the Nativity, Ailred told the worshiper to help the Virgin and to place the Child in the manger. Margery Kempe assisted in her own way, finding "bedding for Our Lady to lie in with her Blessed Son" (p. 12).

Of the Virgin's sorrow at the Crucifixion, Ailred spoke poignantly to his sister: "But you, virgin, who can feel more confidence with the Virgin's son than the women who stand at a distance, draw near to the Cross with the Virgin Mother and the virgin disciple, and look at close quarters upon that face in all its pallor. What then? Will you not weep as her soul is pierced by the sword of sorrow?"[17] Ailred assumed that his sister could not stand dry-eyed at the Cross while the Virgin wept. Margery Kempe certainly could not: "Then she thought Our Lady wept wondrous sore, and therefore the said creature must needs weep and cry when she saw such ghostly sights in her soul . . . " (p. 174). The emphasis on virginity is characteris-

15. Ailred, *A Rule of Life for a Recluse*, tr. Mary Paul Macpherson O.S.C.O., *The Works of Ailred of Rievaulx, Vol. I*, p. 81.

16. *Ibid.*

17. *Ibid.*, p. 90.

tic of monastic meditations; Ailred indicated that his sister's virgin status allowed her to approach the Virgin. That assumption was conventional, and Margery's lament for her own lost virginity is hardly surprising in such a context. She needed the Lord's reassurance that "though the state of maidenhood be more perfect and more holy . . . yet, daughter, I love thee as well as any maiden in the world" (p. 40).

Ailred described the complex relationship of the Incarnation, the ascetic religious life, and affective piety. In his *Speculum caritatis* he wrote: "that a man may not succumb to carnal concupiscence, let him turn his whole affection to the attractions of the Lord's flesh."[18] The Christian, and especially the man or woman vowed to religion, was not supposed to be cold or unfeeling—quite the opposite. Feelings indeed must be controlled, damned up, but only so that they might pour out in the love of God, which should absorb all human senses and affections. Sometimes, Ailred wrote, anchoresses keep a school for small children from the window of their cells. If one of the little pupils is hurt or punished, the recluse takes the child in her arms to kiss and comfort it—and then what happens to the "continual remembrance of God?"[19] Such affections are not bad or harmful in themselves; they do harm only insofar as they confuse priorities.

God became human so that God could be loved by human beings with human emotions, and those who renounce or subordinate human love do so in order to become greater lovers. Every medieval religious thinker believed this, or something like it, but Ailred made it explicit. His understanding of

18. Ailred, *Speculum caritatis* iii, 5, quoted in Aelred Squire, O.P., *Aelred of Rievaulx*, p. 47.

19. Ailred, *A Rule of Life*, p. 50. Mary Paul Macpherson points out in a note that the "memory" of God is an Augustinian theme emphasized in monastic spirituality and that it "does not mean simply a calling to mind but rather a re-presentation and actual living presence of the reality somewhat as we have it in the sacrifice of the Mass in response to Christ's command: 'Do this in remembrance of me.' "

human and divine love, which is essential to an appreciation of Margery Kempe, makes affective piety intelligible to a post-Freudian age. Originally, such meditations were not written for lay people—as Ailred's were not—for the excellent reason that lay people were not in a position to sublimate all their affections in the love of God. But the appeal of such piety spread beyond the cloister, and Margery Kempe's story illustrates the ability and desire of some lay people to love God with all their hearts.

The contribution to the affective tradition of Saint Bernard, Ailred's contemporary and fellow Cistercian, was immeasurable because his influence was so wide and so long-lasting. Bernard's writings were even more popular than those of Anselm in the late Middle Ages.[20] Many pious works were composed directly under his influence, and many more were attributed to him. Bernard's devotion to the humanity of Christ, admittedly a formative influence in late medieval piety, was just one aspect of a complex and sophisticated theology. He regarded the sensory and emotional adoration of the human Jesus as a step toward the rational grasp of Christian truth and the ultimate goal of spiritual union. Through the imaginative recreation of the Christian story, God could be loved first through the Incarnation, but in time human emotions could be transformed into spiritual love: "Your affection for your Lord Jesus should be both tender and intimate, to oppose the sweet enticements of sensual life. Sweetness conquers sweetness as one nail drives out another. No less than this keep him as a strong light for your mind and a guide for your intellect. . . . "[21] In Sermon 20 on the Canticles, Saint Bernard explained the place of attraction to Christ's humanity in prayer and devotion. For the lover

---

20. Giles Constable, "The Popularity of Twelfth-Century Spiritual Writers in the Late Middle Ages," p. 17. Pourrat commented that "the preachings of the Abbot of Clairvaux, taken collectively, form a kind of mystical biography of the Saviour" (Pierre Pourrat, *Christian Spirituality in the Middle Ages,* 2:51).

21. *On the Song of Songs I,* in *The Works of Bernard of Clairvaux* 2:150.

of Jesus, everything about his life is absorbing, and concentration on him makes the soul love virtue and hate vice. That was one purpose of the Incarnation: "I think this is the principal reason why the invisible God willed to be seen in the flesh and to converse with men as a man. He wanted to recapture the affections of carnal men who were unable to love in any other way, by first drawing them to the salutary love of his own humanity, and then gradually to raise them to a spiritual love."[22]

Bernard noted that the disciples loved Jesus' physical presence, followed him, and (being human) could not endure the thought of his death even for their salvation. Margery Kempe struggled with that sorrow when she suffered with Mary Magdalene at "Touch me not" and when she hesitated to marry the Godhead because of her great love for the human Jesus. Saint Bernard preached and helped to inspire the love of Christ's humanity, which he saw as a safeguard against sin: "to love with the whole heart means to put the love of his sacred humanity before everything that tempts us."[23] Such love, as well as a safeguard, was a stepping-stone to a "higher" love, "carnal" only "with comparison to that other love which does not know the Word as flesh so much as the Word as wisdom, as justice, truth, holiness, loyalty, strength. . . . "[24] Carnal love of Christ was desirable, but it "becomes better when it is rational, and becomes perfect when it is spiritual."[25] The "carnal" love of God was only one element of Bernard's theology, but it had extensive influence on his own order, on the Franciscans, the Carthusians, and on late medieval piety in general.

Of all the forces that helped to shape popular devotion in the Middle Ages, none was more significant than the influence of

22. *Ibid.*, p. 152.
23. *Ibid.*, p. 153.
24. *Ibid.*, p. 154.
25. *Ibid.*

the Franciscans—of the saint himself, of the lives and preaching of the friars, and of Franciscan themes in art and literature. Their appeal was to all classes; their approach, according to Heiko Oberman, succeeded so well because it was "psychological rather than metaphysical."[26] The Franciscan ethos and pathos color almost every aspect of the piety of Margery Kempe, from her love of sermons to the meditations that focused on homely details of Nativity and Passion.

The life of Francis, which was transformed almost instantaneously into legend with apocrypha, was perfectly suited to myth making. Whether the hermeneutic be religious or psychoanalytic, the great archetypes were present: the hidden hero recognized only by a "simpleton,"[27] the defiance of the father, the rapid and complete conversion. In relation to Margery's story, it is worth noting that one early mark of sanctity was Francis's sudden attention to lepers, "whereas aforetime not only the company, but even the distant sight, of lepers had inspired him with violent loathing."[28] After his conversion he used to kiss them, even their wounds, as Margery wished to do until discouraged by her confessor.

Francis's response to the Passion was striking and formative. When he was discovered walking and weeping aloud and asked what was wrong, the saint answered: "I ought to go thus weeping and wailing without shame through the whole world for the passion of my Lord."[29] Whether or not that anecdote was ever told or read to Margery, it certainly was known to English friars, and it penetrated the contemporary culture sufficiently to make such a response believable, even admirable. Francis

26. Heiko A. Oberman, "The Shape of Late Medieval Thought," p. 7.

27. "A certain citizen of Assisi, a simpleton as he was believed, yet one taught of God, whensoever he met Francis going through the city, would doff his cloak and spread the garment before his feet, declaring that Francis was worthy of all honor" (*"The Little Flowers" & the Life of St. Francis with the "Mirror of Perfection,"* p. 308).

28. *Ibid.,* p. 310.

29. *Scripta Leonis, Rufini et Angeli,* p. 155.

also was a great exemplum of the gift of tears; "he made declaration that they who keep watch over the perfection of their life ought to cleanse themselves daily with floods of tears."[30] His tears were not, like Margery's, "wells" of virtue; they were floods or rivers "whereby the inner eye is cleansed, that it may avail to see God."[31] The weeping saint, and the fervent emotionalism of his imitators, enshrined tears at the heart of Christian piety.

The legends concerning Francis and his first companions, exemplary in poverty and humility and radiant joy and sorrow, were building blocks in the great edifice of Franciscan spirituality that dominated so much of Christian piety in the thirteenth and fourteenth centuries. Much has been written about Franciscan scholarship in the universities, in theology and philosophy and natural science. The impact of popular Franciscanism was even wider, permeating art, literature, and drama as well as preaching and Christian education. Most people, who could not read the Bible, knew their religion best through Franciscan stories with Franciscan emotion and emphases. The literal story was less important than the penitence it produced; any incident that moved the believer was "true" in the sense that mattered.[32]

One illustration of the Franciscan principle at work on the Christian tradition is the series of legends and works of art concerning the response of the Virgin to the Passion. The synoptic Gospels do not mention Mary among the women at the Crucifixion; Saint John says that she was standing by the Cross, and tells of Jesus' committing her to John's care. Nowhere is there any basis for the elaborate spectrum of response, which ranged from the dignified *Stabat Mater* through a variety of tales of Jesus meeting his Mother on the way to Calvary

30. *"Little Flowers,"* p. 333.

31. *Ibid.*

32. See David L. Jeffrey, *The Early English Lyric and Franciscan Spirituality*, pp. 48–51.

and visiting her after the Resurrection. (Writers of meditations explained, for example, that Jesus called Mary "Woman," and not "Mother," from the Cross—"Woman, behold thy son"—so that her sorrow would not be exacerbated by the tender word, "Mother.")[33] The effect of such stories can be measured by Margery Kempe, who identified her own response to the Crucifixion with that of the Virgin. The most striking feature of Chapter 79 of Margery's book ("The Passion from Betrayal to Scourging") is a full affective meditation on Mary's sorrow. Margery "thought that Our Lady and she were always together to see Our Lord's pains" (p. 174), and it was as Mary's companion that she "saw" the Crucifixion: "Then she thought that Our Lady and she went by another way to meet with Him; and, when they met with Him, they saw Him bearing that heavy Cross with great pain; it was so heavy and so unwieldy that He hardly might bear it. Then Our Lady said unto Him:—'Ah! My sweet Son, let me help to bear that heavy Cross' " (pp. 174–175). The encounter of Mother and Son inspired Margery's intense response to the Passion: "When she heard the words and saw the compassion that the Mother had of the Son, and the Son of His Mother, then she wept, sobbed and cried as though she would have died, for the pity and compassion that she had of that piteous sight, and the holy thoughts that she had in the meantime . . . " (p. 175).

The ghastly details of Scourging and Crucifixion—the drops of bloody sweat, the livid complexion of Jesus, the wounds and the nails—were "facts" made concrete in Franciscan piety, "facts" that Margery Kempe and other Christians could imagine feeling in their own bodies. Freud believed that the drives toward love and death dominate the unconscious hopes and wishes of all people; if this is so, it is not surprising that the Franciscan message was so enthusiastically received. The friars addressed people in what they cared about most deeply—the desire for love and the fear of death—and Margery's book testifies to the

33. *Meditations on the Life of Christ*, p. 336.

resounding success of their mission.

With their enthusiasm for the concrete and tangible, Franciscans were natural guards and guides for pilgrims to the Holy Places. The friars inspired and encouraged the widespread desire for contact with the physical remains of Christ's life, and *The Book of Margery Kempe* testifies to their conspicuous presence and behavior in the Holy Land. When Margery was ostracized by the other pilgrims, "the Grey Friars, who had led her from place to place, received her to them and set her with them at the meat so that she should not eat alone" (p. 62). At Mount Quarentyne, when her companions would not help her, "God, of His great goodness, moved the Grey Friars with compassion, and they comforted her, when her countrymen would not know her" (p. 63).

Saint Francis was a notable advocate of the virtue of humility, especially the extreme humility that seeks public shame and reproof for the love of God. According to legend, the saint felt he had indulged himself during a serious illness even though he had eaten very little. After preaching in the marketplace (still weak from fever), he made another friar "lead him naked before the people; and he ordered another brother to take a bowl full of ashes and go up to the place where he had preached and throw and scatter the ash over his head."[34] Then Francis publicly confessed to "overindulgence" during his illness. The general love and admiration of such behavior must have helped to create—especially in the Holy Land—the climate that inspired Margery to be "more bold to suffer shame and reproof for His sake" (p. 63). Franciscan stories may have helped her to imagine scenes such as the following: "And I would, Lord, for Thy love, be laid naked on a hurdle, all men to wonder on me for Thy love—so that it were no peril to their souls—and they to cast mud and mire on me, and to be drawn from town to town every day of my lifetime, if Thou wert pleased there-by . . . " (p. 168). Obviously this was not the behavior of the friars

34. *Scripta Leonis*, p. 157.

Margery knew, nor was it any part of the role of a good wife of Lynn; the legends, with their glorification of dramatic humility, helped to permit and to nourish such fantasies.[35]

In the fourteenth century, English friars were under attack from such powerful critics as Langland and Wycliffe, and the force of their criticism has contributed to the belief that Franciscan influence had waned by late in the century. However, the evidence of wills suggests that many people were unaware of or unmoved by the critics, and that they followed the friars (especially the popular preachers) with untempered enthusiasm.[36] Certainly Margery Kempe—crushed when she was excluded by the visiting friar in Lynn—reflected no hint of disenchantment with Franciscan preaching. Not many English Franciscan sermons survive from this period,[37] but one that does is particularly relevant to Margery Kempe. It was preached by Nicholas Philipp in Newcastle in 1431, and it may have been written by William Melton, who has been identified as Margery's "Preaching Friar."[38]

The sermon itself, which was delivered on a Good Friday, offers evidence of the kind of preaching Margery admired.

---

35. Anthony Goodman suggested that "the constant experience of popular denigration had become a necessary 'fix' for Margery's spiritual life" ("The Piety of John Brunham's Daughter of Lynn," p. 356). It may be that Margery grew accustomed to humiliation and even sought it out, but she did so within the Christian (and especially the Franciscan) tradition of suffering shame for Christ's sake, which honors the Mocking and Scourging of Jesus.

36. See John Moorman, *A History of the Franciscan Order*, p. 348.

37. Few sermons survive, but there are books of sermons which were compiled by friars for the use of English preachers. These are described in Jeffrey, *Franciscan Spirituality*, p. 189 ff.

38. The sermon is described and reprinted by A. G. Little in *Franciscan Papers, Lists, and Documents*, pp. 244–256. Hope Allen reported a marginal note on the manuscript of Margery's *Book*: "nota contra Melton" is written opposite the following sentence: "My blisful Lord Crist Ihesu wil not latyn me dyspeyryn for noon holy name þat þe good frer hath, for my Lord tellyth me þat he is wroth wyth hym, & he seyth to me it wer better he wer neuyr born, for he despisith hys werkys in me" (Meech and Allen, *Margery Kemp*, p. 155; compare p. 321, n. 148/28–29).

(Like most sermons, except those given to university audiences, it was delivered in English but written in Latin, with French and English phrases mixed in as convenient.) The preacher compared the sorrow of the Passion to a harp and directed the women in the congregation particularly to think of the Virgin's sorrow when she saw her Son's body hanging on the Cross. He described each of the Lord's cries and Mary's responses: "Ecce lugens mater hec audiens dixit: Lord qwat I am wo.myn childe cryse and sayse his fadir has for sakyn hym; and I wolde dye up on þe crose cum eo. . . . O Gabriel, quare dixisti *gracie plena*? I am plena doloris. et omnium mulierum will of soc. Filius meus moritur, A me!"[39] Margery's meditation on the Passion, with its loud weeping and its attribution to biblical persons of familiar emotions in familiar language, was inspired by just such sermons.

Richard Rolle, known to Margery (or her scribe) as "Richard Hampol. hermyte,"[40] is generally classed with Walter Hilton, Julian of Norwich, and the anonymous author of *The Cloud of Unknowing* in a group known as "the fourteenth-century English mystics." From the point of view of literary specialists, the grouping is useful. All of them played an important part in the development of Middle English, and their exclusive focus on religious ideas and experience (in contrast to Chaucer, for example) made them a recognizable group, if not a "school." From the point of view of religious history, however, there were great differences among the four, and Rolle (d. 1349) was in some respects more like Margery Kempe than were the other three. His writings, which were extremely popular in his own time and throughout the fifteenth century, have generally been ignored in modern times, or contrasted unfavorably with those

---

39. Little, *Franciscan Papers*, p. 255. The editor gives the alternate reading "ffull of sorwe" for "will of soc." in the last line.

40. Meech and Allen, *Margery Kempe*, p. 154.

of the other fourteenth-century mystics.[41]

Emotional and enthusiastic, Rolle rhapsodized over the joys of the mystic way and tended to accept and delight in its sensory accompaniments. His best-known work, *The Fire of Love*, opens with his surprise and naive delight at the "real" warmth he felt in contemplation:

> I cannot tell you how surprised I was the first time I felt my heart begin to warm. It was real warmth too, not imaginary, and it felt as if it were actually on fire. . . . I had to keep feeling my breast to make sure there was no physical reason for it![42]

Margery Kempe had a similar experience:

> Our Lord gave her another token . . . and that was a flame of fire, wondrous hot and delectable, and right comfortable, not wasting but ever increasing, of love; for though the weather were never so cold, she felt the heat burning in her breast and at her heart, as verily as a man could feel the material fire if he put his hand or his finger therein. [P. 76]

Rolle experienced sweetness and song as well as heat:

> While I was sitting in that same chapel, . . . I heard, above my head it seemed, the joyful ring of psalmody, . . . in myself I sensed a corresponding harmony at once wholly delectable and heavenly. . . . The effect of this inner sweetness was that I began to sing what previously I had spoken; only I sang inwardly and that for my Creator.[43]

Margery heard wonderful sounds also:

> One was a sort of sound as if it were a pair of bellows blowing in her ear. . . . it was the sound of the Holy Ghost. And then Our

---

41. For a brief description of Rolle's work in English and its influence, see *English Writings of Richard Rolle*, pp. ix–lxiv.

42. Richard Rolle, *The Fire of Love*, p. 45.

43. *Ibid.*, p. 93.

Lord turned that sound . . . into the voice of a little bird which is called a red-breast, that sang full merrily oftentimes in her right ear. And then she would ever have great grace after she heard such a token. [P. 77]

Rolle encouraged his readers to experience similar wonders through solitude and contemplation. They keynote of most of his works is exuberant joy, and in this he resembled the Franciscans, with whom he was much in sympathy.

Like the Franciscans, Rolle hoped to speak not just to the learned but to all devout Christians. In the prologue to *The Fire of Love* he said he wrote for "the simple and unlearned, who are seeking rather to love God than to amass knowledge."[44] Perhaps through Franciscan influence, he spoke fondly of poverty, although the effect of his remarks is somewhat mitigated by his complaints about the deprivations and tribulations he suffered as a hermit dependent on patronage.[45] Like most preachers— Franciscan or Dominican, Lollard or orthodox—he condemned the extreme fashions of the day as worldly, extravagant, and tending to viciousness. Women's headdresses were of special concern to Rolle, as they were to Margery Kempe, who cared intensely about fashion and "wore gold pipes on her head" (p. 3) before she was converted and bitterly repented of it afterward. Rolle said "they put wide-spreading horns on their heads, extremely horrible."[46]

In many of his works Rolle dwelt upon the rewards and pleasures of the contemplative life. However, in his *Meditations on the Passion* (written for beginners), he wrote of pain, sorrow, and tears. Instead of his own joys, he spoke of Christ's pains, hoping to make them real and accessible to other Christians.

44. *Ibid.*, p. 46.

45. The complaints are mentioned in *English Writings*, p. xviii. Rolle changed his cell because of discomfort and noise due to heat and harvesters; he complained of friendlessness and poor food and inadequate blankets supplied by bad patrons. St. Francis would have welcomed these as aids to holiness.

46. Rolle, *Fire of Love*, p. 178.

He introduced the familiar and terrible physical details: the blunt nails, the swollen face of Jesus, the bones and sinews that outlined the tormented body. The aim of his meditations was to acquire for himself some small part of the feeling of those who were present at the Crucifixion. He begged the Virgin for one of her wounds—for a "prikke at myn herte of þat ilke peyne."[47] Saying "I have appetyte to peyne," he asked the Lady for "a sparcle of compassyoun of þat dere passyoun."[48] He knew he was not worthy to stand beside Mary and John, but he was worthy (for his sins) to hang beside the thieves. Pain was the threshold to joy, suffering to bliss, and the aim of spiritual exercise was participation in feeling.

The fullest and most vivid expressions of the affective tradition, and its most influential group of documents, were the various *Meditations on the Life of Christ* produced in many parts of Europe in the thirteenth, fourteenth, and fifteenth centuries. Several of such works were attributed to Saint Bonaventure and borrowed his prestige. Devotion and attention to Christ's humanity inspired the *Meditations*, which in turn inspired artists and playwrights to turn their attention to painful details of the Passion, to tortured crucifixes and pietà. Additions to the biblical story appeared in paint and in stone: detailed Nativities, meetings between Jesus and his Mother before and after the Crucifixion, the Virgin fainting—often into the arms of Mary Magdalene. Domestic details of the life of the Holy Family became popular.[49] The "Christ in Majesty"

47. *English Writings*, p. 23.

48. *Ibid.*, p. 24.

49. In *L'art religieux de la fin du moyen âge en France*, Emile Mâle wrote that the author of the pseudo-Bonaventurian *Meditations* "looked for minute little details which might interest a woman: he spoke of household matters; he almost descended to childishness" (p. 28). Mâle believed that the Gospel meditations of this period, which were intended for women (and thus not, as he thought, for intelligent or educated readers) were required to be only moving and piteous.

who dominated Romanesque art gave way to the pathetic human Jesus of late medieval painting and sculpture. The artistic shift had complex theological and social roots, but one of its most prolific sources was the *Meditations on the Life of Christ.*

An excellent example of late medieval *Meditations* is a fourteenth-century Italian manuscript (Ms. Ital. 115, Paris Bibl. Nat., translated and edited by Isa Ragusa and Rosalie B. Green), which is illustrated with 193 scenes ranging from the childhood of Mary to Christ answering Peter. (The picture cycle was not finished, so there are no scenes of the Passion.) The text was written by a Franciscan for a Poor Clare, to whom the friar offered advice and instruction on the duty and privilege of affective meditation. Although he entered the usual disclaimer of his own ignorance and inadequacy to the task, he did not feel obliged to adhere to the scriptural text. All the things Jesus did and said are not in the Bible, he believed, and: "For the sake of greater impressiveness I shall tell them to you as they occurred or as they might have occurred according to the devout belief of the imagination and the varying interpretation of the mind."[50] Free interpretation of Scripture was not restricted to priests and theologians; readers were encouraged to let their imaginations work on the story. In the context of late medieval disagreement over the vernacular Bible, such freedom is significant: apparently only Scripture itself was reserved to the learned.

In his description of the Nativity the friar emphasized the favorite Franciscan virtue of poverty, exemplified in the birth of Jesus among beasts in a stable. Quoting Saint Bernard, he spoke of "a mother who could not swaddle Him but with the most wretched clothes, who hardly had rags to wrap Him in" (p. 37). In her own meditation Margery Kempe, unable to bear such piteous poverty, begged clothes for the Mother and Child.

---

50. *Meditations on the Life of Christ* (Ms. Ital. 115, Paris Bibl. Nat.) p. 5. The next twelve references are to this work and are indicated by page numbers in the text.

The reader of the *Meditations* was urged to respond as a woman to another woman and a child in all the ways that were "natural": "Pick Him up and hold Him in your arms. Gaze on His face with devotion and reverently kiss Him and delight in Him" (p. 38). Margery, who was experienced in the necessities of childbirth, found clothes and food for the Lady and the Child before she "swathed" him with tears.

Many of the persistent themes of Margery's book are displayed in the *Meditations*. Tears are admired and encouraged, especially the tears of Christ, and the reader is told to "observe Him carefully as He weeps, for you should weep with Him. . . . you must not believe that when He was crying the mother and the other intimates could restrain their tears" (p. 307). The more intimate with Jesus was the believer, the more she would cry—a message that Margery took to heart. The author seems to be speaking directly to her when he says: "Oh, if you could see the Lady weeping . . . but moderately and softly, and the Magdalen frantic about her Master and crying with deep sobs, perhaps you too would not restrain your tears!" (p. 309).

As was usual in works of affective piety, the Virgin's compassion formed a counterpoint to the Lord's Passion. Mary and all those present at the Cross were models for Christians: "What did the faithful Magdalen, the beloved disciple, what did John, beloved above all, what did the other two sisters of the Lady, do now? What could they do, filled with bitterness, overwhelmed with sorrow, drunk with wormwood? Everyone wept unconsolably" (p. 337). The Virgin's sorrow surpassed them all: "out of the abundance of her tears, she washed the face of her Son much more than the Magdalen did His feet" (p. 344). The others tried to comfort her, and the reader was told to do likewise: "If you will use your powers, you too will know how to obey, serve, console, and comfort her, so that she may eat a little, and comfort the others in doing so, for they have all fasted up to now" (p. 347). When Margery Kempe made her "caudle" for the sorrowful Virgin, she was "using her powers" as the friar directed.

In these *Meditations* (and in many similar works), Jesus
appeared first to his Mother after the Resurrection; apparently
this suited the author's sense of propriety and of the relationship of Mother and Son. In this version, the Virgin gave Jesus
permission to leave her to go to the empty tomb to comfort
Mary Magdalene. The author added that "you should know,
however, that nothing is mentioned in the Gospel about the
appearance to the Lady" (p. 365). Special attention is paid to
Mary Magdalene, who always remained with the Virgin. She is
called "beloved disciple and apostle of the apostles" (p. 369):
such extraordinary titles—the equal of those given to John,
Peter, and Paul—might well have made Margery Kempe (or any
medieval woman) wish to emulate her.

At the end of the book, the friar urged his reader to accept the
book "reverently, willingly, and joyfully, and do not be lazy in
using it with all devotion, . . . for this is your way and your life"
(p. 385). He hopes she will use the meditation to shut out
worldly distractions: "Let meditating be your whole and only
intent, your rest, your food, your study" (p. 386). As for the
method of meditation: "it is enough to meditate only on what
the Lord did . . . feeling yourself present in those places as if the
things were done in your presence, as it comes directly to your
soul in thinking of them" (p. 387). That certainly was Margery
Kempe's practice, and her experience.

Franciscan sentiments lingered in affective meditations even
when the authors were not Franciscans. The *Vita Christi* of
Ludolph the Carthusian (d. 1370) is a huge work, larger than
those of the Pseudo-Bonaventure, but its themes and emphases
are almost identical. In the fourteenth and fifteenth centuries
the Carthusian order flourished in many parts of Europe
(Ludolph lived in Saxony). It was a strict contemplative order
dedicated to the mystical life; unlike the friars, the monks lived
in solitary cells within the charterhouses. Particularly in
England, the Carthusians captured the respect and imagination of the godly, and especially of devout noble men and
women. While other orders suffered bitter and continual

criticism, the Carthusians were much admired, but they were never "popular" in the numerical sense or with the widespread enthusiasm of earlier monastic revivals. The friars had been socially and spiritually radical in the thirteenth century, but the Carthusians were conservative. They did not attempt to reach out to new groups of people or into new places; theirs was an ancient style of piety called by David Knowles a "primitive spirit of austerity and seclusion."[51]

The most rapid growth of the English Carthusians took place during Margery Kempe's lifetime: six new charterhouses were founded between 1370 and 1420. Many Carthusians were learned men; a number were priests with late vocations to the monastic life. Most of the charterhouses had fine libraries which included works of mystical theology as well as the lives and writings of contemporary saints. The Carthusians managed to combine the ancient ascetic monastic ideal with the new mystical and devotional enthusiasm of the late Middle Ages. They studied and transmitted the thought of the Flemish mystics, of the *devotio moderna*, and of the contemporary English "school" of Rolle, Hilton, and the *Cloud*.

Of all the English charterhouses, Mount Grace (founded in 1397) best expressed the Carthusian ideals of austerity in life and rapture in devotion.[52] The manuscript of *The Book of Margery Kempe*, which was owned and glossed by monks of Mount Grace, offers a clue to the kind of works the Yorkshire Carthusians appreciated. With their love of learning, their unimpeachable lives, their sponsorship of the new religious "enthusiasm," and their ties to royal and aristocratic circles, the Carthusians were at the center of the movement Hope Allen called the "Counter-Reformation" of the fifteenth century. They fought Lollardy with "true" enthusiasm, enlisting affective piety in the service of orthodoxy.

51. David Knowles, *The Religious Orders in England*, 2:130.

52. *Ibid.*, p. 223. And see James Hogg, "Mount Grace Charterhouse and Late Medieval Spirituality."

In 1410 Prior Nicholas Love of Mount Grace presented to
Archbishop Arundel an English translation of portions of the
Meditations of the Pseudo-Bonaventure. Love's work, written
in support of the archbishop's campaign against the Lollards,
is the only extensive Middle English translation of the *Meditations*; it is somewhat reduced from the original, with fewer
chapters.[53] Entitled *The Mirrour of the Blessed Lyf of Jesu
Christ*, it differs from Continental versions in two important
respects: it was part of a campaign against a specific heresy,
and it was intended for a wide audience of lay as well as
religious persons. Love wrote for "bothe men and wymmen and
euery age and euery dignyte of this worlde ... not onliche to
clerkes in latyn / but alfo in englifh to lewed men and wommen
and hem that ben of fymple underftondynge."[54] According to
the evidence of wills, he achieved his goal: Love's *Mirrour* was
the most popular of all books in fifteenth-century England.[55]

Love wrote near the crest of a great wave of lay piety which
included royal and aristocratic men and women as well as the
urban middle class. Cicely (d. 1495), duchess of York and
mother of Edward IV and Richard III, managed her own life
and a royal household according to a strict schedule of prayer
and meditation. She owned copies of the *Legenda Aurea*, of
Hilton's *Epistle on Mixed Life*, of the *Life* of Saint Catherine of
Siena, of the *Revelations* of Saint Birgitta, and of the *Book of
Special Grace* of Mechthild of Hackborn. (She bequeathed the
Legenda Aurea, the *Book of Special Grace*, and the *Life* of Saint
Catherine to her granddaughter Bridget, whose name probably
was given her in honor of the Swedish saint.) Cicely also
owned a volume described in her will as "Bonaventure," which
was most likely Love's *Mirrour*, and her private devotions may
have been constructed around the prior's suggestions.[56]

53. Salter, "Love's Myrrour," p. 48.
54. Nicholas Love, *The Mirrour of the Blessed Lyf of Jesu Christ*, p. 8.
55. R. W. Chambers, "The Continuity of English Prose," p. cxxviii.
56. C. A. J. Armstrong, "The Piety of Cicely, Duchess of York."

Love agreed with Saint Bernard that for simple people "contemplacioun of the manhede of chrifte is more lykynge more fpedeful and more fiker than is hiʒe contemplacioun of the godhede."[57] The prior of the austere and aristocratic charterhouse did not moderate the tears and affections of the *Meditations*: "Who fo wole than here ynwardely take hede and byholde how oure lorde Jefu wepeth / the fiftres wepen / the Jewes wepen / ʒe and as refoun telleth the difciples wepen / fkilfully he may be ftired to compaffioun and wepynge. . . . "[58] To achieve true compassion, to participate in the Passion, the reader must concentrate on Christ's humanity, "mofte in thy mynde depart in manere for the tyme the myʒt of the godhede fro the kyndely infirmyte of the manhede."[59] This obviously suited Margery Kempe, and presumably also Love himself, as well as the aristocratic and well-educated duchess of York.

The *Mirrour* was a weapon in the battle against Lollardy. Love was very careful to explain transubstantiation in explicit, orthodox language (similar to the language used in Leicester by Margery Kempe), and to denounce heretical views on penance and confession. That issue arose in connection with Christ's forgiveness of Mary Magdalene, and Love pointed out: "But here perauntre fumme men thynken / after the falfe opinioun of lollardes / that fchrifte of mowthe is not nedefulle / but that it fuffifeth only in herte to be fchryuen to god / as this forfaide womman was. . . . "[60] Margery Kempe made that mistake and suffered bitterly for it when she postponed full confession until she feared death, hoping she need only "do penance by herself alone and all should be forgiven, for God is merciful enough" (p. 1). Probably that was a common private sin, resulting (as in Margery's case) from fear of priestly disapproval. However, the Lollards stated publicly that inner repentance was sufficient,

57. Love, *Mirrour*, p. 8.
58. *Ibid.*, p. 176.
59. *Ibid.*, p. 216.
60. *Ibid.*, p. 121.

and that was heresy. Love explained that penitence sufficed for Mary Magdalene because Christ was physically present as man and God and could hear her feelings as a priest hears confession. Without Christ's presence, spoken confession to a priest had to accompany inner repentance.

The primary aim of all meditations on the life of Christ, including Love's *Mirrour*, was "compassion," or sympathetic participation in Christ's saving work. The second aim was moral transformation, the substance of which varied with the time and place of the writer. The Franciscans emphasized poverty, humility, and chastity (the latter especially when writing for religious women). The struggle against Lollardy was central for Love, and he emphasized those points on which the Lollards were teaching heresy. The third aim of affective meditation—the aim most important to Saint Bernard, who wrote for a religious elite—was to build a step toward spiritual union, or "true" contemplation. The Franciscans put that goal aside in favor of the conversion, through compassion and penitence, of large numbers of lay people. Nor did Nicholas Love, a general in a war against heresy, emphasize mystical union, although it is likely that he himself experienced the joys of the contemplative."[61]

The interests and intentions of affective writers naturally changed a great deal over four centuries, but certain moods and themes remained consistent. The first outpourings of private, emotional response in the prayers of Saint Anselm may have influenced Saint Ailred's meditations, in which rapturous emotion was directed toward Jesus and his Mother. With Saint Bernard, adoration of the sacred humanity became the basis of a grand scheme of mystical theology. Bernard's central devotion was adapted by the Franciscans, who transformed it into a popular passion focused on the details of Christ's birth and death and used it to preach penitence to large numbers of lay as

61. *Ibid.*, pp. 208–209.

well as religious people. Writers like Nicholas Love built upon the same fervor to preach orthodoxy, but intense feeling remained the central goal of affective writings. This feeling included the "compassion" that enabled Christians to participate in Christ's life and death, the "contrition" that produced repentance and conversion, and the emotive, sensory accompaniments of an experience of the divine.

Margery Kempe incorporated the major elements of affective piety into her own devotional life, transforming the tradition to the uses of her singular vocation and personality. Her spiritual life was centered, from the beginning and throughout her life, on the human Christ, the object of her prayers and her love. She identified very closely with the Virgin as woman and mother, and her participation in the Passion was enlarged and inspired by sharing Mary's grief. Her enthusiasm, her "boisterous" emotion, and her conspicuous humility were borrowed from the Franciscans and legitimated by their authority. And her method of meditation—that is, her personal involvement in the biblical story, placing herself among the holy figures— was exactly the method prescribed by writers of affective devotion.

Against this background, the religious life of Margery Kempe seems neither aberrant nor even very unusual, but rather a complex personal response to a tradition established by some of the great medieval saints and theologians. Unlike these men, Margery was not an authority or a "professional," and her book testifies to the influence on "ordinary" Christians of their writings, as these were transmitted through the preaching and spiritual direction of the Church. The range and intensity of her emotions, and her concentration on the human feelings and experiences of Christ, his Mother, and the saints, were shared with many devout people of her time. Obviously there were differences between Margery Kempe and these others, but the differences must be sought outside the form, feeling, and content of her prayers. Her meditations belong to a tradition, but the teachers and preachers of that tradition (all men, all clerics, all celibate, all literate) could not be models for her vocation or her way of life. For such models, Margery had to look farther afield, toward people who were more "like" her than an Anselm, a Bernard, or even a Dominican anchorite of Lynn.

Chapter Six

"A MAIDEN IN THY SOUL":

Female Sanctity in
the Late Middle Ages

THE prayers and meditations in the tradition of affective piety which inspired Margery Kempe and other devout people in the later Middle Ages were almost always composed by men in religious life—originally, by abbots for the monks and nuns in their care. These writings were monastic in character as well as authorship, designed to assist those who were free of worldly responsibilities to pour their feelings into the love of God. A few were intended for noble ladies, especially for those who had been kept from the convent by the responsibilities of family and station. But after the middle of the thirteenth century, affective meditations were also intended for lay people; in the wave of popular piety reflected (and stimulated) by the mendicant orders, religious affectivity lost its exclusively monastic character. Nicholas Love, the prior of an austere charterhouse, wrote for lay persons of both sexes.

The tastes and interests of lay women as well as nuns increasingly influenced the style and content of devotional writings. Because women (including many nuns) were not generally taught to read Latin, pious works were written in the vernacular, with significant effect on the development of the European

languages.[1] But despite the obvious influence of women on
their composition, works such as those examined in the previ-
ous chapter can by no means be described as "feminine" piety.
The writers of affective meditations were monks and friars, and
because it has so often been suggested that there is (or was) a
peculiarly—perhaps innately—"feminine" piety,[2] it is important to remember that these authors, without exception, were
men. If Margery Kempe's piety was "feminine," it was not
because she meditated (as they did) on the homely details of the
Virgin's childhood or felt rapture and piteous sorrow at the
Passion. Her religious practices and emotions were shaped (at
least indirectly) by the teaching of Anselm and Bernard and
the activities of the Franciscans. There were feminine influences on Margery's piety and her experience, but these had

---

1. The educational level in convents varied widely, of course, in different
periods and different parts of Europe. Eileen Power believed that except in the
"golden" Anglo-Saxon age, it was generally very low in England: see Power,
Medieval English Nunneries, p. 238 ff. R. W. Chambers, in "The Continuity
of English Prose," p. xciii, makes the following point: "a fact which is
the cause of the composition of so much English prose: the fact that women
recluses would not be expected to be as familiar as men would be with
Latin."

2. Traditionally, the nature and existence of this "feminine" piety has
been suggested in such comments as Emile Mâle's (Chap. 5, n. 49 above),
which state or imply that the religious needs and aspirations of women are
served and expressed by the domestic, the trivial, and the sentimental—that
women's emotions can easily be aroused by the pathetic, but that it is difficult
or dangerous to stimulate their minds. The first serious and significant
discussion of "feminine" piety of which I am aware is by Caroline W. Bynum,
Jesus as Mother, see esp. pp. 14–19, 170–262.

The question of "feminine" piety is not entirely extricable from larger
questions about the existence and nature of "the feminine": does it exist, and
is it biological, social, or a mysterious and innate "principle" above and
beyond biology, society, or history? Arguments and assumptions about "the
feminine" were made in religious language and context during the Middle
Ages; in modern times they occur in relation to education, art, psychology, or
politics. The literature is too vast to summarize: its primary sources include
the writings of many men. Women, on the whole, have been less concerned
about what Woman is.

more to do with her life and vocation than with the content and style of her meditations.

Whether or not piety can be "masculine" or "feminine," ways of living certainly are dictated by gender. As a woman, Margery was not eligible to become a priest or a monk or a friar. She might have become a nun, but apparently she had no vocation in youth to the religious life, and she followed the conventional program of the middle-class girl: marriage and motherhood. After her conversion she might still have entered a convent or cell with her husband's permission; late vocations were likely to cause problems, but they occurred fairly frequently throughout the Middle Ages.

Margery did not, however, choose to retire to a convent or a cell. On the contrary, she traveled widely after her conversion, and she ceased to live with her husband or to keep the needs of her household at the center of her attention. Such behavior (unlike her meditative practices) was neither prescribed nor suggested by the affective writers whose modes of prayer she followed. Her way of life was not dictated by any ecclesiastical authority, neither did she find models among the middle-class families of Lynn. Margery was well acquainted with housewives and mothers, business- and tradeswomen, nuns and anchoresses, but it is improbable that she knew anyone like herself.

However, there were other women whose lives were somewhat like Margery's, and it is certain that their existence helped to shape her vocation and her book. Indeed, by the fifteenth century, the lives and works of a great number of holy women had become part of the Christian story. David Knowles has pointed out that the century 1325–1425 produced many such women saints, "several of whom were, or had been, married women, all of whom led lives of external movement in which the visionary and abnormal elements were strongly in evidence, and most of whom wrote accounts of their experiences."[3] As

3. David Knowles, *The English Mystical Tradition*, p. 142.

far as we know, the only "holy woman" known personally to Margery was Julian of Norwich, and she may have known that Julian had written a book, although she did not speak of it. The other medieval (as opposed to biblical or legendary) women she mentioned were Birgitta of Sweden, Marie d'Oignies, and Elizabeth of Hungary; she certainly knew "Bride's book" and the biographies of Marie and Elizabeth. But her acquaintance was not limited to the female figures who appear by name in her book.

Holy persons—saints and ecstatics and miracle workers—were the celebrities of the Middle Ages. In the merchant-trading communities of northeastern England, with their close ties to the Continent, reports of holy lives and miraculous happenings were circulated along with reports of storms at sea or political unrest abroad. Furthermore, the medieval Church was an international organization, and the friars especially belonged to international associations. They certainly knew about the women saints (particularly those connected to their own orders), and Margery would have heard from them about such lives. Just as important, the friars were not apt to be astounded or totally discouraging about Margery's unconventional way of life. The substantial sympathy and support she received from so many regular and secular churchmen reflects in part their awareness of the lives and reputations of the Continental women saints.

To understand the choices and decisions of any historical figure, we need to discover what varieties of roles and experience were available to her imagination. This is a special requirement of women's history, in which what is "available" is modified by the circumstances and restrictions of women's lives in particular times and places. Margery Kempe was troubled by instances of misunderstanding and persecution and very much afraid of demonic illusion, but she was not afraid that her way of life was wrong or "unnatural" even when others disapproved of it. She knew of the achievements of other visionary women and of the respectful attention accorded them, and that awareness helped her to discover and define as well as persist in her vocation.

Female saints, martyrs, and leaders distinguished the first Christian communities, but with the establishment of Christianity as the official religion of the Roman Empire in the fourth century, women began to disappear from positions of spiritual and administrative leadership. Welcome as martyrs, women were not invited to join the swelling ranks of theologians and administrators. As bishops became local governors and educated men became Christians, office, ordination, and special education became requirements for leadership of the Church. Through the writings of the Church Fathers, the sexual asceticism and profound misogyny of so much of late antique thought were absorbed into Christian theology and ecclesiastical practice. When the Church was no longer a persecuted band of brothers and sisters but the dominant political and intellectual organization of Europe—as "Christendom" came into existence—the ministries of women were discouraged or forgotten.

With certain outstanding exceptions,[4] Christian women did not re-emerge in any number as visionaries or reformers until the twelfth or the thirteenth century. The early stirrings of new attitudes and possibilities were felt in the Low Countries and the Germanies, which remained for years the center of the so-called "women's movement."[5] Hildegarde of Bingen (1098–1179), abbess of Rupertsberg, was only the first of a series of remarkable German nuns. Hildegarde saw visions, prophesied, and corresponded with popes and emperors and church digni-

---

4. In early medieval Europe, and especially in Anglo-Saxon England, women played major roles in religion and society as nuns and abbesses, and in the process of conversion as queens and princesses who converted their royal husbands. Both are exemplified in Bede's *Ecclesiastical History*.

5. The phrase was used by Herbert Gründmann in *Religiöse Bewegungen im Mittelalter*. See also Ernest W. McDonnell, *The Beguines and Beghards in Medieval Culture*, esp. pp. 81–100.

taries (including Saint Bernard). She chided unworthy priests, called for reform of the Church, and cloaked her warnings in the apocalyptic language and imagery of a great seer. Her mission and ministry were prophetic, and her influence enormous: Hildegarde, unique in her time as a public figure, stood as a symbol of divine favor and female power.

The women saints of the next century were no less extraordinary than Hildegarde, but they did not stand alone; they belonged to the great new wave of lay and monastic piety. The popularity of the Cistercians and of the mendicant orders reflected the desire of all kinds of people for intense emotional expression and lives of service in the world. Men and women, lay and religious, wanted more from their religion than the old forms allowed. The beguines of northern Europe (among whom were some of the new saints) exhibited many of the characteristics of the "New Piety"—a fervent, mystical devotion combined with hard work. They lived in the world but apart, in their own homes or in *beguinages* (households of religious women under unofficial rule), and they did not fit traditional models of either active or contemplative life.[6]

No single explanation accounts for such a complex phenomenon as the outburst of mystical, emotional piety of the High and late Middle Ages. Many explanations have been offered, including response to the Schism and to corruption and demoralization of the Church and clergy, disillusion with arid speculative theology, and an outgrowth of the emergence of larger towns, of capitalism, and of a merchant middle class. In relation to the beguines, to the women saints, and to Margery Kempe, it should be said that women may have participated enthusiastically in the "New Piety" in part because it was possible for them to do so. Mystical experience requires no office or ordination: women's experience is as valid as men's. The authority of inspiration—unlike that of theological educa-

---

6. The fullest history of the beguines in English is given by McDonnell, *Beguines and Beghards*. See also Brenda M. Bolton, "Mulieres sanctae."

tion or of the ecclesiastical hierarchy—was available to both sexes.

For these reasons and many others, female saints and visionaries appeared in substantial numbers in thirteenth-century Europe. They had confessors, directors, and secretaries who attended them, transcribed their revelations, and wrote their *Lives*, often for the greater glory of a particular shrine or cathedral. One of the most important of these attendants was Jacques de Vitry (d. 1240), the confessor as well as disciple and biographer of Marie d'Oignies. The influence of de Vitry and of Marie in the writing of *The Book of Margery Kempe* has already been mentioned.

The Saxon convent of Helfta produced three great women saints in the thirteenth century. The nuns of Helfta observed the practices of the Cistercians, but the convent was not formally a part of the Cistercian order, and the nuns had Dominican confessors. Its three great visionaries were mystics who wrote books of their prayers, visions, and revelations. The earliest of the three—Mechthild of Magdeburg (d. 1282)—was a beguine who lived for a time at Helfta; Mechthild of Hackborn (d. 1298) and Gertrude the Great (d. 1302) entered the convent as children. The nuns of Helfta encouraged and even collaborated in their writings, and Caroline Bynum has pointed out that their works not only "reveal the spiritual orientation of the whole group of Helfta nuns but also were a conscious effort to establish and hand on to the next generation of sisters and to readers outside the cloister a spiritual teaching and a collective reputation."[7] By the late thirteenth century, and especially in Germany and the Low Countries, women's mystical experience—and its literary expression—was entirely acceptable; in some circles it was even expected.[8]

7. Bynum, *Jesus as Mother*, p. 180.

8. Felix Vernet reported that the German Dominican nun Christine Ebner of Engelthal identified one of her sisters as the only one in that convent who never experienced ecstasy—and that was surprising, Ebner said, for she was a very holy nun! (Vernet, *La spiritualité médievale*, pp. 49–50).

Female leadership in mystical ecstasy and in holiness of life was not limited to northern Europe. After all, the founders of the two great mendicant orders, the heart of thirteenth-century piety, were an Italian and a Spaniard, and women were among their first and most devoted followers. Because of the order she founded, Saint Clare is the best known of the Franciscan saints, but more relevant to Margery Kempe is the life of Blessed Angela of Foligno, who died in 1309. Angela's scribe (a friar) wrote in the preface to her *Book of Visions and Instructions*: "God Himself hath raised up a woman of the secular state, bound to the world, entangled by ties to husband and children and riches, simple in knowledge, weak in strength, but who, by the power of God . . . hath broken the chains of the world, and mounted up to the summit of evangelical perfection."[9] The friar pointed out that Angela's gender made her life and teachings especially significant:

> Bear in mind . . . that the apostles . . . learnt from a woman that He had risen from the dead: and so too, as most dear sons of our holy Mother Angela, learn along with me the rule. . . . Now this is contrary to the order of God's Providence, and for the shaming of carnal men, to make a woman a doctor . . . for the shame of men who were doctors of the law, but transgressors of what it commanded, the gift of prophecy had been translated unto the weaker sex of women." [P. 3]

Like Margery's scribe, Brother Arnold at first experienced great difficulty in transcribing Angela's visions; he doubted his own skill, found he had to confess his sins before he could write, and feared always that he could write neither clearly nor in order. Nevertheless, he experienced "in the very act of writing a spiritual and new grace" (p. 8).

At the time of her conversion Angela was a prosperous

9. *The Book of the Visions and Instructions of Blessed Angela of Foligno,* p. 1. The next fourteen references are to this work, indicated by a page number in the text.

married woman with children. Without a specific mystical experience, she began to think about her sins and to fear damnation, but (like Margery) she was ashamed to make a full confession. Assured in a dream that she would find a sympathetic confessor, she found one the next day, and after the confession began to sorrow and weep endlessly: "it was somewhat of a consolation to me that I could weep; but it was a bitter consolation" (p. 20). She undertook drastic penances, including physical deprivation, humiliation, and the poverty that was always emphasized in Franciscan writings. Again like Margery Kempe, she began to cut her ties to the world where they touched her vanity; unlike Margery, some of her ties were severed by circumstance:

> I began to lay aside my better kind of clothes and dresses; and the daintier kinds of food, and of head coverings in like manner. But . . . as yet I did not feel much of the love of God, and I was still with my husband. . . . Moreover, God so willing, it happened at that time that my mother died, who was a great obstacle to me in the way of God. And in like manner my husband died, and all my sons, in a short space of time. And because I had entered on the aforesaid way . . . I received a great consolation from their death. [P. 25]

Free of human ties, Angela prayed for a share of the sorrow felt by the Virgin and Saint John at the Crucifixion. She learned to weep more effectively: "my former tears had been as it were forced in comparison" (p. 35). Her love of God grew more intense: "if I heard speak of God, I cried out so loud and shrilly that if any one had stood over me with an axe to kill me, I could not have kept from crying out" (p. 38). Sometimes this attracted unfavorable attention, as when she could not help but cry out in public and was called "inordinate" (p. 38). In these cries, and in her attitude toward them, Angela was like Margery, and also in her response to the Passion: "whenever I saw the Passion of Christ depicted," she said, "I could scarcely contain myself, and fever seized on me, and I became weak"

(p. 39). When she perceived hypocrisy in herself (for example, when she pretended to eat barely enough to stay alive), her self-reproach and desire for exaggerated humiliation is reminiscent of Margery (and of Francis), for she "would wish to go naked through cities and to hang pieces of meat and fish about my neck, and to say, 'This is that most vile woman' " (p. 46).

Angela was rewarded by marvelous illumination and holy comfort. The Holy Ghost promised to stay with her, calling her "my sweet daughter. . . . And he added in an underbreath, 'I love thee more than any woman in the valley of Spoleto' " (p. 57). When the Spirit did leave her, àt the door of Saint Francis's church in Assisi, she "fell down in a sitting position, and began to cry with a loud voice, and to scream, and to call out" (p. 64). Walking home from Assisi, she "went along the way, speaking of God, and it was to me the greatest punishment to be silent. But I tried to abstain from speaking on account of the company" (p. 65).

There is a hint in that abstinence "on account of the company" of the kind of disapproval encountered by Margery Kempe, but for the most part, Angela's cries and conversation seem to have been received with respect and reverence. She was perceived as a very holy woman, perhaps because the spiritual atmosphere of thirteenth-century Umbria (like that of the Low Countries) tolerated and encouraged much that was discouraged in fifteenth-century England. Angela's behavior was in fact much more extreme than Margery's: Margery suffered from demonic visions of priests exposing themselves, but Angela's pains and temptations were greater: "Even those vices which have never existed are raised up. And in my body I suffer at least in three parts: for in those parts which for shame I dare not mention, the fire is so great that I was wont to apply material fire to extinguish that other fire of concupiscence, until my confessor forbade me" (p. 42).

Many of Angela's visions were centered on the physical torments of the Passion, but they were more abstract and intellectual than those of Margery Kempe. Angela was a teacher, and much of her book is phrased in a didactic style totally unlike Margery's: for example, "Further, the soul knoweth that God is in her beyond all doubt in many ways, of which we will only mention two" (p. 178). Angela was also the "mother" of a spiritual *famiglia*—not an international figure of the stature of Birgitta of Sweden or Catherine of Siena, but a woman of considerable local importance and reputation, especially among Franciscans. English friars probably knew of the Umbrian woman whose life and work were so closely tied to that of their founder, and spoke of her to their congregations and penitents. Her story must have helped to form their expectations of what a holy woman could be.

The greatest of the Italian women saints was Catherine of Siena (d. 1380), whose story is too well known to need repetition here. Her life and achievements are relevant to the *Book of Margery Kempe* not because (like Angela of Foligno) she was similar to Margery, for she was not, but because of her enormous prestige. Born one of twenty-five children of a Sienese dyer, Catherine was a visionary from early childhood. She resisted marriage, lived for a time in prayer and meditation in a "cell" in the family home, and eventually became a Dominican tertiary. Her devoted *famiglia* included Raymond of Capua, who became her confessor and first biographer and Provincial of the Dominicans. The goals of Catherine's later years were peace and reform within the Church and in Italy, the return of the pope to Rome, and a crusade against the Muslims. Because she was an international political and ecclesiastical figure of great importance, her image and reputation were of the highest value to Dominicans and Urbanists, and her real story and achievements were shrouded in legend even before her death. The "Venetian Process" for her canonization, with its fervent saint-making and excitement, was conducted in 1411–13, just before Margery's first visit to Italy.[10]

Catherine's *Dialogue*, dictated to secretaries while the saint was in ecstasy, was extremely influential all over Europe. In the early fifteenth century it was translated into English for the Birgittine nuns of Syon Abbey. Syon was a center of visionary piety, and obviously the work of this outstanding saint was regarded as appropriate and valuable for English nuns. Certainly the authority and reputation of Saint Catherine contributed to the new (for England) respect for holy women who wrote books. The English Austin friar William Flete, a member of Catherine's *famiglia*, wrote letters about her to his brothers in England.[11] And during the 1390s, Raymond of Capua corresponded with William Bakthorpe, prior of Lynn. No Dominican confessor (or his female penitent) could fail to be aware of Catherine's life and work.

The *Dialogue* was a great formative work of late medieval mystical theology. Catherine's visions and her preaching were both tender and terrible, ranging from the tears of the humble soul, to fierce denunciation of unworthy clerics, to the majesty of the Trinity. Her life and legend, transported throughout Europe by Dominican preachers and confessors, became a powerful force in the spiritual imagination of medieval Christians.

Of all the Continental women saints, Birgitta of Sweden (1303–1373) exerted the most direct influence on the life and work of Margery Kempe. As we have seen, Margery was well aware of Birgitta and her *Revelations*, and she and her advisers

10. For a thorough study of St. Catherine and her canonization, see Robert Fawtier, *Sainte Catherine de Sienne*. See also R. Fawtier and Louis Canet, *La double expérience de Catherine Benincasa*. For the influence of Catherine's *Dialogue*, see Phyllis Hodgson, *"The Orcherd of Syon" and the English Mystical Tradition*.

11. See W. A. Pantin, *The English Church in the Fourteenth Century*, pp. 246–247.

were much affected by the furor over visionary women and their writings occasioned by the Swedish saint. The spheres in which Margery and Birgitta moved were very dissimilar, but the resemblances between the two women are nevertheless more striking than their differences.

Birgitta belonged to a noble family related to the ruling dynasty of Sweden. As with so many holy persons, her sanctity was obvious even in childhood; as a young girl she saw a vision of the crucified Christ.[12] At thirteen she was married to Ulf Gudmarsson, and she used the example of Saint Cecilia to persuade him that they should remain chaste until it was time for them to conceive and raise children. They lived "as brother and sister" for two years, and (according to the testimony of their daughter Saint Catherine of Sweden) maintained strict sexual morality throughout their lives: "each time before they came together carnally they would always pray the same prayers to God, that He would not permit them to sin in the carnal act and that God would give them fruit who would always serve Him."[13] During the next twenty years, the couple had eight children.

Birgitta's first director-biographer was Canon Matthias of Linköping Cathedral, who shared with her not only his Swedish Bible and stories about pilgrimages in Europe and the Holy Land but his interest in the contemporary European mood of apocalyptic excitement. Birgitta took up an increasingly strict life, fasting, sleeping in straw on the floor, even burning herself with a wax candle on Fridays in memory of the Passion. She grew more and more dissatisfied with ordinary married life—with physical comfort and sexual pleasure—but remained at home until she left (in the late 1330s) to serve at the court of the king of Sweden and his French bride, where she was shocked at the prevalence of vice and corruption.

In 1341 Birgitta and her husband set out for Saint James,

12. Johannes Jorgensen, *Saint Bridget of Sweden*, 1:47.
13. *Acta et Processus Canonizacionis Beate Birgitte*, p. 305.

their first distant pilgrimage. Ulf became ill on the return journey, and Birgitta took the opportunity to secure his consent to a mutual vow of chastity. Ulf died in 1343, leaving Birgitta free to take up a vocation as a seer, reformer, pilgrim, and founder of a religious order. She began her new life with a long stay at the Cistercian monastery of Alvastra, where she found her second important director, Petrus Olai, who was ordered by God to write down Birgitta's revelations. When he hesitated, he was supernaturally knocked to the ground, after which he felt no further doubts. He remained with the saint until her death.

During her visit to Alvastra, Birgitta clarified her vocation, focusing her concern on the war raging in Europe, on the Babylonian Captivity of the pope, and on corruption in the ecclesiastical hierarchy. Both Christ and the Virgin came frequently to speak to her, and Jesus directed her to found a religious order. She went to the king in Stockholm, stopping along the way at Vadstena, where the mother house of the Birgittines would later be built. There she received detailed instructions and a Rule (the Rule of Saint Saviour) for an order of nuns to be dedicated to the glory of the Virgin. Although the foundations would include men, it was not a double order but a women's order ruled by an abbess. The women were to be served by monk-priests and lay brothers who would have their own buildings and chapel. Priests were necessary to celebrate the sacraments, and lay brothers for manual labor, but the Birgittine order existed for women and in honor of the Virgin, and its rule and organization were designed to that end.[14] Whether through personal force, social standing, or a combination of these and other factors, Birgitta had no worries about the right

14. In *The History and Antiquities of Syon Monastery, the Parish of Islesworth, and the Chapelry of Hounslow*, George James Aungier reprints the Rule of Saint Saviour and discusses both the Birgittine order and the intentions of its founder.

and ability of women to lead. She had set the tone and conditions of her own marriage, and wherever she went she exerted personal, spiritual, and social authority—at home, at the Swedish court, or in Rome. Her visions tended to enhance her confidence, stressing the willing obedience and love of Christ toward his Mother.

In 1350, at the age of forty-seven, Birgitta left Sweden for Rome, where she remained until the end of her life. She felt some guilt and anxiety about her children, some of whom were still young and unsettled. However, she was constantly reassured by the Virgin, and warned that excessive love of her children (excessive if it kept her from God's work) came from the devil.[15] Like Saint Catherine, Birgitta became the "mother" of a *famiglia* devoted to her and committed to the reform of the Church and the return of the pope to Rome. She obeyed a divine command to study Latin, which was necessary for ecclesiastical correspondence and conversation, and was comforted by Saint Agnes when she complained that her lessons interfered with her prayers and that the study of Latin was a difficult and tedious task for an older person.

In 1371 Birgitta was ordered by Christ to visit the Holy Land; when she protested her age and infirmity, Christ said: "I will be with you and I will direct your road, and I will lead you thither and lead you back to Rome, and I will provide you more

---

15. Once when she was worried about her children's welfare, Birgitta had a vision: "And she saw in a vision a pot placed above a fire and a boy blowing on the coals so that the pot would catch fire. Blessed Birgitta said to him: 'Why do you try so hard to blow so that the pot will be set aflame?' The boy answered: 'So that the love of your children will be kindled and set on fire in you.' Blessed Birgitta asked: 'Who are you?' He said to her: 'I am the agent.' Then, realizing that an inordinate love for her children arose in her heart, she immediately corrected herself, so that nothing would interfere with the love of Christ" (*Den Heliga Birgittas Revelaciones Extravagantes*, p. 218).

amply with what you need than ever before."[16] When Margery Kempe was sent to Germany at about sixty years of age, she complained that she had not money enough for the journey and that her daughter-in-law did not want her. Christ said: "I shall provide for thee, and get thee friends to help thee. Do as I bid thee, and no man of the ship shall say nay to thee" (p. 207).

In an early vision (1347), Birgitta saw the kings of England and of France as two wild beasts devouring France in their greed and hatred. Christ told the saint that peace would be achieved eventually through the issue of a royal marriage, but that the kings must first make peace in their hearts.[17] Perhaps it is not surprising that much later—after the marriage of Henry V and Catherine of Valois in 1420 and the birth of the infant Henry VI—the English Crown was counted among the most enthusiastic supporters of the cult of Saint Birgitta. The Lancastrian kings and their retainers, shadowed with the taint of the usurper, were anxious for heavenly legitimation and delighted with the wide dissemination of the saint's revelation.

Houses of the Birgittine order were gradually established throughout Europe during the century after the saint's death. The Birgittines came to England under the sponsorship of

16. Translated and quoted in Jorgensen, *Bridget*, 2:238–239. Birgitta's pilgrimage was an important event in Christian art history; her visions of the Nativity and the Passion were extremely influential. In her revelation of the Nativity, the Virgin told Birgitta of the bloodless birth of the Child, from whom shone forth an extraordinary radiance—a light so bright that it obscured the candle Joseph brought into the stable. Immediately after Birgitta returned to Italy and reported her vision, artists began to depict the Nativity as revealed to the saint: the first such work was a Neapolitan fresco painted before 1380 (see Aron Andersson, *St. Birgitta and the Holy Land* [Stockholm, 1973], p. 112). At Calvary, Birgitta experienced a detailed, concrete revelation of Jesus's suffering and emaciated body on the Cross, and her description, which was widely circulated, contributed to the contemporary style of graphic, tortured crucifixes.

17. "And if these two kings of France and England do indeed desire peace I will give everlasting peace," tr. and quoted in Jorgensen, *Bridget*, 1: 197.

Henry V, who laid the first stone of Syon Abbey at Twickenham in 1415. Monks and nuns came from Sweden (by way of Lynn)[18] to instruct the English candidates. Their rule had not then been confirmed by the pope, and the Schism complicated the official establishment of the order in England, but the first nuns were professed in 1420. In 1431 the Abbey was moved to Islesworth, across the Thames from the Carthusian house at Sheen. On her return from Germany in 1434, Margery Kempe visited "Schene," glossed "syon" in the margin by the annotator of the manuscript: Syon Abbey was often named in contemporary records as "Mount Sion of Sheen." Margery went there, she said, "to purchase her pardon" (p. 225), that is, the "Pardon of Syon," an indulgence made available to pilgrims by the pope.[19]

Syon was a center of mystical devotion, of Continental influence, and of "feminine" piety—meaning, in this instance, the piety of devout women living under female religious

18. Princess Philippa, sister of Henry V, was married to King Eric of Denmark and Sweden in 1406; she passed through Lynn on the way to her wedding: see *The Incendium Amoris of Richard Rolle of Hampole*, p. 99. A member of the princess's retinue visited Vadstena and announced that he intended to give land in England for a Birgittine convent: he never did so, but the king took up the project. Swedish Birgittine monks and nuns also traveled through Lynn on their visits to Syon Abbey: see *Incendium*, p. 107, and Aungier, *Antiquities*, p. 46. The royal wedding and the building of Syon took place while Margery was living in Lynn; she would have been aware of the excitement over the new order. The most complete account of the establishment of Syon Abbey is given in *Incendium*, pp. 91–130; it is summarized in David Knowles, *The Religious Orders in England*, 2:175–181.

19. The "Pardon of Syon" was celebrated in John Audelay's poem "A Salutation to St. Brigitte," written in the 1420s. It praised Pope Urban's grant of an indulgence for pilgrims to the abbey and said that Jesus himself would have granted the pardon if the pope had not done so. The pardon was available at Lammas time, which was the season of Margery's visit in 1434. Audelay's poem is reprinted in *The Revelations of Saint Birgitta*, pp. xxxiii–xxxv.

leadership.[20] Certainly it exemplified a contemporary mood in which the spirituality of women was highly valued. The model for Birgittine convents might have been the founder's vision of the Nativity, in which Mary—the numinous figure— was attended by Joseph, who served God through serving the Virgin. English churchmen were prominent in the struggle for the Birgittine rule and order, which was carried on in Rome in the 1420s. They encountered some very powerful opposition, not only to the acceptance of Birgitta's *Revelations* but to the existence of religious houses for both women and men. Double monasteries were out of favor by the fifteenth century for a number of reasons, including the decline of some of the older orders and the chronic suspicion of cohabitation.[21] Also, Birgitta's emphasis on the abbess as superior was unpopular and perceived to be in conflict with the traditional understanding of 1 Timothy 2:12 ("I permit no woman to teach or to have authority over men; she is to keep silent"). Supporters of the Birgittines held that Paul's words applied within marriage, but that women might hold positions of authority outside of the marriage bond.

The cult of Saint Birgitta in fifteenth-century England was

20. The central purpose of the Birgittine order, as dictated by Christ, was the worship of the Virgin. See A. J. Collins, *The Bridgettine Breviary of Syon Abbey* (Worcester, 1963). *The Myroure of Oure Ladye*, an explanation and translation into English of the Hours and masses of the Virgin used at Syon, exemplifies the devotion to Mary which dominated Birgittine piety.

Hope Allen called Syon "a great centre of mystical piety in England, a bulwark of faith in indulgences and pilgrimages. . . . The early Bridgettines of Syon would seem to have been particularly extreme feminists, a fact which will have been influential for English feminine piety at the time" (Meech and Allen, *Margery Kempe*, p. 349, n. 245–31). Allen refers to the controversy over the authority of the abbess, outlined in *Incendium*, pp. 91–130, and in Knowles, *Religious Orders*, 2:175–181. Syon was a center of mystical piety and of admired religious women, but the phrase "extreme feminists" is misleading in this context.

21. A full account of this struggle is given in Hans Cnattingius, *Studies in the Order of St. Bridget of Sweden*, 1:138–146 and *passim*.

widespread and influential.[22] The large number of surviving manuscripts and early printed copies of *Lives* of the saint and of fragments of her *Revelations* testifies to the enthusiasm for Birgitta, and many of the manuscripts of English versions of the *Revelations* were owned by aristocratic women. Syon Abbey was popular and prosperous right up until the Dissolution; rich (often royal) patrons endowed it with money and land and gave books to the monastery library—usually, of course, to the brothers' library. Whatever Saint Birgitta's views of female leadership, and despite her own struggles, the nuns were not expected to read Latin. Syon was an important religious center, but the real heart of the cult of Birgitta in England was not there but at Oxford, where the chancellor of the university, Thomas Gascoigne, dedicated himself and his pen to her cause. Syon Abbey had an important place in contemporary mystical piety, but both the abbey and the *Revelations* may have had more influence on bookish men than on "ordinary" women.[23] It is interesting to find Margery Kempe visiting Syon, but it is also clear that the model of Saint Birgitta's life was more important in Margery's career than were the *Revelations* or the order.

Margery knew a great deal about Saint Birgitta and may have been aware of their common experience of conflict and distress over sexuality and family life. Birgitta's aristocratic birth and family tradition of sanctity made her much less vulnerable than Margery Kempe, and the Swedish saint apparently was not criticized for her way of life. But like all Christian women, Birgitta had to confront within herself the conflict of sanctity with sexuality, marriage, and motherhood—perhaps even with women's "nature" as defined and understood in the Christian tradition. In childhood, Birgitta hated to give up singularity and holiness for the ordinariness of marriage. She obeyed her

22. The most complete account is F. R. Johnston, "The Cult of St. Bridget of Sweden in Fifteenth-Century England."

23. *Ibid.*, pp. 133, 147.

family by marrying, but attempted to preserve continence within marriage, first by a vow of chastity, then by separating "lust" from the duty of procreation. At the first opportunity she returned to continence. The incompatibility of sexual activity and sacred power constituted an obvious and obdurate dilemma: Christ himself addressed the subject in several revelations, rationalizing Birgitta's wedded and widowed state.[24]

Not only Jesus, but members of Birgitta's *famiglia* were anxious to explain away the taint of sexuality. At the beginning of his *Life* of the saint (the basis for later *Lives*), Birger Gregorius pointed out that there are three ways to holiness—that of the virgin, of the widow, and of the wife. Virginity might be the best, but married persons also could please God through their faith and good works. Birgitta, although wife of Ulf, was the *Sponsa* (or bride) of Christ, and she is usually referred to by that name in the *Revelations*. After all, the Virgin herself had been wife, widow, and virgin, and a humble widow is more pleasing to God than a proud virgin. Birger's *Life* of the saint is noticeably, almost primarily, attentive to Birgitta's sexual attitudes and behavior, which obviously were matters of major concern for the noble Swedish saint as well as the English woman.[25]

In her book, Margery mentioned the births of some of her children, but never the children themselves. The one exception is the son whom she turned away from an evil life, who married overseas, came to her in England with his wife and child at the end of his life, and may have been her first scribe. While he still lived in Lynn and was a sinner, Margery kept urging him to "leave the world and follow Christ, insomuch that he fled her company and would not gladly meet with her" (p. 201). A lecherous young man (in his mother's opinion), he returned from a trip diseased, "his face waxed full of weals and blubbers as if he were a leper" (p. 202). He told people that his

24. See, for example, *Revelaciones Extravagantes*, p. 218.
25. See, for example, *Birgerus Gregorii Legenda Sancte Birgitte*, p. 9.

mother had cursed him and sent him away, and they said "she had done right evil, for through her prayer, God had taken vengeance on her own child" (p. 202). Margery ignored the criticism and felt justified when he begged forgiveness and changed his way of life. Obviously he believed that his mother's curse had caused his illness and that her prayers could cure him, and Margery must have agreed: "When she came to her meditation, not forgetting the fruit of her womb, she asked forgiveness for his sin and release from the sickness. . . . So long she prayed, that he was clean delivered of the sickness and lived many years after . . . " (pp. 202–203). He ascribed not only the cure but his conversion to his mother's prayers, and Margery thanked God for it, although she was skeptical at first. When she realized the change was permanent, however, she was delighted, and when he died within a month of his return to England, she praised God that he had died "in good life and right belief" (p. 205).

Margery's experience with her son is reminiscent of that of Saint Birgitta with her son Karl, the only one of her eight children to provoke tears and worry. In trouble from boyhood, Karl's last sin was the worst: he became the lover of Joanna, the evil queen of Naples. Karl was "punished" by dying of tuberculosis in 1372, just before his mother's pilgrimage to the Holy Land, and Birgitta was tormented by anxiety over the state of his soul. She was reassured by an extraordinary vision in which the Virgin told her that she herself had stood by Karl's deathbed: "as a womman that standith by another womman when sche childeth, to help the chylde that it dye not of flowying of bloode ne be no slayne in that streight place were it cometh oute."[26] (The image of Mary as midwife to the dying soul, revealed to a woman with eight children, is a graphic contribution to "feminine" piety.)

Mary helped Karl because he used to say a prayer to her

26. *Revelations*, p. 117.

taught him by Birgitta.[27] The Virgin and the devil fought over his soul, and his many sins were weighed against Mary's intercession and Birgitta's tears and prayers and holy deeds. An angel arguing for Karl's soul said to the devil: "The teres of his madre haue spoiled [thee] . . . so moche hir teeres plesed God."[28] The coincidence of the two sons, dying earlier than their mothers and saved from eternal punishment by their mothers' prayers and tears, is too striking to be overlooked. Both sons, in the eyes of their mothers, were sexual sinners, and their mothers fought their sins—perhaps literally—to the death. It may be that any woman who left her children in order to serve God needed to believe that she could save them through her own sanctity, that her maternal power could be enlarged and transformed.[29] Margery's story, played out on the domestic and local level, is almost a parody of Birgitta's, which took place on a much larger stage, but the shared themes are striking.

Unfortunately for Margery, she did not, like Birgitta, produce a child whose existence could justify the married state. One of Birgitta's daughters, Saint Catherine of Sweden (1331–1381), was another woman saint, and a remarkable one. Like her mother, Catherine was married at about twelve years of age; having observed her parents' continence, she persuaded her husband not to consummate the marriage. But she outdistanced her mother, for she was still a virgin at eighteen, when she left her husband for a visit to her mother in Rome. In her own words, "I longed so much for Mother that I could neither eat nor drink nor sleep, and I could no longer find a joy in

27. Such an intercession is characteristic of much medieval Marian piety, in which the Virgin serves as an advocate for the members of her own *famiglia*.

28. *Revelations*, p. 121.

29. Despite their very different context, recent studies of maternal power (often the most significant form of power available to women) support this point of view. See esp. Nancy Chodorow, *The Reproduction of Mothering* (Berkeley, 1978), Dorothy Dinnersteen, *The Mermaid and the Minotaur* (New York, 1976), and Adrienne Rich, *Of Woman Born* (New York, 1976).

anything."[30] Birgitta urged Catherine to remain with her in Rome although her husband was ill in Sweden, and God agreed: "Tell your daughter . . . that it is more useful for her to stay in Rome than to go home. . . . I will have a care for her husband and bestow upon him the gifts that are best for his soul, for soon I will call him to Me."[31]

The young husband died, and Catherine, with the enviable status of virgin-widow, remained with her mother for the rest of Birgitta's life. Catherine's life was not simple, however, for at eighteen it was attachment to her mother, and not a religious vocation, that brought her to Rome. After her husband's death she forced herself, by horrifying methods, to discover a vocation that would keep her by her mother's side.[32] When Birgitta died, Catherine became abbess of Vadstena, but she spent most of her time and energy in the cause of her mother's canonization and in the fight for the Birgittine order and rule.

Dorothea of Montau (1347–1394) was the Continental holy woman closest to Margery Kempe in time, place, and spirit, and Hope Allen believed that her life may have had a direct influence on the English woman.[33] Like most of the other saints (but unlike Margery), Dorothea was exceptionally holy all her life; at six she indulged in severe penitential practices. Married at sixteen, she had nine children, most of whom died at birth or in early childhood. In 1378 she began to experience ecstatic states and raptures; like Margery (but with a much less sympathetic man), she fought and achieved a vow of chastity.[34]

30. Tr. and quoted in Jorgensen, *Bridget*, 2:57.

31. *Ibid.*, 58–59.

32. *Ibid.*, 69–72.

33. Meech and Allen, *Margery Kempe*, pp. 378–380 and pp. 266 (19/37), 269 (27/20), and 280 (46/29).

34. I am indebted to Richard Kieckhefer for allowing me to read his unpublished manuscript "Dorothy of Montau: Housewife and Mystic," which was helpful in pointing up some of the differences as well as the similarities in the experiences of Margery and Dorothea.

She also won permission for weekly Communion, and she went on pilgrimages—to Aachen (where Margery went in 1433) and to Rome. When her husband died in 1390, Dorothea became a recluse attached to the cathedral at Marienwerder. She was attended by Canon John of Marienwerder, who wrote her *Life* and revelations: in fact he wrote four versions of her story, one soon after her death and three some time later, in the service of her canonization.

Dorothea's revelations, and Canon John's account of them, were influenced by the Dominicans, by the Teutonic Order (to which the canon belonged), and most of all by the *Revelations* and contemporary Process of canonization of Saint Birgitta.[35] Birgitta's relics were carried in solemn procession through Danzig in 1374, on the way to burial at Vadstena, and the excitement surrounding that event may have affected the early stages of Dorothea's life as a visionary and ecstatic. Dorothea became very well known in her own region, through the influence of the Cathedral canons of Marienwerder and the Teutonic Order. A Process of canonization was begun in 1396, and although it was never successful, her local fame and reputation remained significant. On her last pilgrimage in 1433, Margery Kempe "abode in Danske [Danzig] in Ducheland about five or six weeks, and had right good cheer of many people for Our Lord's love" (p. 211). Dorothea lived in Danzig during her married life, and her fame must have been alive there even forty years after her death: Canon John did not die until 1417.

Margery's resemblance to Dorothea is not limited to the circumstances of their lives as middle-class married women with many children. More significant are their shared habit of tears and the emphasis in their lives and writings on tears as evidence of sanctity. Four chapters (28–31) of the long Latin *Life* of Dorothea are devoted to her tears. Like Margery, Dorothea referred often to the tears of the Magdalene which bought the

---

35. Hans Westpfahl, "Dorothée de Montau."

saint forgiveness.[36] She also wept with compassion, compunction, and devotion[37]—the three kinds of "holy tears"—as did Margery, to whom God said: "tears of compunction, devotion, and compassion are the highest and surest gifts that I give on earth" (p. 23). Dorothea also knew that her tears were not entirely her own, but a gift of the Lord.[38] Sometimes she wept for many hours at a time (up to ten hours);[39] Margery at times wept "nearly all day both forenoon and afternoon also" (p. 20), and "every Good Friday in all the aforesaid years she was weeping and sobbing five or six hours together" (p. 128). Dorothea wept sometimes for herself, sometimes for the people,[40] as did Margery: "sometimes for her own sin, sometimes for the sin of the people, sometimes for the souls in Purgatory, sometimes for them that were in poverty and dis-ease, for she desired to comfort them all" (p. 12). The description of Dorothea's crying in Canon John's dignified Latin text is more detached (more liturgical and objective) than Margery's account of her own experiences, but the content of the descriptions is similar. It may be that Margery was moved to complete her book through the influence of Dorothea's reputation; she never mentioned the Prussian woman by name, but their inspiration and experience were very much alike.[41]

The flowering of female sanctity in the Middle Ages did not end with the fourteenth century. Among Margery Kempe's

---

36. Hans Westpfahl, ed., *Vita Dorotheae Montoviensis*, p. 257.

37. *Ibid.*, p. 258.

38. *Ibid.*, p. 259.

39. *Ibid.*, p. 261.

40. *Ibid.*

41. Hope Allen pointed out that Margery's journey to Danzig took place when she had lost her first scribe and had not yet persuaded the second scribe to write. The visit to Danzig (where Dorothea's reputation survived) may have encouraged her to press to finish the *Book*. (Meech and Allen, *Margery Kempe*, p. 341 n. 221/9–11).

closest contemporaries were Joan of Arc (d. 1431),[42] Lydwine of Schiedam (d. 1433), Francesca Romana (d. 1440), and Colette of Corbie (d. 1444), to name only a few of the closest in chronology and most significant in context. In Italy in particular, but to some extent in all of Europe, the fifteenth century brought a continuing elaboration and expansion of female piety, mystical experience, and good works. However, the connections and mutual influences among these women became very complex and diffuse after about 1400, by which time the stream of women's sanctity had grown too large and complex to be confined in any specific channel. It is more helpful to an understanding of Margery Kempe to retrace some chronological steps, remembering that none of the women discussed so far was English, to try to discover an English tradition of female sanctity. Margery's piety and self-understanding were shaped to a great degree by Continental influences, and English priests were inclined to be sympathetic toward her because they were aware of the Continental women. Nonetheless she was an English woman, and we need to discover the extent to which she was unique in her own country.

Fourteenth-century England had almost no tradition of ecstatic piety or religious "singularity" among women. Since the time of Saint Hilda in the seventh century, no English woman held a major public religious role, prophetic or administrative, nor were English priests eager to serve as disciples, biographers, or secretaries of holy women. Whether or not they were experienced, mystical trances were not often reported from English convents. But the spiritual development of women was not

42. Joan of Arc was unlike the other women saints of the late Middle Ages: her vocation was unique, and she was always a political figure. Although she was better known in the noble and military class than in other levels of society, it still is somewhat surprising that stories carried by soldiers did not circulate in England more than apparently they did. Margery Kempe never mentioned her, although Joan's execution in 1431 took place just before Margery's journey to Prussia. See W. T. Waugh, "Joan of Arc in English Sources of the Fifteenth Century."

neglected, nor did women lack models for ecstatic forms of piety.

Nuns and anchoresses existed in substantial numbers in England, as in all of Europe, throughout the Middle Ages. There were nuns of every order, and they shared in all the triumphs and failings of their kind.[43] They appear in English literature from Aldhelm and Bede to Chaucer and beyond: Chaucer included two nuns among his Canterbury pilgrims. Despite all the criticism and satire directed against them, they were generally respected as holy women. Margery visited the convent at Denny at the abbess's request, and she had opportunities there and elsewhere to observe the sisters' lives and piety. A more exotic phenomenon (because it ended with the Reformation) was the institution of anchorites and anchoresses, well established in England, and especially in Norfolk.[44] Margery's principal confessor was a Dominican anchorite, and she visited Dame Julian at her cell in Norwich. The possibility of an enclosed, solitary life must always have been available to her imagination.

The importance of the female recluse in the English religious tradition is apparent in the several rules written for them, from Ailred's *A Rule of Life for a Recluse* in the twelfth century through Rolle's *Form of Perfect Living* and Hilton's *Scale of Perfection* in the fourteenth. But the most renowned is the *Ancrene Riwle*, an early thirteenth-century work by an anonymous author written for three sisters who had chosen to live apart from the world.[45] The *Riwle*, which greatly influenced later rules for women and has been celebrated as a formative

43. Material about nuns and convents is scarce in general histories of medieval monasticism, for example, in Knowles, *Religious Orders*. Some older books by women scholars are helpful; for example, Power, *Medieval English Nunneries*; Lina Eckenstein, *Woman Under Monasticism*; Sr. Mary Byrne, *The Tradition of the Nun in Medieval England*.

44. See Rotha Mary Clay, *The Hermits and Anchorites of England*, pp. 234–237.

45. Gerald Sitwell, Introduction to *The Ancrene Riwle*, p. ix.

stage in the development of English prose,[46] is traditionally regarded as the normative description of what English holy women should be and do. In certain respects it is characteristic of much writing for and about religious women, with its kindly, avuncular approach and the conventional yet horrifying misogyny that lies below. Using the Old Testament analogy of the man who left a pit uncovered and became responsible for the death of any animal that fell into it, the author insists that a woman who lets men see her is responsible for their lust:

> The pit is her fair face, and her white neck, . . . and further, her speech is a pit, if it is not controlled, . . . if the man is tempted in such a way that he commits mortal sin through you in any way, even though it is not with you, but with desire for you, . . . be quite sure of the judgment: you must pay for the animal because you laid open the pit.[47]

The usual virtues urged by men on women are here: women are not to teach or rebuke men, they are to be silent—like the Virgin, who "spoke so little that we find her words recorded in Holy Scripture only four times."[48] The monk who wished Margery "enclosed in a house of stone, so that, there, no man should speak with thee" (p. 20) had ample precedent for his wish. Over all, the *Riwle* exemplifies the English ideal of women's piety: the religious woman is to be quiet, enclosed, hard working, and humble. The portrait is not that of Margery Kempe.

No account of English religious women, no matter how brief, would be complete without mention of an atypical example—

46. R. W. Chambers, "The Continuity of English Prose," p. c: " . . . whoever the maidens were for whom the *Riwle* was written, they were the cause of great things in English prose." See also *Riwle*, p. xxiv.

47. *Riwle*, p. 25. This attitude lingers in the twentieth century, especially in trials for rape in which the defendant is excused because the victim was "seductive."

48. *Ibid.*, p. 33.

Christina of Markyate, a twelfth-century rebel, runaway, and recluse.[49] Her story is reminiscent of the lives of the legendary early saints, for it is presented in terms of dramatic conflict between the defense of her virginity (which is identified, to a great extent, with her vocation), and the concerted efforts of family, society, and villains to despoil her of that prize. A related theme of great importance is rejection of the married state in favor of a "higher" sphere by a holy woman—a rejection achieved with divine assistance. Christina's perils and triumphs constitute a medieval melodrama, with the rich and mighty Ranulf Flambard (favorite bishop of the wicked king William Rufus) as villain, and Christina's parents as co-conspirators. Christina was heroic: she lived for four years after her escape in a cell so small she could neither stand up nor lie down, and at the end of her life became the prioress of a convent with an extensive reputation for sanctity.

The thirteenth-century treatise *Hali Meidenhad* is among the most extreme of all the antisexual and antimarital polemics in the Christian tradition. It was written to persuade young women to a celibate religious life, and its picture of the married state is unrivaled for nastiness and gloom. Sexual feelings as well as sexual behavior are perceived as filthy:

> the impure deed that begat thee of thy mother, that same inde-
> cent burning of the flesh, that same flaming itch of carnal lust,
> before that loathsome act, that beastly copulation, that shame-
> less coition, that fullness of stinking ordure and uncomely
> deed.[50]

Maidenhood was the most valuable of all God's gifts: "a virtue above all virtues, and to Christ the most acceptable of all" (p. 15). Marriage was second best, if that: "a bed for the sick, to catch (in their fall) the unstrong, who cannot stand in the high

49. See *The Life of Christina of Markyate*.

50. *Hali Meidenhad*, p. 12. The next thirteen references are to this work, indicated by page numbers in the text.

hill, and so near to heaven, as the virtue of maidenhood"
(p. 28). Margery Kempe (like most other children) grew up from
a marriage and within a family, and she probably saw marriage and family as a "natural" way of life. However, this
ancient (and for Christians, dangerously Manichean) view of
marriage remained alive and powerful in her culture, and she
adopted many of its assumptions. In relation to her vision of
Christ dancing with his Mother and the holy maidens in
Heaven, it is interesting to find the same image in *Hali
Meidenhad*: "In their circle is God himself; and his dear
mother . . . leads in that blessed band of gleaming maidens: nor
may any but they dance and sing, for that is ever their song, to
thank God . . . that for him they renounced every earthly man,
and kept themselves clean ever from carnal defilements in
body and in breast. . . . This song, none but they may sing"
(p. 30). Virginity—and by implication, the hymen itself—is the
virgin's link to God; in extraordinarily direct language, the
maiden is warned: "break not thou that seal that sealeth you
together!" (p. 14).

The author expressed not only his admiration of virginity
and disgust at sexuality but his view of domestic life as an
abomination. In the rare cases in which a man and woman are
happy together they must fear each other's death; most couples
are miserable, and the housewife's lot is unhappy always, for
she must "be more worried than any drudge in the house, or
any hired servant" (p. 40). The life of the woman who hates her
husband is worst of all: "While he is at home, all thy wide
dwellings seem too narrow for thee; his looking on thee makes
thee aghast; his loathsome mirth and his rude behavior fill
thee with horror. He . . . maketh mock at thee, as a lecher [does]
his whore; he beateth thee and mawleth thee as his bought
thrall and patrimonial slave" (p. 43). There is no escape from
this life of horror: "if the knot of wedlock be once knotted, let
the man be an idiot or a cripple . . . thou must keep to him"
(p. 45). If the woman has no children she is denounced as barren;
if she has children, further miseries await her: "In the gestation,

is heaviness and hard pain in every hour; in the actual birth is of all pangs the strongest, and occasionally death; in the nourishing the child, many a miserable moment" (p. 47). A healthy, sound child brings with it the terror of its death, a deformed child is a shame and a sorrow, and "often it occurs that the child most loved . . . most sorrows and disturbs his parents at last" (p. 47). But perhaps the most revolting of all of this description of marriage and motherhood concerns the physical deterioration of pregnancy:

> The ruddy face shall turn lean, and grow green as grass. Thine eyes shall be dusky, and underneath grow pale; and by the giddiness of thy brain thy head shall ake sorely. Within thy belly, the uterus shall swell and strut out like a water bag; thy bowels shall have pains, and there shall be stitches in thy flank. . . . Thy mouth is bitter, and nauseous is all that thou chewest, and whatever thy stomach disdainfully receives; that is, with want of appetite, throws it up again. [Pp. 49–50]

The thesis argued by this catalogue of horrors is that the bride of Christ is infinitely happier than the wife of a mortal man—that God exceeds any husband in beauty and wealth, that the virtues born in the soul of the chaste woman make nonsense of mortal children. In spite of his warning that pride, even pride in virginity, is a great sin—that "a mild wife or a meek widow is better than a proud maiden" (p. 61)—the author returns again and again to his major theme. He offers as examples Saints Katherine, Margaret, Agnes, Lucy, Cecilia, and Juliana, and all those who "revel now in God's arms as Queens of Heaven!" (p. 64). Margery Kempe, too, believed that the virgin saints were with God in Heaven, admitted to center stage by virtue of their virginity and their heroic defense of that state. She was painfully aware, as were Birgitta and the other married women who aspired to sanctity, that they had lost the pearl beyond price—"a loss that is beyond recovery" (p. 15)—and that special graces were required to admit them to that heavenly company.

The defense of virginity was among the most popular subjects of medieval English literature. Among the surviving evidence of its popularity are the "Katherine group" (three
thirteenth-century legends of Saints Katherine, Margaret, and
Juliana), many of the tales in the *Legenda Aurea*, John Capgrave's
Life of Katherine, Osbern Bokenham's *Legendys of Hooly
Wummen*, and many other single tales and groups of stories.
The maiden who fought and (usually) died to preserve her
virginity for Christ was obviously a heroic figure. Most often
these were royal or noble women whose outstanding common
characteristic was defiance: defiance not only of demons and
villains but of all forms of civil and familial authority. Most of
them had to defy fathers and magistrates as well as seducers—in
fact, it was not unusual for magistrate and seducer to be the
same man.

The prototypical example of the legendary female saint was
Margaret of Antioch, rebellious virgin and daughter of a proud
father. Katherine of Alexandria, the other favorite, had to debate and defeat the lords of her own kingdom and assembled
philosophers in order to defend her marriage to Christ. The
rulers, magistrates, and philosophers so confronted were pagans,
and thus not legitimate Christian authorities, but the obdurate
resistance and open defiance of the women is still remarkable
in light of the conventional "feminine" virtues of meekness
and silence. Saint Christina, in archetypical heroics, had her
tongue cut out by a judge who wanted her to sacrifice to pagan
gods. Instead of giving in, she spat a piece of her tongue in his
face, blinding him, and did so "wyth a mychty entent,"[51] that
is, deliberately and powerfully. Her namesake, Christina of
Markyate, showed the same fighting spirit when she resisted
her (nominally) Christian parents and the bishop.

The strength and aggression set forth as desirable womanly

---

51. *Bokenham's Legendys of Hooly Wummen*, p. 84. Osbern Bokenham
was an Augustinian of East Anglia (Stoke Clare, in Suffolk); he was born
about 1392, and thus was a younger contemporary of Margery Kempe.

virtues in the saints' *Lives* help to clarify certain aspects of the lives of historical (late medieval) saints. The determination and defiance displayed by women who were seen or saw themselves as holy or special was derived in part from these remarkable models. Such women were able to defy the conventions of their own time partly because, from earliest childhood, they heard stories of extraordinary women. It is known, for example, that Birgitta had a special devotion to Saint Agnes, that Joan of Arc was guided by Saints Margaret and Katherine, that Margery Kempe wished to emulate Mary Magdalene. Saint Birgitta and Christina of Markyate used the story of Saint Cecilia in their arguments over chastity and marriage. In the fourteenth century these were not mere names in a litany but powerful individuals who gained Heaven despite—or even because of—social nonconformity. The lesson of their *Lives* was not lost, and it was not simple.

Unhappily, the legends of the saints were steeped in violence as well as virtue, and when the subjects were female, the most brutal episodes were sexual. Men as well as women were beaten and burned, but women saints were also sexually humiliated and assaulted. In many stories they were stripped naked (their hair generally grew long in an instant, to cover them, or a white garment appeared), and taken to brothels (where their chastity was protected by supernatural means).[52] Almost inevitably, their breasts were mauled or torn off, an attack upon them as women as well as Christians: it should be noted that male saints were spared corresponding tortures. Writers of the *Lives* lingered over these episodes, making it difficult to avoid the conclusion that such passages were experienced as erotic. In Bokenham's story of Saint Agatha, for example:

Sum wyth pynsouns blunt & dulle

52. Saint Agnes, for example, was stripped by her persecutors, but her hair instantly grew long and thick enough to cover her; when she was taken to a brothel, a miraculous light blinded those who looked at her, and then a white stole appeared, which fit her exactly. See *Bokenham's Legendys*, pp. 199–120.

> Her tendyr brestys begunne to pulle
> Full boystously; summe in here hondys
> Browhtyyn brennyng hoot fyr-brondys,
> And therwyth hyr pappes al to-brent;
> Sum wyth yirnene forkys out rent
> The flesh þer-of, that grete pyte
> How þe blood owt ran yt was to se
> On euery syde ful plenteuously.[53]

Saints' legends, an extremely popular form of oral and written literature, obviously served more than one function in medieval culture. On the highest level they inspired faith and courage, perhaps especially in women, for whom these were the only models of active and heroic femininity. (The protagonists of epic and romance, from Beowulf to Lancelot, were male.) But on the lowest level, their indulgence—perhaps even delight—in the details of sexual abuse can only be described as pornographic.[54]

In relation to Margery Kempe, it seems clear that the stories of female saints helped her to live out her vocation by placing before her a group of holy women who not only defied their society but won closeness to Christ by doing so. In a less positive vein, the legends may have exacerbated her fear of sexual violence, a fear that was to some extent a realistic response to the dangers of an unconventional life. It may be, however, that on the unconscious level at least, she feared abuse almost as an adjunct to her vocation and perhaps even as a punishment for its singularity.

Probably because its author lived in the world, and not at home or in a convent, the *Book of Margery Kempe* is populated largely by men. Apart from an occasional figure like the sympathetic jailer's wife of Leicester, Margery encountered only men on her travels. She wrote about her father, her husband, and her son, but said nothing of her mother, of sisters, or of daugh-

53. *Ibid.*, p. 234.

54. Erotic writings are designed to arouse sexual feelings; pornographic writings arouse such feelings through suggestion or portrayal of violence, abuse, or degradation of the sexual "object."

ters (except for the unsatisfactory daughter-in-law). She visited the nuns at Denny and comforted the woman who went insane after childbirth, but these were exceptions. Margery departed from the conventional female roles of housewife or nun, and as a result, she lived among men or remained solitary. Of course her confessors and advisers were men, as were all the spiritual authorities to whom she turned, with one notable exception: the anchoress Julian of Norwich. Margery knew Julian by reputation as a spiritual counselor and an expert in the discernment of spirits. When she visited her, they spoke together at length of spiritual matters: "Much was the holy dalliance that the anchoress and this creature had by communing in the love of Our Lord Jesus Christ the many days that they were together" (p. 34).

Julian of Norwich is unique in English religious history. She was a mystic, a theologian, and an educated woman: her description of herself as "unlettered" is an expression of conventional humility.[55] She was deeply learned but not university trained; no hint of scholastic argument enters her book. After about 1403 she lived in a cell in the church of Saints Julian and Edward in Norwich, and she may have been a nun before she became an anchoress. In 1373, at the age of thirty, she fell desperately ill (in response to her own prayer for a serious illness); when she recovered, she received the sixteen "showings" that comprise her revelations. She wrote a short account of her experiences soon after the event; twenty years later, after profound reflection and meditation, she produced an expanded and revised longer version.[56] Her writings are orthodox in content, unorthodox in style—informal, experiential, and written in the first person, characteristics of mystical confession and not of theological argument. Beginning with the revela-

---

55. Edmund Colledge and James Walsh, "Editing Julian of Norwich's *Revelations*." This article summarizes the full description of Julian's "intellectual formation" given in the introduction to their edition of *A Book of Showings to the Anchoress Julian of Norwich*, 1:43–59.

56. Colledge and Walsh compare the two versions in their introduction. See also B. A. Windeatt, "Julian of Norwich and Her Audience."

tion of Christ's humanity and Passion, and without departing
from her experience, Julian moved toward a spiritual intellectual appreciation of who God is.

Julian's *Book of Showings* consists of description and contemplation of the sixteen revelations, which were vivid, graphic
experiences of Christian doctrine, centered on the Passion. The
central theme is love, and the central theological problem, or
argument, is that of sin and evil. The last "showing" sums up
Julian's belief, and her experience: "What, woldest thou wytt
thy lordes menyng in this thyng? Wytt it wele, loue was his
menyng. Who shewyth it the? Loue. (What shewid he the?
Love.) Wherfore shewyth he it the? For loue."[57] To Julian, sin
was nothing, for God does everything: "ther is no doer but he"
(p. 340), and God does not sin. Sin does cause pain, however,
and thus Christ's pain and Passion—revealed to her by direct
"showing"—became the resolution of the problem of evil. Unlike sin, "payne is somthyng . . . for it purgyth and makyth vs
to know oure selfe and aske mercy" (pp. 406–407). In her own
way, Margery Kempe also struggled with the question of sin
and evil, and received from God a very different resolution.
When she refused to believe that some souls were damned, she
was punished with demonic visions of sexual abominations
until she learned to believe God's word as it was spoken to her
soul (see Book I, chapter 59, of Margery's *Book*). The problem of
evil became a problem of authority, and Margery's God—a stern
Father in this instance—settled her doubts by exerting his power.

Unlike Margery Kempe, whose God was always Father or
beautiful young man or boy-child, Julian of Norwich was
supreme among those Christian thinkers who have perceived
God (and God's relationship to the soul) unrestricted by patriarchal language and masculine imagery. For Julian, God is "the
maker, the keper, the louer" (p. 300). In the Trinity she "saw
and vnderstode these thre propertes: the properte of the faderhed,

---

57. *Showings*, 2:732–733. The next eight references, indicated by page
numbers in the text, are to this volume.

and the properte of the mother hed, and the properte of the lordschyppe in one god" (pp. 583–584). Christ is "oure moder in kynd . . . and he is oure moder of mercy . . . " (p. 586). The point is repeated again and again: "As verely as god is oure fader, as verely is god oure moder . . . " (p. 590). This is so for good reason, as Julian explained: "The moders servyce is nerest, rediest and suerest: nerest for it is most of kynd, redyest for it is most of loue, and sekerest for it is most of trewth. This office ne myght nor coulde nevyr none done to þe full but he allone. We wytt that alle oure moders bere vs to payne and to dyeng. A, what is that? But oure very moder Jhesu, he alone beryth vs to joye and to endlesse levyng, blessyd mot he be" (p. 595). Christ died on the Cross in childbirth.

The appreciation of Christ as Mother is not limited to the Cross; it includes the familiar image of Christ as nursing mother: "The moder may geue her chylde sucke hyr mylke, but oure precyous moder Jhesu, he may fede vs wyth hym selfe, and doth full curtesly and full tendyrly with the blessyd sacrament, that is precyous fode of very lyfe . . . " (pp. 596–597). The recognition of God as Mother, experienced directly through mystical revelation and expressed in the ancient imagery of the maternal Saviour, enabled Julian to incorporate the pains of Christ into a profound theology of love and suffering.

Julian of Norwich was an imposing exception to Margery's isolation from other women. Apart from the anchoress, Margery knew about other holy women through story and legend and reputation gathered in church, in pious conversation, and on her travels. The friars of Lynn shared tales of the saints of their orders; in Germany and the Low Countries, where Margery's friends and relatives were merchants and traders, almost every town and cathedral had its special saint, and many of these were women. From the life of Saint Birgitta in particular, Margery was aware that a special sanctity was accessible even to married women, despite the persistent Christian emphasis on virginity. In the lives of such women as Birgitta or Dorothea or Margery Kempe, the ancient saints' battle for virginity was transformed into a struggle for chastity within marriage, and for sufficient freedom from the marriage bond to permit intimacy with Christ. Free of the burdens of marriage and family, women could move out into the world as prophets and reformers, and a woman might hope for a special vision or divine revelation. Despite persistent disparagement of the female sex (and of sexuality itself), there were new possibilities of spiritual leadership and adventure for women in the later Middle Ages. Special promises were made to chosen women, and one of these was Margery Kempe, to whom God spoke explicitly to comfort and to reassure: "Daughter, when thou art in Heaven, thou shalt be able to ask what thou wilt, and I shall grant thee all thy desire. I have told thee beforetime that thou art a singular lover, and therefore thou shalt have a singular love in Heaven, a singular reward, and a singular worship" (p. 42). In a remarkable eschatological vision, Margery and others like her were linked by a promise to the legendary virgin saints: "And, forasmuch as thou art a maiden in thy soul, I shall take thee by the one hand in Heaven, and My Mother by the other hand, and so shalt thou dance in Heaven with other holy maidens and virgins, for I may call thee dearly bought, and Mine own dearworthy darling" (p. 42).

The holy women of late medieval Europe, who began to appear in substantial numbers after the middle of the thirteenth century, characteristically saw visions, communicated directly with God, and found scribes or biographers who publicized their experiences. Some of them, in the tradition of Christian female sanctity, were lifelong virgins, but an increasing number were married women and mothers who struggled with the married state and eventually "transcended" it, becoming in effect "honorary" virgins through their own holiness and the special favor of God. These women saints, who traveled widely, spoke out publicly, and departed from the traditional roles of Christian women, were a new creation of the late Middle Ages. Their lives and works form a context in which to recognize and appreciate Margery Kempe, her book, and her vocation.

Chapter Seven

"ORDAINED TO BE A MIRROR":

Interpretations of Margery Kempe

MARGERY KEMPE and her book pose intriguing questions for students of medieval religion and society, for historians of the English Church, and for those who attempt to discover and interpret women's experience in premodern times. The book is a wonderfully rich source: above all, a firsthand account of what it was like to be a mystic and a pilgrim—and a woman—in the Middle Ages. It discloses in lavish detail the particularities of an unusual life and vocation, and the ways in which Margery Kempe and her career were regarded by her lay and clerical contemporaries. Neither the author, her calling, nor her book fit conventional categories, and for that reason they are more instructive than conventional sources. The very eccentricity of Margery Kempe and her autobiography makes them invaluable to historians.

We have been able to "see" *The Book of Margery Kempe* within the several traditions and contexts set forth in the preceding chapters. But Margery was "ordained to be a mirror" for our time as well as her own, and before we summarize the results of our investigations, it may be enlightening to review what has been seen in the mirror since the book reappeared in 1934. The historiography of *The Book of Margery Kempe* is the latest chapter in her story; our responses shed light on the twentieth century, just as the responses of Margery's acquaintances shed light on the fifteenth. Like autobiographers, historians work with more than one agenda, and the reception of the *Book* reveals much about our attitudes toward the past, toward various forms of religious expression, and toward extraordinary women.

The discovery of *The Book of Margery Kempe* caused great excitement among historians and students of the English language. It was not only a substantial work in Middle English (and the first autobiography in English), but it provided new insights into various aspects of fifteenth-century religion and society. It also introduced a new historical character—Margery Kempe, who had been known only (and inaccurately) as an "anchoress" of Lynn through the extracts from her book made in the sixteenth century.

When Colonel Butler-Bowdon took his manuscript to the Victoria and Albert Museum for identification, the task was given to Hope Emily Allen, an American scholar who was working in England on a study of the history and influence of the *Ancrene Riwle*.[1] Allen announced the discovery in a letter to the *Times Literary Supplement* of December 27, 1934, and arranged with the owner and with the Early English Text Society to publish a critical edition of the book. A coeditor, Sanford B. Meech, was chosen to study the language and chronology, while Hope Allen herself was to discuss "the mysticism and mystics of Margery Kempe's narrative"[2] in footnotes and appendixes. That edition was published in 1940.

1. Allen's earlier work included an authoritative book on the Richard Rolle corpus and several studies of English mystical writings of the fourteenth century and earlier. See Bibliography.

2. Meech and Allen, *Margery Kempe*, p. liii.

Meanwhile, Colonel Butler-Bowdon brought out his own translation of the book in 1936; an American edition was published in 1944. The translation was introduced by R. W. Chambers, who hailed the discovery of Margery's book as "of the very greatest importance for the history of English literature" (p. xv). Chambers recognized its unique place in religious and social as well as literary history, and was also the first to describe its author as a "difficult and morbid religious enthusiast" (p. xxii). *The Book of Margery Kempe* came to light in an age conscious of abnormal psychology and unsympathetic to religious "extremism," and its publication provoked a wave of similar opinions. In a prefatory note to the critical edition, Hope Allen quoted Herbert Thurston's diagnosis of "terrible hysteria,"[3] and that response was widely shared.

Hope Allen at first accepted "hysteria" as sufficient explanation for Margery's deviation from the traditional piety of English women. Regarding the *Ancrene Riwle* as the devotional norm for such women, Allen believed that Margery Kempe was the first since Christina of Markyate to indulge in a more emotional style of religious experience, and that her "neuroticism" accounted for her beliefs and behavior. But before the 1940 edition of the book was published, Allen discovered that even if Margery Kempe was unique among English women, her autobiography bore substantial resemblance to various Continental works of piety written by or about religious women. Allen's notes and appendixes contain many references to such resemblances, especially to the *Revelations* of Saint Birgitta of Sweden and to the experience of Dorothea of Montau. Before 1937, when she urged the Early English Text Society to publish their edition without waiting for her own researches to be completed, Allen realized that Margery Kempe occupied an

3. *Ibid.*, p. lxv.

important place in a distinctive tradition of piety within the larger story of medieval Christianity.[4]

Because Hope Allen's work was not finished, *The Book of Margery Kempe* appeared in 1940 as "Volume One" of a projected two-volume series. The second volume was to include further notes and appendixes by Hope Allen, including lengthy extracts from Middle English translations of various Continental religious writings, especially from the *Revelations* of Saint Birgitta, the *Orcherd of Syon* (the translation of the *Dialogue* of Saint Catherine of Siena), and the *Book of Special Grace* of Mechthild of Hackborn. Allen believed that these works were sponsored by a circle of influential English persons with ties to the Lancastrian court and to Henry V's foundations at Shene and Syon. The writings appealed to educated, devout lay men and women as well as to those in religious life, and their sponsors may have hoped to satisfy, incorporate, and render harmless certain contemporary forms of religious "enthusiasm"—the "Fifteenth-century Counter-Reformation" mentioned above. By this time, Allen recognized a dual tradition in English women's piety: the disciplined devotion of enclosed women represented by the *Ancrene Riwle*, and a new wave of visionary, ecstatic piety influenced by Continental women and their admirers. Margery Kempe's book, she believed, was a product of the newer spirit, and its social and geographical origins were predictable, given the close ties to the Continent of the merchant class of Lynn.

Unfortunately, Hope Allen was not able to finish Volume Two before her death in 1960. At first she was isolated by the World War from European sources and materials; later, the task as she had conceived it, which included elements of much

4. "When I undertook this work I saw Margery in an entirely different light from what I do now" (letter from Hope Emily Allen to Dr. Pollard, Dec. 21, 1937, Allen papers, Bryn Mawr College Archives).

of her earlier work, was too large and diffuse to accomplish. In the mid-1950s, although she still hoped to produce a second volume, Allen realized that her scheme was "more suited to a beginning career than to one well on toward the end."[5] Her inability to complete the ambitious assignment—tragic for herself and a great loss to students of medieval history and religion—is entirely understandable, for her vision was too grand and original to be realized by one historian working alone.[6] Hope Allen was a pioneer of women's history: one of the first scholars to perceive the existence of a distinct female tradition and to value the special experience of women.[7]

Despite the initial excitement over the discovery of the *Book* and the continuing interest in Margery Kempe, no full-scale interpretive study has been published. Martin Thornton wrote a short appraisal in 1960, and two retellings of Margery's story have appeared.[8] (In the 1980s, with the renewed appreciation of women's history and the increasing sophistication in the study of medieval spirituality, we have a much richer background for understanding Margery Kempe. Scholars are taking

5. Letter from Hope Allen to unnamed correspondent, June 14, 1955. In an earlier (March 12, 1949) letter to Dr. Onions of the Early English Text Society, Allen called her work on Margery Kempe "the most ideally congenial subject that I could imagine which also gathers up all that I have ever done before" (Allen papers).

6. Throughout her papers, Allen makes frequent reference to the difficult circumstances of her own life and work, including illness and isolation, and more particularly to the special problems encountered by women scholars who have family responsibilities and no "wives" to take care of them.

7. In the field of medieval English women's history, Hope Allen had a notable contemporary colleague in Eileen Power (1889–1940). For a rare note of appreciation of Allen's work on Margery Kempe, see Robert Karl Stone, *Middle English Prose Style*. See also Wolfgang Riehle, *The Middle English Mystics*, esp. pp. ix and 165.

8. Martin Thornton, *Margery Kempe*; Katharine Cholmeley, *Margery Kempe*; Louise Collis, *The Apprentice Saint*.

a new and rewarding look at the *Book* and its context.)[9] Before the 1980s, although almost every historian of late medieval England, or of English mysticism or church history, mentioned the *Book* in a few paragraphs or a chapter, their notices tended to convey a sense of dislike or discomfort; they told the story as rapidly as possible and moved on to more congenial subjects.[10]

Margery has often been compared (usually unfavorably) to Julian of Norwich: a natural comparison, given the conjunction of time, place, and gender, and the women's acquaintance with one another, but not always useful in terms of the two authors and their writings.[11] Julian's theological reflections have been regarded as more significant than Margery's account of her experiences; her life and work have been accepted as valid when Margery's have not. Also, Julian stayed in one place

9. See esp. Caroline Walker Bynum, *Jesus as Mother*; Susan Dickman, "Margery Kempe and the English Devotional Tradition"; Anthony Goodman, "The Piety of John Brunham's Daughter, of Lynn"; André Vauchez, *La spiritualité du moyen âge occidental*.

10. In *The English Church in the Fourteenth Century*, W. A. Pantin devoted five pages to Margery Kempe. More sympathetic and interested than many historians, he described Margery as "sincere, generous, and affectionate, and completely lacking in that harshness which has sometimes marked the pious laity" (p. 261). David Knowles, in *The English Mystical Tradition*, included a chapter on Margery but concluded that her book had "little in it of deep spiritual wisdom, and nothing of true mystical experience" (p. 148). Knowles also commented that "Margery herself, however interesting a figure she may be to the student of religious sentiment or psychology, is clearly not the equal of the earlier English mystics in depth of perception or wisdom of spiritual doctrine, nor as a personality can she challenge comparison with Julian of Norwich" (p. 139). In *Pre-Reformation English Spirituality*, Edmund Colledge praised Margery's sincerity and compassion but suggested that "she was a hysteric, if not an epileptic" (p. 222). In their learned introduction to *A Book of Showings to the Anchoress Julian of Norwich*, Colledge and Walsh refer to Margery's "morbid self-engrossment" (1:38).

11. Some of the useful comparative studies of the two women are by literary scholars: see Mary G. Mason, "The Other Voice"; Karl Robert Stone, *Middle English Prose Style*; E.I. Watkin, *On Julian of Norwich and In Defense of Margery Kempe*. (I am indebted to Susan Dickman for allowing me to read her interesting unpublished work on Margery Kempe and Julian of Norwich.)

while Margery wandered, and an early review of *The Book of Margery Kempe* struck a note that has persisted in later histories: "If she had really been an ancress, living secluded in her cell, these peculiarities would not have mattered. But she insisted on going everywhere, following, as she believed, the special call of God."[12] That reviewer, from a modern perspective, echoed the wish of the infuriated monk of Canterbury who wished that Margery were "enclosed in a house of stone" so that no one could speak with her. By her habit of wandering and her claims to special attention, Margery Kempe provoked many of her contemporaries and has baffled or dismayed historians. With significant exceptions, her story (and her personality) have not until very recently appealed to reviewers of her book or to church historians, with the unfortunate result that it has not been fully appreciated as a historical document.

Obviously, it is not simply Margery's personality or her eccentricity which for so long discouraged historians from serious attempts to incorporate her book into their picture of the fifteenth century. Part of the problem lies with the common distaste for aspects of late medieval religious expression, of which *The Book of Margery Kempe* seemed an exaggerated example. Her vocation, with its visions, weeping, and "self-centered" meditations, appalls historians who look to medieval Christianity for the roots of their own faith, and is easily disregarded by those who look to the past for confirmation of a secular perspective. The discovery of Margery's book was much more welcome to students of the English language than to historians of religion and society, who generally have found it trivial or not "serious." Margery Kempe has been dismissed by sophisticated critics as a "hysteric," by traditionalists as an aberration in the history of English piety.

---

12. Herbert Thurston, review of Butler-Bowdon edition in the *Tablet*, October 24, 1936, p. 570. Thurston also found it "impossible to forget the hysterical temperament revealed in every page of the narrative portions."

The historiography of *The Book of Margery Kempe* must be seen against the background of established attitudes of historians toward the later Middle Ages in general. Until the latter half of this century, widespread dislike or "disapproval" of the entire period prevailed—perhaps a natural response to an era of war, plague, unrest, and confusion. Especially in the nineteenth century (and such attitudes linger past their time), most European and American historians believed in the continuing progress of human beings and their cultures, especially of Western people and of Western civilization. With confidence in progress still unshaken by holocaust and cataclysm, these historians viewed the fourteenth and fifteenth centuries as an unfortunate setback in the long upward march of "Western man." Civil and dynastic wars, economic recession, unchecked disease, and the chronic protest of the poor were the stuff of the miserable interlude between the practical and spiritual triumphs of the High Middle Ages and the glory of the Renaissance. Not even the great fourteenth-century cathedrals or the new vernacular European literature redeemed the late Middle Ages: these successful creations were perceived as vestiges of Gothic civilization or precursors of the sixteenth century. For northern Europe at least, much of late medieval culture was seen as febrile, superficial, and tainted by fascination with the grotesque.[13]

Until fairly recently, the accusation of decadence was leveled against the religion as well as the art, politics, and economy of the late Middle Ages. Schism, heresy, and corruption in the Church matched war and unrest in the body politic, while the scholastic synthesis collapsed under the pressure of new movements in faith and philosophy. Late medieval Christian thought was regarded as sterile and mechanistic; popular piety as

13. The classic interpretation of late medieval cultural "decadence" is Johan Huizinga, *The Waning of the Middle Ages.*

"arithmetical" and overscrupulous.[14] It is true that aspects of late medieval piety do appear complicated in comparison to (for instance) the twelfth century—partly because of the development of techniques of moral casuistry during the twelfth century. Examination of conscience certainly was complicated for Margery Kempe and her confessors, but that does not mean that it was trivial or insincere.

In an unusual application of the Weber-Tawney thesis, the mercantile spirit of the late Middle Ages has been blamed for an apparently "mercantile" piety: the new bourgeoisie made a bourgeois God in their own unattractive image—a divine Bookkeeper who added and subtracted credits toward salvation. The late medieval Church, with its sales of indulgences and benefices, and its corrupt and overnumerous clergy, has been castigated as an excessively sacerdotal, top-heavy, and avaricious institution that did little to check the depredations of vicious or foolish clerics. The "automatic" grace of the sacraments (*opus operatum*) defeated their true meaning and inhibited real piety and penitence.

We have seen the language and imagery of the counting-house in *The Book of Margery Kempe*, but her faith was no less passionate for that. Her God was less a bookkeeper than a merchant prince, but more than either of those, a parent and a lover. And the many regular and secular clerics who inhabit her book reveal on the whole a care for pastoral duties and the individual soul which would be impressive in any era. The negative image of the late medieval Church, which is quite unsupported by the evidence of Margery Kempe, was in part the product of partisan Reformation scholarship. Both Catholic and Protestant historians have assigned to the shortcomings of the Old Church the primary responsibility for the Reform.

In relation to the English Church, historians have distinguished between the fourteenth century and the fifteenth,

14. See, e.g., Etienne Delaruelle et al., *L'église au temps du Grand Schisme et de la crise conçiliare*, pp. 870–875.

acknowledging the marvelous mystical writings, splendid churches, and successful preaching of the earlier period. The later century stands alone accused of late medieval "decadence." The great Benedictine scholar David Knowles wrote this of the fifteenth century: "Yet it was an age singularly barren in great issues and great men. Rarely, if ever, between the Conquest and the present day, has a space of seventy years passed over an England so devoid of men of distinction in any walk of life as the age between the death of Henry V and the adolescence of More and Wolsey."[15] The widespread assumption that only "great men" and "men of distinction" reward the historian's energy and attention made it unlikely that much significance would be attached to Margery Kempe.

Knowles noted the contrast between fourteenth- and fifteenth-century spirituality. Praising the fourteenth-century writings of Walter Hilton and the author of *The Cloud of Unknowing*, he pointed to their "intellectual and emotional austerity, and sense of the transcendence of supernatural reality, which are derived from some of the purest sources of theological and ascetical tradition."[16] Like most historians of mysticism, Knowles regarded the Dionysian tradition of the *via negativa*, exemplified at its finest in Saint John of the Cross, as the "highest" form of spirituality. He perceived affective mysticism, with its emphasis on the humanity of Christ, as a "stage" in progress toward a purer contemplation, dangerously sentimental in the hands of practitioners less sophisticated than Bernard of Clairvaux. Naturally, Knowles's assumptions and values colored his judgment of the fifteenth century and of Margery Kempe.

David Knowles's comments convey not only his own but the "classic" view of late medieval English religion:

> This stream [of pure spirituality] continued to flow till the reign of Henry VIII, but there is some evidence that from the beginning of the fifteenth century onwards it was *contaminated* by

15. David Knowles, *Religious Orders*, 2:361.
16. *Ibid.*, 222.

another current, that of a more emotional and idiosyncratic
devotion, manifesting itself in visions, revelations and *unusual
behavior*, deriving partly . . . from the influence of some of the
women saints of the fourteenth century, such as Angela of
Foligno, Dorothea of Prussia and Bridget of Sweden. The most
familiar example of this type in England is Margery Kempe.
[Italics mine][17]

The attitude of most church historians toward "emotional and
idiosyncratic" religion, with its "unusual behavior," is perfectly
expressed by the word "contaminated." Margery's spiritual life,
with its "foreign" flavor and associations, was not expected of
an English woman. Her book, which uncovered a native English
outcropping of ecstatic religion, has left historians silent.

A revision of the religious history of the late Middle Ages is
under way, stimulated in part by a new appreciation of its
philosophy and theology. In his study of the thought of Gabriel
Biel and in other writings, Heiko Oberman has not only
reappraised late medieval nominalism, but demonstrated the
compatibility of nominalism and mysticism.[18] Oberman emphasized the "richness of deep pastoral and searching theological concern"[19] of Biel's writings, which are not abstract or
sterile treatises. Oberman's view of the creativity of late scholas-
ticism is complemented by his appreciation of the Franciscan
piety that shaped so much of medieval culture. Oberman is
also a leader of the school of historians who examine the unity
instead of exaggerating the differences of late medieval and
Reformation Christianity. Martin Luther was a medieval monk
before he became a reformer, and the quest for the "young
Luther" and the sources of his thought has led scholars toward
a new appreciation of Franciscan preaching, medieval mysticism,

17. *Ibid.*, 222–223.

18. Heiko A. Oberman, *The Harvest of Medieval Theology*; see also his
article "The Shape of Late Medieval Thought."

19. Oberman, *Harvest*, p. 5.

and many other aspects of fifteenth-century piety and practice.[20]

In relation to popular religion and spirituality, Oberman has pointed out that in the late Middle Ages, "mystical experience is no longer regarded as the privilege of a few elect aristocrats of the Spirit."[21] In the writings of Jean Gerson, whose interests and career ranged through the varieties of medieval religious experience, mystical communion was valued above scholastic philosophy. Despite Gerson's anxiety about the discernment of spirits, about women, and about the *Revelations* of Saint Birgitta, he celebrated the mystical rapture in which even "young girls and simpletons"[22] could excel. The "democratization of mysticism"[23] described by Oberman—that is, the extension of mystical ecstasy and divine communion to many people outside a spiritual elite—may be valued or deplored, but our attitude toward the phenomenon of "democratization" is bound to affect our response to Margery Kempe.

A flowering of interest in popular religion (even "superstition")[24] has persuaded historians to examine popular piety with the care traditionally reserved for theological treatises or the *Acta* of Church Councils. For historians of women's experience, for whom conventional sources may be limited or irrelevant, popular piety is of central concern. Their problem has not been lack of interest, but scarcity of sources, and for them *The Book of Margery Kempe* is a document of enormous value. The official records of the Church and the writings of its

20. Besides Oberman's writings, see, e.g., Scott H. Hendrix, *Ecclesia in Via* (Leiden, 1974); and Steven E. Ozment, *The Age of Reform 1250–1550, Homo Spiritualis* (Leiden, 1969), and *The Reformation in Medieval Perspective.*

21. Oberman, "Shape of Late Medieval Thought," p. 19.

22. Jean Gerson, *De mystica theologia speculativa,* quoted by Ozment in "Mysticism, Nominalism and Dissent," p. 84.

23. Oberman, "Shape of Medieval Thought," p. 19.

24. Natalie Zemon Davis has written persuasively of the need to avoid artificial distinctions between popular religion and "superstition": see "Some Tasks and Themes in the Study of Popular Religion."

learned men are actually, of course, sources for the history of an elite—and such history, while important, is not identical with "history" itself. New materials, evidence of the experience of people outside the elite, are scarce and difficult to find and to interpret, but they make possible a reshaping of the images and constructs in which historians think about the past. We have discovered, for example, that periods and phenomena traditionally defined as "progressive," or productive of freedom or achievement, are not necessarily progressive or liberating for all people. (During the Italian Renaissance, women actually lost freedom and status in relation to the men of their own class.)[25] The converse may also be true: late medieval disorder or "decadence" may have permitted unprecedented opportunity to a woman like Margery Kempe. Her book opens a window on the religious experience of medieval people outside the educated or monastic or clerical elite whose stories we have been accustomed to accept as "church history."

Many systems of interpretation can be applied to *The Book of Margery Kempe*: insights from the study of literature, psychology, and anthropology (among other disciplines) assist our understanding of the text. In any system, the book must be appreciated first of all as a product specifically of a woman's experience and placed within the context of a distinct tradition of women's history. Scholars are beginning to appreciate the crucial and complex role of gender in the creation of cultural constructs, including religion, and the radical revisions of conceptual structures implied in the recognition that the experience of women cannot be subsumed under that of "man."[26] Traditionally, studies of autobiography make "man" the measure of their analysis; the "individuality" assumed to be the

25. Joan Kelly-Gadol has argued that "there was no renaissance for women—at least, not during the Renaissance" (Kelly-Gadol, "Did Women Have a Renaissance?," p. 139).

26. An important discussion of this question is presented in Joan Kelly-Gadol, "The Social Relations of the Sexes."

subject of autobiography has typically been male. Indeed, we are not accustomed to notice the gender of a male author, whose first-person singular pronoun is accepted as the normative "I," comparable to the "generic he" of third-person writings. But like any other creative endeavor, autobiography is shaped by gender in ways so fundamental that they are seldom recognized or discussed. A fifth-century North African woman, a convert to Christianity, would not have lived the life of the young Augustine, certainly would not have become bishop of Hippo, and would not have written anything like the *Confessions*. Shakespeare's sister wrote her poetry only in the imagination of Virginia Woolf. A devout layman of fifteenth-century Lynn might serve as Margery's first scribe, but he could not have been the author of *The Book of Margery Kempe*.

As Mary G. Mason has pointed out, Margery's book is in some respects a prototype of later books by women, especially stories of factual or fictional journeys and pilgrimages and accounts of spiritual education.[27] Linguists and literary scholars, whose predecessors contributed so much to the story of Middle English religious writings, discover in Margery's book an early and substantial expression of the female imagination. Both book and author (as a literary protagonist) can be studied in relation to other female figures in medieval literature, and such work illuminates the mystery plays, the *fabliaux*, and *The Canterbury Tales* as well as assisting in the interpretation of Margery Kempe.

Although the contributions of modern psychology and psychoanalysis are difficult and hazardous to apply to the minds and hearts of people in the distant past, Margery Kempe is extraordinarily attractive to the psychohistorian. The candor of her narrative and the quality of her experience lend themselves without undue distortion to psychoanalytic categories. The distinctions between meditation and fantasy, vision and wish fulfillment, religious ecstasy and hysteria—never simple—are

27. Mary G. Mason and Carol Hurd Green, eds., *Journeys*, pp. xiii–xv.

wonderfully blurred in the autobiography of Margery Kempe. Beginning with its opening pages, much of her book is susceptible to psychological interpretation. Indeed, given the manifest content of much of the author's experience, such interpretation is almost irresistible.

The insights of modern psychology are helpful, for example, in interpreting the illness that Margery suffered after the birth of her first child. The description resembles "postpartum psychosis," a condition that is distinguished from the common depression that afflicts many new mothers and usually is mild and short-lived. In the rarer psychoses, endocrinological vulnerability permits a regression to childhood and adolescent conflicts.[28] In severe cases there may be a "peculiar sad delirium" characterized by a "profound quandary about one's role as a new mother."[29] The condition tends to occur in patients who have rejected their own mothers as unloving, leaving them with no satisfactory model to help them to become parents. Such a patient is likely to turn against herself, her child, or her husband, as did Margery Kempe, and the situation is complicated when the birth seems to trap the patient in an undesired role or marriage— which may also have been true of Margery Kempe. Margery recovered with the aid of her vision of Christ, whose appearance helped her to establish a new perception of herself as a much-loved child. Like an effective therapist, Christ functioned as the loving mother and model parent necessary for Margery's recovery.[30] The erotic overtones of the experience were less significant than the parental.

Margery was punished by God for refusing to believe in the reprobation of sinners; the account of her punishment is better

28. Karnosh and Hope, "Puerperal Psychoses," *American Journal of Psychiatry* 94 (1937): 208.

29. Frederick T. Melges, "Postpartum Psychiatric Reactions," pp. 445–446.

30. *Ibid.*, pp. 448–449. Suggestions for therapeutic treatment of postpartum psychosis include "the use of future-oriented psychotherapy, focussed on building a self-image and rehearsing plans of action specific to the patient's chosen model of mothering."

suited to the couch than the confessional: "And, as she before
had many glorious visions and high contemplation in the Manhood of Our Lord, in Our Lady and in many other holy saints,
even right so had she now horrible sights and abominable,
for aught she could do, of beholding men's members, and such
other abominations. She saw . . . divers men of religion, priests
and many others . . . so that she might not eschew them or put
them out of her sight, shewing their bare members unto her"
(p. 132). From this distance we cannot discover the psychological antecedents of Margery's experience. What the quotation
does illustrate is the existence in a woman's imagination of a
mood and fantasy analogous to those of Saint Anthony and
other Christian men, who were tormented by diabolical ugliness in female form. As is so often the case, the psychohistorical lens is most effective in the examination of groups and
generations.[31] In the interpretation of an individual, the method
has serious limitations, and particularly for those for whom
childhood material is fragmentary or nonexistent.

With whatever difficulties and reservations, readers of *The
Book of Margery Kempe* have consistently turned to psychology
for help with its interpretation. Reviewers of the first edition,
basing their notions in part on the popular Freudianism of the
1930s, wrote of Margery's "hysteria," and as recently as 1980,
she was dismissed as "quite mad—an incurable hysteric with a
large paranoid trend."[32] This concept of "hysteria" was shaped
by misunderstandings of Freud and also by a much older
constellation of ideas around the ancient association of women
and hysteria—the "wandering womb" of antiquity. At least as
early as Plato's *Timaeus*, the condition was associated with
women and with sexual problems: "the matrix or womb in
women . . . is a living creature within them which longs to

31. Among the valuable group studies making use of psychohistorical
evidence and techniques are John Demos, *A Little Commonwealth* (New
York, 1970) and "Underlying Themes in the Witchcraft of Seventeenth-Century
New England," *American Historical Review* 75 (1970): 1311–1326.

32. Donald R. Howard, *Writers and Pilgrims*; p. 35.

bear children. And if it is left unfertilized long beyond the
normal time, it causes extreme unrest, strays about the body,
blocks the channels of the breath and causes in consequence
acute distress and disorders of all kinds."[33] This alarming
picture, which is not obviously suited to the mother of fourteen
children, has been the source of much nonsense. It is a very
early expression of centuries of concern over women who are
not actively engaged in reproduction or who neglect or aban-
don family life. Even today, hysteria is vaguely associated in
the popular imagination with female sexual disorders, dis-
function, deprivation, or excess. Such a woman as Margery
Kempe, who wept and threw herself on the ground, who first
enjoyed and then despised sex, and who became temporarily
insane after childbirth, is still a likely candidate for the label.

However, if we called "hysterical" all those who detested or
feared the opposite sex, or sexuality itself, few martyrs, saints,
or Fathers of the Church would escape the name. Modern
judgments about "normal" and healthy sexuality are not appli-
cable to medieval Christians, whose values, socialization, and
world view were so unlike our own. (For the Church Fathers,
after all, sexual passion itself was abnormal; Augustine believed
that lust was one of the dismal consequences of the Fall.)
Historians sometimes share the popular misunderstandings of
"hysteria," which they may use to dismiss or trivialize certain
kinds of experience. In modern psychology, however, hysteria
is generally understood as a conversion of psychic tension into
"unnatural" physical activity, and primarily as a "means of
obtaining ego-satisfaction."[34] It is also described as "liberation
from an unresolvable conflict" or "flight from an intolerable
situation into an abnormal mental state."[35] These definitions
are less colorful than ancient or modern ideas about wandering

33. *Plato: Timaeus and Critias*, ed. and tr. Desmond Lee (London, 1965),
p. 120.
34. Ilza Veith, *Hysteria*, p. 274.
35. Ernst Arbman, *Ecstasy or Religious Trance*, 3:75.

wombs, but much more helpful in the interpretation of Margery Kempe.

On the simplest level, it is not hard to understand that married life and difficult childbirth might produce an "unnatural" psychic state in a woman who accepted contemporary sanctions against sexual desire and sexual activity. Margery Kempe believed herself to be an unusually sinful, lustful woman; she remembered in middle age the "fleshly lusts and inordinate loves" (p. 166) she once had felt. The memory may have been conventional—any degree of lust might have been described as "inordinate"—but it reveals an awareness of sexual wishes that were incompatible with her desired self-image. As a young woman, when she first experienced the joy and suffering of conversion, she was "afflicted with horrible temptations of lechery and despair" (p. 9). To a medieval woman with aspirations to holiness, lechery and despair were inseparable.

In one form or another, the next question is bound to arise in any psychohistorical approach to an individual: why did she react so strongly and specifically to attitudes and sanctions that were common in her society? If certain medieval Christian attitudes promoted sexual anxiety, and if many (or even most) first childbirths were dangerous and difficult, why was her response so extreme? Ultimately there is no satisfactory answer to that question: she was special because she left a record of her experience that has survived to become an object of our curiosity. But there may be another answer, which can be applied to more than one individual, and to which we are assisted by the definition of hysteria as a product of "unresolvable conflict."

The tension experienced by Margery Kempe was not exclusively religious, neither was it confined to the realm of the intrapsychic. In the "real" world outside, there was obvious conflict between the social (and domestic) role of John Kempe's wife and John Burnham's daughter and the ambitious, restless, powerful personality of Margery Kempe. Middle-class women in late medieval England were in many respects more free and more active than most women of premodern times, but the laws that govern rising expectations must have made restriction no less irksome. Margery Kempe was the daughter of a public figure. Her brother followed their father into public office, with all of the real and symbolic authority and significance attached to public power in medieval Lynn. It must have been obvious very early that Margery's energies could not be expressed in commercial or political life. (Her attempts at brewing and milling, which she called "housewifery," were not on the level of merchant trading dominated by John Burnham and his peers.) Burnham's son became a Member of Parliament; his daughter found autonomy, power, and significance in another place.

The social anthropologist I. M. Lewis, in a valuable cross-cultural study of ecstatic religion, has described the function of religious "extremism" (trance, possession, ecstasy, and the like) in the lives of individuals and groups for whom it provides a sanctioned form of resistance or aggression or escape from narrow and unsatisfactory lives. For women in particular, but also for men in certain disadvantaged groups, "peripheral possession cults" serve as "thinly disguised protest movements directed against the dominant sex. . . . To a considerable extent they protect women from the exactions of men, and offer an effective vehicle for manipulating husbands and male relatives."[36] The "victims" of possession are not held responsible for their behavior, for the spirits are blamed for any inconvenience or distress caused by the afflicted person.

Possessed persons, known to anthropologists as "shamans," live in close communication with the spirits who direct their activity and who may provide them with special powers of healing, prophecy, or mediation. Bizarre behavior (trance, babbling, "fits," or possibly tears) manifests the closeness of the spirits. Shamans are not revolutionaries or even reformers; most often they are not conscious of dissatisfaction in themselves or in their group or class. Lewis points out that possessed

36. I. M. Lewis, *Ecstatic Religion*, p. 31.

persons do not necessarily (or characteristically) question authority or attack the status system in which they find themselves.
Their anger or rage is expressed without conscious awareness of
the effects of hierarchy.[37]

Very often, the shaman is distinguished by some special
affliction or illness. According to Lewis, "what begins as an
illness, or otherwise deeply disturbing experience, ends in
ecstasy; and the pain and suffering of the initial crisis are
obliterated in its subsequent re-evaluation as a uniquely effica-
cious sign of divine favour."[38] Margery's tears constituted such
an affliction and became a mark of special favor. From the first
"cry that ever she cried in any contemplation," her tears brought
her "much despite and much reproof" (p. 57). But that sorrow
and pain was a channel of grace, and testified to grace, as she
was constantly assured by holy, and even by divine, persons.
The special relationship of affliction and holiness, which began with Christ's Passion, was one of the enduring traditions of
Christianity. Martyrs were transported by suffering into the
company of saints; ascetics insisted on mortification of the
flesh as education for the spirit. The tears and pains of Margery
Kempe made her eligible for holiness.

In many of the tribal religions studied by Lewis, the shaman
is tied to the spirits or to the god by a mystical union that may
be symbolized in a marriage metaphor. In the case of female
shamans, "the spirit partners of such women regularly come to
lie with them and tend to monopolize their affections. . . . while
giving the woman increased status and freedom, this also
renders her a formidable marriage partner to ordinary men."[39]
With God's help, Margery Kempe became a formidable partner
indeed: "On the Wednesday in Easter week, after her husband
would have had knowledge of her, she said:—'Jesus Christ,
help me,' and he had no power to touch her at that time in

37. *Ibid.*, p. 33.
38. *Ibid.*, p. 71.
39. *Ibid.*, p. 61.

that way, nor ever after with any fleshly knowledge" (p. 14).

The vocation of the shaman is not ordinarily compatible with maternity. The powers of female shamans often fade or disappear when they are bearing children, and return when they have ceased to do so. Margery could not begin fully to live out her vocation until she could be chaste and have no more children. More than once in the early years, Jesus had to reassure her about her maternal status, for practical as well as spiritual reasons. When God informed her of a new pregnancy, she first asked: "Ah! Lord, what shall I do for the keeping of my child?" Christ promised first to "arrange for a keeper," then soothed her anxiety about the incompatibility of her sexual and spiritual roles when she protested: "Lord, I am not worthy to hear Thee speak, and thus to commune with my husband" (p. 39). Despite heavenly reassurance, it is clear that God and Margery Kempe agreed that active indulgence in the married state impeded spiritual growth. In a late meditation, Christ reminded Margery of her good fortune, saying: "Daughter, if thou knewest how many wives there are in this world, that would love Me and serve Me right well and duly, if they might be as free from their husbands as thou art from thine, thou wouldst see that thou wert right much beholden unto Me" (p. 193).

According to Lewis's notion of the social and psychological functions of ecstatic religion, the creation and continuing legitimation of the shamanistic vocation permits its adepts to experience a sense of power, significance, and liberation from unsatisfactory lives. Such ecstasy may or may not be "hysterical"; it certainly is not a maladaptive neurotic state but an effective and fairly common means by which depressed or deprived people improve their lives. Obviously it is not a conscious strategy. The shaman is a true believer and may not even be aware of social or personal deprivation. The sufferings of the afflicted are as genuine as their ecstasy.

Cross-cultural studies by anthropologists help us to "see" and interpret Margery Kempe and her strange vocation, so frequently dismissed as religious "extremism." To perceive her calling in relationship to the experience of the shaman permits us to appreciate the creativity of religious ecstasy and to recognize the extraordinary achievement of Margery Kempe. Lewis's interpretation helps us to relate her vocation to her circumstances: social, economic, geographic, and domestic. Neither anthropology, psychology, nor literary criticism can "explain" Margery Kempe, but the work of scholars in all these fields enriches our understanding.

As we look into the mirror of *The Book of Margery Kempe*, we inevitably see reflections of our own time and our own values and concerns. Our primary aim, however, has been to "see" the historical figure Margery Kempe, to look at her and her book from the several points of view which illuminate the image. We looked first at the book itself—our single source of information about her life, her character, and her calling. We determined that the book *is* an autobiography, according to the intention and achievement of the author, if not according to canons that restrict the genre to the life stories of modern "selves." Margery's scribes certainly influenced her work, as did her literary and religious models, but essentially she reconstructed her own life with honesty and attention to significant detail. She referred to herself as "this creature," her "self" was of the fifteenth century, but she told her own story. Obviously the book leaves out much that we would like to know and tells us much that we cannot interpret, but it does provide a sufficient basis for the study of Margery Kempe.

Margery discovered and lived out a complicated and unusual vocation as a mystic and a pilgrim, called to weep and to pray—in the world—for the sins of other people. She found ways to know God's will directly through lively meditation and direct discourse with divine beings, and she established herself as a holy person by adopting the practices that characterized sanctity in her world—fasting, prayer, celibacy, and pilgrimage. She traveled great distances to enter physically into the land

and.to visit the relics of Christ's life and death; she made the transition from her old life to her new one through the "liminal" state of pilgrimage. And her tears—that special, trying gift of the Spirit—marked her as something more than an ordinary devout lay person. She was a "chosen soul," with a special, conspicuous habit that has been difficult for her admirers as well as her detractors to accept.

Margery Kempe was a "creature" of a particular time and place and community as well as a "creature" of God. She was born to a powerful upper-middle-class family of an East Anglian city in the late fourteenth century. She grew up socially and economically secure, sufficiently privileged and self-confident to defy convention and to speak up to bishops. In King's Lynn she was exposed to Continental trends, persons, and events in the religious world that attracted her. She was raised according to a powerful and specific set of norms and conventions for women; to defy those norms she had to depart—psychologically —from conventional attachments. She did not leave the world for a convent, but she found another "family" in Heaven to love and appreciate her. She grew up at a juncture of bourgeois solidity, Continental "extremism" in religion, and a set of domestic models for women which could not contain her rest-less and powerful spirit. If we apply Lewis's insights to Margery Kempe, we can see her break through conventional restrictions into a life of power, autonomy, and freedom. Such an interpreta-tion helps us to understand why a woman might choose a dangerous, uncomfortable, and psychically distressing life over the comfort and security of middle-class domesticity.

Margery's vocation, so often suspected of "hypocrisy" by her neighbors, was generally accepted as valid by her Church. On the whole, she got along well with clergy, choosing her confes-sors according to God's will and her own sense of their interest and sympathy. She was troublesome and annoying, but high churchmen listened to her and protected her. She lived at a time of intense anxiety over Lollardy and was arrested more than once and accused of heresy, but the charges were never proved: her theological orthodoxy and social position averted disaster. Margery was much less afraid of persecution for heresy than of diabolical suggestion; her "dread of illusions" kept her visiting clergy to "show her feelings" and to win their approval and support. The vocation of the shaman, with its liberation from ordinary responsibilities, was paid for in part with lifelong anxiety.

Margery's orthodoxy, which secured clerical support, extended beyond matters of faith and doctrine into her prayers and meditations, in which she concentrated on Christ's humanity and entered into the intimate lives of the Holy Family and the saints. Her style of prayer was a direct and conventional response to the instructions of respected medieval authorities on the spiritual life. Because Margery could not read such instructions, her book serves as evidence of the permeation of these teachings throughout fifteenth-century piety. She did just what the great Cistercian and Franciscan writers had directed the devout to do: loved Christ in his humanity, attended the Virgin, participated with all her emotions in the joy and grief of the Christian story. She followed closely the example set forth by authors of *Meditations on the Life of Christ*. The distinct and specific influence of such works in the prayers of an illiterate woman shows us how religious instruction was transmitted (and transformed) in the Middle Ages. Margery's book is especially valuable because it is a *response*. Generally, our sources are limited to the writings of the experts—teachers and professionals; here we find some of the results of their work.

Obviously, neither Margery Kempe nor her vocation can be understood simply as a product of conventional piety. Her strange way of life was not dictated by her bishop, by any Franciscan preacher, or by the writers of *Meditations*. Her life was strange in King's Lynn, unfamiliar in England, but intelligible within a context of Continental women saints, who for some time (and increasingly, in the century before Margery Kempe) attracted attention and recognition for lives of "extreme" holiness. Christ reminded Margery Kempe that many wives would envy her, and we have seen that some wives in fact preceded her—Saint Birgitta, for example, and Dorothea of Montau. Margery Kempe knew of women who left home, lived chaste lives although they were married, saw visions, talked with God, and wrote books about their experiences. She had models across the Channel in her own time, and models from the past in the Lives of saints—standards of female heroism, singularity, and adventure.

Margery Kempe was a problem for many of her acquaintances, probably for her family, and certainly for historians, who have found her character and her vocation difficult or tiresome. Religious enthusiasm is not attractive to everyone, and until fairly recently, the image of late medieval religion has not been widely appealing.[40] But with all their strange manifestations and repellent "extremism," the fourteenth and fifteenth centuries witnessed a new phenomenon in the history of Christianity: holy women who were wives and mothers, whose success and significance challenged ancient assumptions about women and holiness. For at least a thousand years, virginity had been a major component of holiness for Christian women.[41] The concept and valuation of virginity is extremely complicated, but among its many meanings is an implication that adult womanhood is unclean or unholy, that a woman must be like a child—or a man—to be close to God. That ancient ideal survived (and survives), and the new saints of the late Middle Ages struggled with it, but in their own lives they evaded ancient restrictions and achieved new status as prophets,

40. In the foreword to *A Distant Mirror: The Calamitous Fourteenth Century* (New York, 1978), Barbara Tuchman noted: "Difficulty of empathy, of genuinely entering into the mental and emotional values of the Middle Ages, is the final obstacle. The main barrier is, I believe, the Christian religion as it then was ... " (p. xix).

41. In the first Christian centuries, before the Peace of the Church and before the writings of such Fathers of the Church as Jerome and John Chrysostom, virginity was prized, but marriage—and even pregnancy—was no barrier to holiness for women. See the stories of SS. Perpetua and Felicitas.

visionaries, and religious leaders. If the late medieval centuries were chaotic or horrifying in certain respects, they were not so for everyone in all respects. For certain women, wives and mothers of families, the period provided unprecedented opportunities to achieve autonomy, power, and freedom through the life of the spirit. Ordained to be a mirror, Margery Kempe and her book reflect not only a singular life but an image of possibility.

Selected Bibliography

I. MEDIEVAL SOURCES

"The Abbey of the Holy Ghost." *Religious Pieces in Prose and Verse*, ed. George Perry. London, 1867.

AILRED OF RIEVAULX. *Jesus at the Age of Twelve.* Tr. Theodore Berkeley, O.C.S.O. In *Treatises: The Pastoral Prayer*, vol. 1 of *The Works of Aelred of Rievaulx*, ed. David Knowles. Spencer, Mass., 1971.

———. *A Rule of Life for a Recluse.* Tr. Mary Paul Macpherson, O.C.S.O. In *Treatises: The Pastoral Prayer*, vol. 1 of *The Works of Aelred of Rievaulx*, ed. David Knowles. Spencer, Mass., 1971.

———. *De spirituali amicitia.* Ed. and tr. Mary Eugenia Laker, S.S.N.D. Washington, D.C., 1974.

The Ancrene Riwle. Ed. and tr. M. B. Salu. London, 1955.

ANGELA OF FOLIGNO. *The Book of the Visions and Instructions of Blessed Angela of Foligno.* Ed. and tr. A. P. J. Cruikshank. New York, 1903.

ANSELM OF CANTERBURY. *Orationes sive meditationes.* Vol. 3 of *S. Anselmi opera omnia*, ed. F. S. Schmitt. Edinburgh, 1946.

AUDELAY, JOHN. *The Poems of John Audelay.* Ed. E. K. Whiting. London, 1931.

BEDE. *Bede's Ecclesiastical History of the English People.* Ed. Bertram Colgrave and R. A. B. Mynors. Oxford, 1969.

BERNARD OF CLAIRVAUX. *On the Song of Songs I.* Vol. 2 of *The Works of Bernard of Clairvaux.* Tr. Kilian Walsh, O.C.S.O. Spencer, Mass., 1971.

BIRGITTA OF SWEDEN. *Acta et Processus Canonizacionis Beate Birgitte.* Ed. Isak Collijn. Vol. 1 of *Samlingar utgivna av Svenska Fornskriftsällskapet.* Uppsala, 1924–1931.

———. *Birger Gregerssons Birgitta-Officium.* Ed. Carl-Gustaf Undhagen. Vol. 6 of *Samlingar utgivna av Svenska Fornskriftsällskapet.* Uppsala, 1960.

———. *Birgerus Gregorii Legenda Sante Birgitte.* Ed. Isak Collijn. Vol. 4 of *Samlingar utgivna av Svenska Fornskriftsällskapet.* Uppsala, 1956.

———. *Den Heliga Birgittas Revelaciones Extravagantes.* Ed. Lennart Hollman. Vol. 5 of *Samlingar utgivna av Svenska Fornskrift-*

sällskapet. Uppsala, 1956.

——. *The Revelations of Saint Birgitta.* Ed. William Patterson Cumming. London, 1929.

Bokenham's Legendys of Hooly Wummen. Ed. Mary S. Serjeantson. London, 1938.

The Book of the Knight of La Tour-Landry. Ed. and tr. Thomas Wright. London, 1868.

BUTLER-BOWDON, W. See Kempe, Margery.

CAPGRAVE, JOHN. *The Life of St. Katherine of Alexandria.* Ed. Carl Horstmann and F. J. Furnivall. London, 1893.

——. *Ye Solace of Pilgrimes.* Ed. C. A. Mills. London, 1911.

CASSIEN, JEAN. *Conférences.* Ed. E. Pichery. Vol. II. Paris, 1958.

CATHERINE OF SIENA. *The Dialogue of St. Catherine of Siena.* Ed. and tr. Algar Thorold. London, 1925.

The Chastising of God's Children. Ed. Joyce Bazire and Eric Colledge. Oxford, 1957.

CHAUCER, GEOFFREY. *The Complete Works of Geoffrey Chaucer.* Ed. F. N. Robinson. Boston, 1933.

The Cloud of Unknowing and the Book of Privy Counselling. Ed. and tr. Phyllis Hodgson. London, 1944.

"De arte lacrimandi." Ed. Robert M. Garrett. *Anglia* 32 (1909): 269–294.

Egeria: Diary of a Pilgrimage. Ed. and tr. George E. Gingras. New York, 1970.

GERSON, JEAN. "De probatione spirituum." In *Oeuvres complètes,* vol. 9. Ed. Mgr. Glorieux. Paris, 1973.

——. *Traité de Jean Gerson sur la Pucelle.* Ed. J.-B. Monnoyeur. Paris, 1910.

The Goodman of Paris. Ed. and tr. Eileen Power. London, 1928.

Hali Meidenhad. Ed. F. J. Furnivall. London, 1922.

HILTON, WALTER. *The Scale of Perfection.* Ed. Evelyn Underhill. London, 1923.

JULIAN OF NORWICH. *A Book of Showings to the Anchoress Julian of Norwich.* Ed. Edmund Colledge, O.S.A., and James Walsh, S.J. 2 vols. Toronto, 1978.

KEMPE, MARGERY. *The Book of Margery Kempe.* Ed. and tr. William Butler-Bowdon. New York, 1944.

——. *The Book of Margery Kempe.* Ed. Sanford B. Meech and Hope Emily Allen. London, 1940.

The Life of Christina of Markyate: A Twelfth-Century Recluse. Ed. and tr. Charles H. Talbot. Oxford, 1959.

The Life of St. Mary Magdalene. Ed. and tr. Valentina Hawtrey. London, 1904.

"The Little Flowers" & *the Life of St. Francis with the "Mirror of Perfection."* Ed. and tr. Thomas Okey. New York, n.d.

LOVE, NICHOLAS. *The Mirrour of the Blessed Lyf of Jesu Christ.* Ed. Lawrence F. Powell. Oxford, 1908.

LUDOLPHUS DE SAXONIA. *Vita Jesu Christi.* Ed: L. M. Rigollet. 4 vols. Paris, 1870.

MANDEVILLE, JOHN. *The Marvelous Adventures of Sir John Maundeville, Kt.* Ed. Arthur Layard. London, 1895.

MECHTHILD OF MAGDEBURG. *The Revelations of Mechthild of Magdeburg.* Ed. and tr. Lucy Menzies. New York, 1953.

Meditations on the Life of Christ: An Illustrated Manuscript of the Fourteenth Century (Ms. Ital. 115, Paris Bibl. Nat.). Ed. and tr. Isa Ragusa and Rosalie B. Green. Princeton, 1961.

MEECH, SANFORD B. AND HOPE EMILY ALLEN. See Kempe, Margery.

MIRK, JOHN. *Instructions for Parish Priests by John Myrc.* Ed. Edward Peacock. London, 1868.

____. *Mirk's Festial: A Collection of Homilies.* Ed. Theodor Erbe. London, 1905.

The Myroure of Oure Ladye. Ed. John Henry Blunt. London, 1873.

The Orcherd of Syon. Ed. Phyllis Hodgson and Gabriel M. Liegey. London, 1966.

The Paston Letters A.D. 1422–1509. Ed. James H. Gairdner. 6 vols. New York, 1965.

"Prosalegenden: Die Legenden des ms. Douce 114." *Anglia* 8 (1865): 102–196.

The Register of Bishop Philip Repington 1405–1419. Ed. Margaret Archer. Hereford, 1963.

ROLLE, RICHARD. *English Writings of Richard Rolle.* Ed. Hope Emily Allen. Oxford, 1931.

____. *The Fire of Love.* Ed. and tr. Clifton Wolters. London, 1972.

____. *The Incendium Amoris of Richard Rolle of Hampole.* Ed. Margaret Deanesly. Manchester, 1915.

____. *The "Melos Amoris" of Richard Rolle of Hampole.* Ed. and tr. E. J. F. Arnould. Oxford, 1957.

The Sarum Missal Edited from Three Early Manuscripts. Ed. J. Wickham Legg. Oxford, 1916.

Scripta Leonis, Rufini et Angeli. Ed. and tr. Rosalind B. Brooke. Oxford, 1970.

Seinte Marherete. Ed. Francis Mack. London, 1934.

The South English Legendary. Ed. Charlotte D'Evelyn and Anna J. Mill. London, 1956.

Speculum christiani. Ed. Gustaf Holmstedt. London, 1933.

"The *Speculum Devotorum* of an Anonymous Carthusian of Sheen." Ed. James Hogg. *Analecta Cartusiana* 12–13 (1973).

The Stacions of Rome and the Pilgrims Sea-Voyage. Ed. F. J. Furnivall. London, 1867; rev. ed. New York, 1969.

The St. Albans Chronicle 1406–1420. Ed. V. H. Galbraith. Oxford, 1937.

TANNER, NORMAN P., ed. *Heresy Trials in the Diocese of Norwich 1428–1431.* London, 1977.

Vita Dorothea Montoviensis Magistri Johannis Marienwerder. Ed. Hans Westpfahl. Cologne, 1964.

VITRY, JACQUES DE. *Lettres de Jacques de Vitry.* Ed. R. B. C. Huygens. Leiden, 1960.

———. "Vita Maria Oigniacensis." *Acta Sanctorum,* vol. 25, pp. 542–572. Paris and Rome, 1867.

VORAGINE, JACOBUS DE. *The Golden Legend of Jacobus de Voragine.* Ed. and tr. Granger Ryan and Helmut Ripperger. New York, 1941.

II. MODERN SOURCES

ALLEN, HOPE EMILY. "The Mystical Lyrics of the Manuel des Pechiez." *Romanic Review* 9 (1918): 154–193.

———. "On the Author of the Ancren Riwle." *PMLA* 44 (1929): 635–680.

———. *Writings Ascribed to Richard Rolle, Hermit of Hampole, and Materials for His Biography.* New York, 1927.

ANDERSON, M. D. *Drama and Imagery in English Medieval Churches.* Cambridge, 1963.

ARBMAN, ERNST. *Ecstasy or Religious Trance.* 3 vols. Uppsala, 1963–1970.

ARMSTRONG, C. A. J. "The Piety of Cicely, Duchess of York: A Study in Late Medieval Culture." In *For Hilaire Belloc,* ed. Douglas Woodruff, pp. 68–91. New York, 1942.

ASTON, MARGARET E. "Lollards and Literacy." *History* 62 (1977): 347–371.

———. "Lollardy and Sedition." *Past and Present* 17 (1960): 1–44.

———. *Thomas Arundel.* Oxford, 1967.

AUNGIER, GEORGE JAMES. *The History and Antiquities of Syon Monastery, the Parish of Islesworth, and the Chapelry of Hounslow.* London, 1840.

BAKER, JOHN, ed. *English Stained Glass.* New York, 1960.

BATESON, MARY. *Catalogue of the Library of Syon Monastery, Islesworth.* Cambridge, 1898.

BÉDIER, JOSEPH. *Les fabliaux.* Paris, 1893.

BELL, ROBERT. "Metamorphoses of Spiritual Autobiography." *Journal of English Literary History* 44 (1977): 108–126.

BELOE, EDWARD MILLIGEN. *Our Borough: Our Churches (King's Lynn, Norfolk).* Cambridge, 1899.

A BENEDICTINE OF STANBROOK. "Margery Kempe and the Holy Eucharist." *Downside Review* 56 (1938): 468–482.

BENNETT, H. S. *Six Medieval Men and Women.* Cambridge, 1955.

BENZ, ERNST. *Die Vision.* Stuttgart, 1969.

BIHLMEYER, KARL. "Die Selbstbiographie in der deutschen Mystik des Mittelalters." *Theologische Quartalschrift* 114 (1933): 504–544.

BLENCH, J. W. *Preaching in England in the Late Fifteenth and Sixteenth Centuries.* New York, 1964.

BODENSTADT, SR. M. IMMACULATA. "The Vita Christi of Ludolphus the Carthusian." *Catholic University of America Studies in Medieval and Renaissance Latin* 16 (1944): 1–160.

BOLAND, PASCHAL. *The Concept of Discretio Spirituum in John Gerson's "De Probatione spirituum" and "De Distinctione verarum visionum a falsis."* Washington, D.C., 1959.

BOLTON, BRENDA M. "Mulieres sanctae." In *Sanctity and Secularity: The Church and the World.* Studies in Church History, No. 10, ed. Derek Baker, pp. 77–95. Oxford, 1973.

_____. "Vitae Matrum: A Further Aspect of the *Frauenfrage.*" In *Medieval Women,* ed. Derek Baker, pp. 253–273. Oxford, 1978.

BOND, FRANCIS. *Dedications and Patron Saints of English Churches.* London, 1914.

BOSWELL, JOHN. *Christianity, Social Tolerance, and Homosexuality.* Chicago, 1980.

BROWN, W. A. AND P. SHERESHEFSKY. "Seven Women: A Study of Postpartum Psychiatric Disorders." *Psychiatry* 35 (1972): 139–159.

BUGGE, JOHN. *Virginitas: An Essay in the History of a Medieval Ideal.* The Hague, 1975.

BUTKOVITCH, ANTHONY. *Revelations: St. Birgitta of Sweden.* Stockholm, 1972.

BYNUM, CAROLINE WALKER. *Jesus as Mother: Studies in the Spirituality of the High Middle Ages.* Berkeley, 1982.

BYRNE, SR. MARY. *The Tradition of the Nun in Medieval England.* Washington, D.C., 1932.

CARTER, E. H. *Studies in Norwich Cathedral History.* Norwich, 1935.

CARUS, PAUL. *The Bride of Christ.* Chicago, 1908.

CARUS-WILSON, ELEANORA. "The Medieval Trade of the Ports of the Wash." *Medieval Archeology* 6–7 (1962–1963): 182–201.

CHAMBERS, R. W. "The Continuity of English Prose." Introduction to *Harpsfield's Life of More.* London, 1932.

CHOLMELEY, KATHARINE. *Margery Kempe: Genius and Mystic.* London, 1947.

CLAY, ROTHA MARY. *The Hermits and Anchorites of England.* London, 1914.

CNATTINGIUS, HANS. *The Crisis in the 1420's.* Vol. 1 of *Studies in the Order of St. Bridget of Sweden.* Stockholm, 1963.

COLLEDGE, EDMUND, O.S.A. "Margery Kempe." In *Pre-Reformation English Spirituality.* Ed. James Walsh, S. J. New York, 1965.

――――, and James Walsh. "Editing Julian of Norwich's *Revelations*: A Progress Report." *Medieval Studies* 38 (1976): 404–427.

COLLEDGE, ERIC. "*Epistola solitarii ad ₹eges*: Alphonse of Pecha as Organizer of Birgittine and Urbanist Propaganda." *Medieval Studies* 18 (1956): 19–49.

――――. *The Medieval Mystics of England.* New York, 1961.

COLLIS, LOUISE. *The Apprentice Saint.* London, 1964.

CONSTABLE, GILES. "The Popularity of Twelfth-Century Spiritual Writers in the Late Middle Ages." In *Renaissance Studies in Honor of Hans Baron,* ed. Anthony Molho and John A. Tedeschi. Florence, 1971.

――――. "Twelfth-Century Spirituality and the Late Middle Ages." In *Medieval and Renaissance Studies,* vol. 5, ed. O. B. Hardison, Jr. Chapel Hill, 1971.

COOK, G. H. *The English Mediaeval Parish Church.* London, 1954.

COX, C. J. "The Carmelites of King's Lynn." In *Memorials of Old Norfolk,* ed. H. J. D. Astley. London, 1908.

CROSS, CLAIRE. *Church and People 1450–1660: The Triumph of the Laity in the English Church.* Atlantic Highlands, N.J., 1976.

―――― "Great Reasoners in Scripture": The Activities of Women Lollards 1380–1520." In *Medieval Women,* ed. Derek Baker, pp. 359–380. Oxford, 1978.

DARBY, H. C. *The Medieval Fenland.* Newton Abbot, Devon, 1974.

DAVIES, RICHARD G. "Thomas Arundel as Archbishop of Canterbury, 1396–1414." *Journal of Ecclesiastical History* 24 (1973): 9–21.

DAVIS, NATALIE ZEMON. *Society and Culture in Early Modern France.* Stanford, 1975.

――――. "Some Tasks and Themes in the Study of Popular Religion." In *Pursuit of Holiness in Late Medieval and Renaissance Religion,* ed. Charles Trinkaus and H. A. Oberman, pp. 307–336. Leiden, 1974.

DEANESLY, MARGARET. *The Lollard Bible.* Cambridge, 1966.

DE FONTETTE, MICHELINE. *Les religieuses à l'âge classique du droit canon.* Paris, 1967.

DE LAGARDE, GEORGES. *La naissance de l'ésprit laïque au declin du moyen âge*. 5 vols. Paris, 1956.

DELARUELLE, ETIENNE, ET AL. *L'église au temps du Grand Schisme et de la crise conçiliare*. Paris, 1964.

_____. "La spiritualité de Jeanne d'Arc." *Bullétin de la littérature écclesiastique* 65 (1964): 17–33, 81–98.

DICKMAN, SUSAN. "Margery Kempe and the English Devotional Tra- ✓ dition." In *The Medieval Mystical Tradition in England*, ed. Marion Glasscoe, pp. 156–172. Exeter, 1980.

DOOB, PENELOPE. *Nebuchadnezzar's Children: Conventions of Madness in Middle English Literature*. New Haven, 1974.

DOUGLASS, JANE DEMPSEY. "Women and the Continental Reformation." In *Religion and Sexism*, ed. Rosemary Ruether. New York, 1974.

DOWNING, CHRISTINE. "Re-Visioning Autobiography: The Bequest of Freud and Jung." *Soundings* 60 (1977): 210–228.

DUGGAN, LAWRENCE G. "The Unresponsiveness of the Late Medieval Church: A Reconsideration." *Sixteenth Century Journal* 9 (1978): 3–26.

ECKENSTEIN, LINA. *Woman under Monasticism*. Cambridge, 1896; rev. ed. New York, 1963.

FAWTIER, ROBERT. *Sainte Catherine de Sienne: Essai de critique des sources*. 2 vols. Paris, 1921–1930.

_____, and LOUIS CANET. *La double expérience de Catherine Benincasa*. Paris, 1948.

FINGARETTE, HERBERT. "The Ego and Mystic Selflessness." *Psychoanalysis and Psychoanalytic Review* 45 (1958): 552–583.

FINUCANE, RONALD C. *Miracles and Pilgrims: Popular Beliefs in* ✓ *Medieval England*. London, 1977.

_____. "The Use and Abuse of Medieval Miracles." *History* 60 (1975): 1–10.

FREUD, SIGMUND. *The Future of an Illusion*. Ed. and tr. James Strachey. London, 1961.

_____, AND JOSEF BREUER. *Studies on Hysteria*. Ed. and tr. James Strachey. New York, 1957.

GARTH, HELEN M. "Saint Mary Magdalene in Medieval Literature." *Johns Hopkins Studies in Historical and Political Science* 67 (1950): 7–114.

GOODICH, MICHAEL. "Contours of Female Piety in Later Medieval Hagiography." *Church History* 50 (1981): 20–32.

_____. "A Profile of Thirteenth-Century Sainthood." *Comparative Stud-* ✓ *ies in Society and History* 18 (1976): 429–437.

GOODMAN, ANTHONY. "The Piety of John Brunham's Daughter, of

Lynn." In *Medieval Women,* ed. Derek Baker. Oxford, 1978.

GRANSDEN, ANTONIA. "A Fourteenth-Century Chronicle from the Grey Friars at Lynn." *English Historical Review* 72 (1957): 270–278.

GRAY, DOUGLAS. *Themes and Images in the Medieval English Religious Lyric.* London, 1972.

GRÜNDMANN, HERBERT. *Religiöse Bewegungen im Mittelalter.* Berlin, 1935.

GUSDORF, GEORGES. "Conditions and Limits of Autobiography." In *Autobiography: Essays Theoretical and Critical,* ed. James Olney. Princeton, 1980.

HANNING, ROBERT W. "From Eva and Ave to Eglentyne and Alisoun: Chaucer's Insights into the Roles Women Play." *Signs* 2 (1977): 580–599.

HARTMANN, HEINZ. *Ego Psychology and the Problem of Adaptation.* New York, 1958.

✓ HASKELL, ANN S. "The Portrayal of Women by Chaucer and His Age." In *What Manner of Woman?,* ed. Marlene Spronger. New York, 1977.

HEATH, PETER. *The English Parish Clergy on the Eve of the Reformation.* London, 1969.

HILLEN, HENRY J. *History of the Borough of King's Lynn.* 2 vols. Norwich, 1907.

✓ HIRSCH, JOHN C. "Author and Scribe in *The Book of Margery Kempe.*" *Medium Aevum* 44 (1975): 145–150.

HODGSON, PHYLLIS. *"The Orcherd of Syon" and the English Mystical Tradition.* London, 1964.

HOGG, JAMES. "Mount Grace Charterhouse and Late Medieval English Spirituality." *Analecta Cartusiana* 82 (1980): 1–43.

✓ HOWARD, DONALD R. *Writers and Pilgrims: Medieval Pilgrimage Narratives and Their Posterity.* Berkeley, 1980.

HUDSON, ANNE. "A Lollard Compilation and the Dissemination of Wycliffite Thought." *Journal of Theological Studies* NS 23 (1972): 65–81.

――――. "Some Aspects of Lollard Book Production." In *Studies in Church History,* vol. 9. Oxford, 1972.

HUIZINGA, JOHAN. *The Waning of the Middle Ages.* London, 1924.

JACOB, E. F. *The Fifteenth Century.* Oxford, 1961.

JACOBS, BETTY. "Aetiological Factors and Reaction Types in Psychoses Following Childbirth." *Journal of Mental Science* 89 (1943): 242–256.

JEFFREY, DAVID L. *The Early English Lyric and Franciscan Spirituality.* Lincoln, Neb., 1975.

JOHNSTON, F. R. "The Cult of St. Bridget of Sweden in Fifteenth-Century England." Master's thesis. Manchester, 1947.

JONES, W. R. "Lollards and Images." *Journal of the History of Ideas* 34 (1973): 27–50.

JONES, RUFUS M. *Studies in Mystical Religion.* London, 1919.

JORGENSEN, JOHANNES. *Saint Bridget of Sweden.* Tr. Ingeborg Lund. 2 vols. London, 1954.

JULIAN OF NORWICH 1973 Celebration Committee. *Julian and Her Norwich.* Norwich, 1973.

KAUFMAN, MICHAEL W. "Spare Ribs: The Conception of Women in the Middle Ages and the Renaissance." *Soundings* 56 (1973): 139–163.

KELLY-GADOL, JOAN. "Did Women Have a Renaissance?" In *Becoming Visible: Women in European History,* ed. Renata Bridenthal and Claudia Koonz. Boston, 1977.

——. "The Social Relations of the Sexes: Methodological Implications of Women's History." *Signs* 1 (1976): 809–823.

KNOWLES, DAVID. *The English Mystical Tradition.* London, 1961.

——. "The Religion of the Pastons." *Downside Review* 42 (1924): 143–163.

——. *The End of the Middle Ages.* Vol. 2 of *The Religious Orders in England.* Cambridge, 1957.

KOLVE, V. A. *The Play Called Corpus Christi.* Stanford, 1966.

LECLERCQ, JEAN. *Bernard of Clairvaux and the Cistercian Spirit.* Kalamazoo, Mich., 1976.

——. "Modern Psychology and the Interpretation of Medieval Texts." *Speculum* 48 (1973): 476–490.

——, LOUIS BOUYER AND FRANÇOIS VANDENBROUCKE. *The Spirituality of the Middle Ages.* London, 1968.

LE STRANGE, HAMON. *Norfolk Official Lists.* Norwich, 1890.

LEWIS, I. M. *Ecstatic Religion.* London, 1971.

LEYERLE, JOHN. "Marriage in the Middle Ages: Introduction." *Viator* 4 (1973): 413–418.

LITTLE, A. G., ed. *Franciscan Papers, Lists, and Documents.* Manchester, 1943.

——. *Studies in English Franciscan History.* Manchester, 1917.

LOVATT, ROGER. "The Imitation of Christ in Late Medieval England." *Transactions of the Royal Historical Society,* 5th ser., 18 (1968): 97–122.

MAKOWSKI, ELIZABETH M. "The Conjugal Debt and Medieval Canon Law." *Journal of Medieval History* 3 (1977): 99–114.

MÂLE, EMILE. *L'art religieux de la fin du moyen âge.* Paris, 1949.

MARTZ, LOUIS. *The Poetry of Meditation.* New Haven, 1954.

MASON, MARY G. "The Other Voice: Autobiographies of Women Writers." In *Autobiography: Essays Theoretical and Critical,* ed. James Olney, pp. 207–235. Princeton, 1980.

_____, and CAROL HURD GREEN. *Journeys: Autobiographical Writings by Women.* Boston, 1979.

MATTHEWS, WILLIAM. "The Wife of Bath and All Her Sect." *Viator* 5 (1974): 413–443.

MAZLISH, BRUCE. "Autobiography and Psycho-analysis." *Encounter* 35 (1970): 28–37.

MCDONNELL, ERNEST W. *The Beguines and Beghards in Medieval Culture.* New Brunswick, N.J., 1954.

MCFARLANE, K. B. *John Wycliffe and the Beginnings of English Non-conformity.* New York, 1953.

_____. *Lancastrian Kings and Lollard Knights.* Oxford, 1972.

MCKISACK, MAY. "The Parliamentary Representation of King's Lynn before 1500." *English Historical Review* 42 (1927): 583–589.

MCLAUGHLIN, ELEANOR C. "Christ My Mother: Feminine Naming and Metaphor in Medieval Spirituality." *Nashotah Review* 15 (1975): 228–248.

_____. "Women and Medieval Heresy: A Problem in the History of Spirituality." *Concilium* 3 (1976): 73–90.

MCLAUGHLIN, MARY M. "Abelard as Autobiographer: The Motives and Meaning of His 'Story of Calamities.'" *Speculum* 42 (1967): 463–488.

MELGES, FREDERICK T. "Postpartum Psychiatric Reactions." In *International Encyclopedia of Psychiatry, Psychology, Psychoanalysis and Neurology,* 1977 ed., vol. 8.

MISCH, GEORG. *Geschichte der Autobiographie.* 4 vols. Frankfurt am Main, 1949–1969.

MOLINARI, PAUL. *Julian of Norwich.* London, 1958.

MOORMAN, JOHN. *A History of the Franciscan Order.* Oxford, 1968.

NELSON, ALAN H. *The Medieval English Stage.* Chicago, 1974.

OAKLEY, FRANCIS. *The Western Church in the Later Middle Ages.* Ithaca, N.Y., 1979.

OBERMAN, HEIKO A. "Gabriel Biel and Late Medieval Mysticism." *Church History* 30 (1961): 259–287.

_____. *The Harvest of Medieval Theology.* Grand Rapids, Mich., 1967.

_____. "The Shape of Late Medieval Thought: Birthpangs of the Modern Era." In *The Pursuit of Holiness in Late Medieval and Renaissance Religion,* ed. Heiko A. Oberman and Charles Trinkaus, pp. 3–25. Leiden, 1974.

OLNEY, JAMES. *Metaphors of Self.* Princeton, 1972.

ORIGO, IRIS. *The Merchant of Prato.* London, 1963.

———. *The World of San Bernardino.* New York, 1962.

OSBORN, J. M. *The Beginnings of Autobiography in England.* Los Angeles, 1959.

OWST, G. R. *Literature and Pulpit in Medieval England.* Cambridge, 1913; repr. New York, 1961.

———. *Preaching in Medieval England: An Introduction to the Sermon Manuscripts of the Period c. 1350–1450.* Cambridge, 1926.

OZMENT, STEVEN E. *The Age of Reform 1250–1550.* New Haven, 1980.

———. "Mysticism, Nominalism and Dissent." In *Pursuit of Holiness in Late Medieval and Renaissance Religion,* ed. Charles Trinkaus and Heiko A. Oberman, pp. 67–92. Leiden, 1974.

———. *The Reformation in Medieval Perspective.* Chicago, 1971.

PANTIN, W. A. *The English Church in the Fourteenth Century.* Cambridge, 1955.

———. "Instructions for a Devout and Literate Layman." In *Medieval Learning and Literature: Essays Presented to Richard William Hunt,* ed. J. J. G. Alexander and M. T. Gibson. Oxford, 1976.

———. "The Merchants' Houses and Warehouses of King's Lynn." *Medieval Archeology* 6–7 (1962–1963): 173–181.

PASCAL, ROY. *Design and Truth in Autobiography.* Cambridge, Mass., 1960.

PEACOCK, JAMES L. "Mystics and Merchants in Fourteenth-Century Germany." *Journal for the Scientific Study of Religion* 8 (1969): 47–59.

PETROFF, ELIZABETH. *Consolation of the Blessed.* New York, 1979.

PFAFF, R. W. *New Liturgical Feasts in Later Medieval England.* Oxford, 1970.

POSTAN, M. *Medieval Trade and Finance.* Cambridge, 1973.

POURRAT, PIERRE. *Christian Spirituality in the Middle Ages.* Vol. 2. Tr. S. B. Jacques. Westminster, Md., 1927.

POWER, EILEEN. *Medieval English Nunneries c. 1275–1535.* Cambridge, 1922.

———. *Medieval Women.* Ed. M. M. Postan. Cambridge, 1975.

PROSSER, ELEANOR. *Drama and Religion in the English Mystery Plays.* Stanford, 1961.

PRUYSER, PAUL W. "Psychoanalytic Method in the Study of Religious Meanings." *Psychohistory Review* 6 (1978): 45–52.

RAPAPORT, DAVID. *Emotions and Memory.* New York, 1950.

RAPP, FRANÇOIS. *L'église et la vie religieuse en occident à la fin du moyen âge.* Paris, 1971.

RIEHLE, WOLFGANG. *The Middle English Mystics*. Tr. Bernard Standring. London, 1981.

ROBINSON, IAN. *Chaucer and the English Tradition*. Cambridge, 1972.

ROISIN, SIMONE. "L'efflorescence Cisterçienne et le courant féminin de piété au XIIIᵉ siècle." *Revue d'histoire écclesiastique* 39 (1943): 342–378.

ROTH, FRANCIS. *The English Austin Friars 1249–1538*. New York, 1966.

ROTH, NATHAN. "The Mental Content of Puerperal Psychoses." *American Journal of Psychotherapy* 29 (1975): 204–211.

ROWLAND, BERYL, ed. *Chaucer and Middle English Studies*. London, 1974.

RUSSELL, G. H. "Vernacular Instruction of the Laity in the Later Middle Ages in England: Some Texts and Notes." *Journal of Religious History* 2 (1962): 98–119.

SALTER, ELIZABETH. "Ludolphus of Saxony and His English Translators." *Medium Aevum* 33 (1964): 26–35. See also Zeeman, Elizabeth.

———. "Nicholas Love's 'Myrrour of the Blessed Lyf of Jesu Christ.'" *Analecta Cartusiana* 10 (1974): 55–118.

SAXER, VICTOR. *La culte de Marie Madeleine en occident des origines à la fin du moyen âge*. 2 vols. Paris, 1959.

SHEEHAN, MICHAEL S. "The Formation and Stability of Marriage in Fourteenth-Century England: Evidence of an Ely Register." *Medieval Studies* 33 (1971): 228–263.

SOUTHERN, R. W. *St. Anselm and His Biographer*. Cambridge, 1963.

SQUIRE, AELRED, O. P. *Aelred of Rievaulx*. Kalamazoo, Mich., 1981.

STENTON, DORIS MARY. *The English Woman in History*. London, 1957.

STICCA, SANDRA. "Drama and Spirituality in the Middle Ages." *Medievalia et humanistica*, NS 4 (1973): 69–87.

STONE, KARL ROBERT. *Middle English Prose Style: Margery Kempe and Julian of Norwich*. The Hague, 1970.

SUMPTION, JONATHAN. *Pilgrimage: An Image of Medieval Religion*. London, 1975.

TENTLER, THOMAS N. *Sin and Confession on the Eve of the Reformation*. Princeton, 1977.

THOMPSON, E. MARGARET. *The Carthusian Order in England*. London, 1930.

THOMSON, JOHN A. F. *The Later Lollards 1414–1520*. Oxford, 1965.

THORNTON, MARTIN. *English Spirituality*. London, 1963.

———. *Margery Kempe: An Example in the English Pastoral Tradition*. London, 1960.

THRUPP, SYLVIA L. "The Problem of Conservatism in Fifteenth-Century England." *Speculum* 18 (1943): 363–368.

TOUSSAERT, JACQUES. *Le sentiment religieux en Flandre à la fin du moyen-âge*. Paris, 1963.

TURNER, VICTOR, and EDITH TURNER. *Image and Pilgrimage in Christian Culture*. New York, 1978.

UNDERHILL, EVELYN. "A Franciscan Mystic of the Thirteenth Century." In *Franciscan Essays*. British Society of Franciscan Studies, ES 1 (1912): 88–107.

_____. *Mysticism*. New York, 1955.

UTLEY, FRANCIS LEE. *The Crooked Rib*. Columbus, Ohio, 1944.

VANDENBROUCKE, FRANÇOIS, et al. "Discernement des esprits." In *Dictionnaire de spiritualité*, vol. 3, cols. 1222–1291. Paris, 1967.

VAUCHEZ, ANDRÉ. *La spiritualité du moyen âge occidental VIIIᵉ–XIIᵉ siècles*. Paris, 1975.

VEITH, ILZA. *Hysteria: The History of a Disease*. Chicago, 1965.

VERNET, FELIX. *La spiritualité médievale*. Paris, 1929.

The Victoria History of the County of Norfolk. Vol. 2. Ed. William Page. London, 1906.

WATKIN, E. I. *On Julian of Norwich and In Defence of Margery Kempe*. Exeter, 1979.

WAUGH, W. T. "Joan of Arc in English Sources of the Fifteenth Century." In *Historical Essays in Honour of James Tait*, ed. J. G. Edwards, V. H. Galbraith, and E. F. Jacob, pp. 387–398. Manchester, 1933.

WEBER, SARAH APPLETON. *Theology and Poetry in the Middle English Lyric*. Columbus, Ohio, 1969.

WEINTRAUB, KARL J. "Autobiography and Historical Consciousness." *Critical Inquiry* 1 (1975): 821–848.

WEISSMAN, HOPE P. "Antifeminism and Chaucer's Characterization of Women." In *Geoffrey Chaucer*, ed. George Economou, pp. 93–110. New York, 1975.

WESTPFAHL, HANS. "Dorothée de Montau." In *Dictionnaire de spiritualité*, vol. 3, cols. 1664–1668. Paris, 1967.

WHITE, HELEN C. *Tudor Books of Saints and Martyrs*. Madison, Wis., 1963.

WINDEATT, B. A. "Julian of Norwich and Her Audience." *Review of English Studies*, NS 27 (1977): 1–17.

WOLPERS, THEODOR. *Die englische Heiligenlegende des Mittelalters*. Tübingen, 1964.

WOODFORDE, CHRISTOPHER. *The Norwich School of Glass Painting in the Fifteenth Century*. Oxford, 1958.

Selected Bibliography

WOOLF, ROSEMARY. *The English Mystery Plays.* London, 1972.

ZACHER, CHRISTIAN K. *Curiosity and Pilgrimage.* Baltimore, 1978.

ZEEMAN, ELIZABETH. "Continuity and Change in Middle English Versions of the Meditationes Vitae Christi." *Medium Aevum* 26 (1957): 25–31. See also Salter, Elizabeth.

———. "Nicholas Love: A Fifteenth-Century Translator." *Review of English Studies,* NS. 6 (1955): 113–127.

Index

Hagiography. *See* Saints' *Lives*
Hali Meidenhad, 185–186
Hanseatic League, 57n., 74
Hayles, 56, 118–119
Heaven, 80, 83–84, 86, 101, 119,
    186, 194
Helfta, 66n., 163
Henry V, king of England, 172–173,
    198
Henry VI, king of England, 118n.,
    172
Heresy, 18, 103, 107, 112–113
    See also Lollardy
Hildegarde of Bingen, 161–162
Hilton, Walter, 144, 151–152, 183,
    204
Holy Family, 16, 93, 96
    See also Christ; Heaven; Virgin
Holy Land, 17, 54–55, 61, 63n.,
    106, 142, 171
    See also Jerusalem; Pilgrimage
Holy Week, 93–94, 112
Hypocrisy, 13, 61–62, 108, 117,
    166, 217
Hysteria, 13, 197, 201, 210–212,
    215

Illumination, 41, 44, 46–47,
    166
    See also Mysticism
Incarnation, 40, 136, 138
    See also Christ
Incendium Amoris. See Rolle,
    Richard
Indulgences, 55, 60, 173
Italy, 48n., 54, 67, 166

Jacob, E. F., 105
Jerome, Saint, 59, 64, 134, 219n.
Jerusalem, 17, 54–55, 61, 63, 67,
    113
    See also Holy Land; Pilgrimage
Jesus. *See* Christ
Joan of Arc, 18, 36, 65, 122n., 182,
    189

John of the Cross, 46–47, 204
John the Evangelist, 56, 135, 140
John, king of England, 75
John of Marienwerder, 180–181
Julian of Norwich, 126, 160,
    191–193, 200–201
    meeting with Margery Kempe,
        26, 31, 54, 64, 124–125, 183
Juliana, Saint, 187–188

Katherine of Alexandria, 48n.,
    83–84, 187–189
"Katherine group," 188
Kempe, John, 15, 17–18, 26–27,
    49–50, 80–82, 88, 110
Kempe, Margery
    children of, 16, 80, 92, 109, 215
    daughter-in-law, 29, 56, 83
    education, 25, 79, 91–94, 101
    illnesses, 15, 63n.
    pregnancies, 15, 28, 41, 80, 149,
        209, 215
    son, 18, 29–30, 80, 82, 176–178
    See also entries under Chastity;
        Confession; Conversion;
        Lollardy; Marriage;
        Meditation; Mysticism;
        Tears; Visions; Vocation
King's Lynn. *See* Lynn
Knight of La Tour-Landry, 87–88
Knowles, David, 87n., 151, 159,
    173n., 174n., 183n., 200n., 204
Kolve, V. A., 94, 96n.

Lancastrian kings, 35, 172, 198
    See also Henry V; Henry VI
Lay people, 130–131, 134, 137,
    152, 155–157, 162, 198
Legenda aurea, 152, 188
Legendys of Hooly Wummen. See
    Bokenham, Osbern
Leicester, 109–110, 112, 153
    abbot of, 112
    mayor of, 108–110
    steward of, 110

Mystic and Pilgrim

Designed by G. T. Whipple, Jr.
Composed by Superior Type
in 10½ point Olympus Medium, 2½ points leaded,
with display lines in Zapf Demi Swash.
Printed offset by Thomson-Shore, Inc.
on Warren's Number 66 Text, 50 pound basis.
Bound by John H. Dekker & Sons
in Holliston book cloth
and stamped in Kurz-Hastings foil.

Library of Congress Cataloging in Publication Data

ATKINSON, CLARISSA W.
    Mystic and pilgrim.

    Bibliography: p.
    Includes index.
    1. Kempe, Margery, b. ca. 1373.   2. Authors, English—
Middle English, 1100–1500—Biography.   3. Mysticism—
England.   4. Christian pilgrims and pilgrimages.
I. Title.
PR2007.K4Z54   1983   248.2'2'0924   82-22219
ISBN 0-8014-1521-7

does analogy yield any insight?
difference / similars?
involved

<u>milk</u> →(peanuts, pizza)
stimonism

1) Is analogy illusming abstractly
it involves differ
similars)

2) Thomistic principle with
analogous instances.

3) subtheological not verbal
(Docus Joseph)

4) Precise definitions (of algebraic
families :

5) insight → the oneness
of the different

5) feminine studies, womanizing
studies

6. in control of food and good spirit